THE BOARD MEMBER'S BOOK

Making a Difference in Voluntary Organizations

BRIAN O'CONNELL

THE FOUNDATION CENTER

1985

Library of Congress Cataloging in Publication Data

O'Connell, Brian, 1930–
    The board member's book

    Bibliography: p.
    Includes index.
    1. Endowments—United States—Officials and employees.
2. Voluntarism—United States. I. Title.
HV97.A3033   1985   361.7'068   85–6911
ISBN 0–87954–133–4

This book is dedicated to the board members of America's voluntary organizations.

It is you who make the difference for so many important causes, and it is you who build the caring spirit of our society.

Contents

Foreword

THIS BOOK IS DEDICATED to the board members of America's voluntary organizations. It is also written for them—to try to match their spirit and determination with some hard-won lessons from thirty years as a community organizer.

Board members can make an enormous difference for organizations, causes and crusades. Much of the progress of America is testimony to the power of what Richard Carter calls "the gentle legions."

Board membership can also be agonizingly ineffective and disheartening. People care passionately about causes or institutions and they want the best for them *now*, but human institutions are all less than perfect and voluntary organizations in particular can require more interaction than most of us can bear. This book begins with the observation that "people who get involved with public causes open themselves to frustration and disappointment...", but it goes on to make the much more important point that "... through it all and after it all—those moments of making change happen for the better are among our lasting joys. There is something wonderfully rewarding in being part of an effort that does make a difference."

The book is an attempt to talk to board members who want to make the very most out of their volunteer efforts. I want to assure them that they can make a tremendous difference for their causes and organizations.

Part I attempts to make clear the impact of volunteers and voluntary organizations. Part II, the body of the book, talks about the effectiveness of boards and board members in planning, evaluation, fundraising, and in their many other essential functions. Part III is an extensive reading list for those who want more information about specific functions. And, because volunteering should be fun as well as inspirational and effective, I've added an Appendix, "Minutes of Our Last Meeting," which I hope provides a lighter moment. Indeed, I have tried hard to give the whole book an upbeat tone to go along with what should be the positive character of voluntary effort.

Most of all, I've tried to make it the board member's book.

I'm grateful to Sam Walker of Walker & Company, current publishers of my book *Effective Leadership in Voluntary Organizations* (originally published by Association Press), for allowing me to use and adapt material from that book. Appreciation also goes to the Durfee, Joyce and Rosenberg foundations which have provided a small fund for research and editorial assistance for this and other writings on the independent sector.

Tom Buckman, President of The Foundation Center, and Pat Read, Director of Editorial Services and editor of both this book and *America's Voluntary Spirit*, have been wonderfully encouraging and helpful—a particularly important combination for this very part-time writer with a very full-time job.

Largest thanks go to Ann Brown O'Connell who has served as research assistant, co-author of the Reading List and partner in everything else. Without the effectiveness and kindness that she brings to her many professional and personal roles, the book—and I—would be undone.

With acknowledgment and appreciation,

Brian O'Connell
McLean, Virginia
January 1, 1985

Part I

The Power of Volunteers and Voluntary Organizations

1

The Personal Meaning of Volunteering

PEOPLE WHO GET INVOLVED with public causes open themselves to frustration and disappointment, but—through it all and after it all—those moments of making change happen for the better are among our lasting joys. There's something wonderfully rewarding in being part of an effort that does make a difference. And there's something rewarding, too, in being among other people when they're at their best.

When we take inventory of the meaning of our lives, these special experiences have to be among the high points. Happiness is, in the end, a simple thing. Despite how complicated we try to make it or the entrapments we substitute for it, happiness is caring and being able to do something about it.

In the community sense, caring and service are giving and volunteering. As far back as the twelfth century, the highest order and benefit of charity was described by Maimonides in the Mishna Torah: "The highest degree, than which there is nothing higher, is to take hold of a Jew who has been crushed and to give him a gift or a loan or to enter into partnership with him or to find work for him, and then to put him on his feet so he will not depend on his fellow man."

In a world just forty years removed from the slaughter of six million Jews, and still rampant with diseases and other indignities of the vilest form and breadth, there is room for concern and caring, for charity and volunteering. Indeed, in this still young democracy there is a total dependence on citizen determination to preserve the freedoms so recently declared and to extend them to all.

The problems of contemporary society are more complex, the solutions more involved, and the satisfactions more obscure, but the basic ingredients are still the caring and the resolve to make things better. From the simplicity of these have come today's exciting efforts on behalf of humanitarian causes ranging from equality to environment and from health to peace.

In the course of these efforts there is at work a silent cycle of cause and effect which I call the "genius of fulfillment"; that is, the harder people work for others and for the fulfillment of important social goals, the more fulfilled they are themselves. Confucius expressed it by saying, "Goodness is God"; that is, the more good we do, the happier we are, and the totality of it all is a supreme state of being. Thus, he said, God is not only a Supreme Being apart from us, but a supreme state of being within us.

Aristotle, too, caught an important part of it when he said, "Happiness is the utilization of one's talents along lines of excellence."

A simpler way of looking at the meaning of service is a quotation from an epitaph:

> What I spent is gone
> What I kept is lost
> But what I gave to charity
> Will be mine forever.

How we want to express the meaning of service doesn't really matter. It can be charity or enlightened self-interest or simple humanity to other people. These are all ways of describing why we volunteer, why volunteering provides some of our happiest moments, and why the good that we do lives after us.

2

The Impact of Volunteers and Voluntary Organizations

THE UNITED STATES is the only country in the world where giving and volunteering are pervasive characteristics of the total society. In "American Philanthropy and the National Character," the Pulitzer Prize historian Merle Curti said, "Emphasis on voluntary initiative . . . has helped give America her national character." In his introduction to my book *America's Voluntary Spirit*, former Health, Education and Welfare Secretary John W. Gardner wrote, "Virtually every significant social idea in this country has been nurtured in the nonprofit sector."

Think back to the sources of ideas and energy responsible for our vast public education system; the abolition of slavery; the settlement of refugees; the creation of our national park system; the galaxy of different local churches; the public libraries; women's suffrage; clean water; public social services; historical societies; the vast cultural networks of museums, orchestras, and dance companies; prevention of contagious disease; humane care of the mentally ill; social security; child labor laws; employment of handicapped; fire and other emergency services; and on and on.

For almost all of us and our parents and grandparents, too, our lives have been shaped substantially by voluntary institutions; beginning with the church, including church-related schools and hospitals, the local Y, visiting nurses, the grange, scout camp, college, community chest, volunteer fire company, community improvement societies, homes for the aged, and the cemetery.

The great private foundations, too—like Rockefeller and Carnegie—were influential in providing the dollars and roadmaps for our pioneering work in everything from education and health to agrarian reform and international understanding.

Many of us remember those earlier days fondly and worry about what's happened to all that neighborliness and charity. There is a generally accepted notion that people don't help out the way they used to. Actually, the truer picture and the good news is that today a greater proportion of our population is involved in volunteering and giving than was true at any time in our history.

Americans are organizing to influence every aspect of the human condition. Increasingly, we are willing to stand up and be counted on almost any public issue. We organize to fight zoning changes, approve bond issues, oppose or propose family planning, improve garbage collection, expose overpricing, enforce equal rights, and protest wars.

One doesn't have to go back in history to come up with encouraging examples of the ways that citizens have enormous effect on their neighborhoods, communities, nation, and even the world. In very recent times, we have organized associations in an array of new efforts on behalf of the rights of women, conservation and preservation, learning disabilities, refugees, Hispanic culture and rights, the aged, voter registration, mental retardation, native Americans, the dying, experimental theater, international understanding, population control, neighborhood empowerment, new religions, control of nuclear power, consumerism, and on and on.

It's important to our orientation and morale and it's important to the volunteers who look to us for leadership, to know that America's voluntary spirit is alive and well.

Beyond the number of volunteers and the causes served, it is important to recognize what this participation and pluralism mean to the kind of society we are. Merle Curti ended his article about our national character by saying, "All these philanthropic initiatives give support to the thesis that philanthropy has helped to shape our national character—[by] implementing the idea that America is a process rather than a finished product."

In *How to Succeed with Volunteers*, David Church makes the case that the health of a society can be equated with the degree of citizen involvement. He quotes Professor Marshall E. Dimock of New York University: "When voluntarism is vigorous, the country is vigorous. When it shows signs of decline, we are in trouble."

In preparation for *America's Voluntary Spirit*, I examined most of the great citizen crusades in our history. What comes through again and again is that the participation, the caring, and the evidences that people can make a difference do add wonderfully to the spirit of our society. In Inez Haynes Irwin's "The Last Days of the Fight for Women's Suffrage" (in *The Story of Alice Paul: And the National Woman's Party*), again and again she comes back to the *spirit* of those women, not only in deciding on the task and accomplishing it, but what their success meant to them as human beings. She says, for example, that "they developed a sense of comradeship for each other which was half love, half admiration and all reverence. In summing up a fellow worker, they speak first of her 'spirit,' and her 'spirit' is always beautiful, or noble, or glorious—."

She describes a moment in 1917 when a group of women, just arrested for picketing at the White House, are shoved into a prison room and, because the experience is so foreign, are terrified about both the immediate and the long-term consequences of their arrests. At the far end of the room is the wave of women who were arrested the day before—but no verbal communication between the two contingents is allowed. In a gesture to calm, encourage, and salute, the veterans "raised their water glasses high, then lowered them and drank to their comrades."

That spirit comes through in each of the great reform movements. It becomes clear that when people make the effort not only are causes and people helped, but something special happens for the giver, too; and the community and the nation take on a *spirit* that is so much a part of our national character.

It is interesting and instructive to realize that when one thinks of the giants of the independent sector, one is as likely to think of women's names—at least in the last 150 years—such as Clara Barton, Jane Adams, Mary McLeod Bethune, Susan B. Anthony, Dorothea Dix, Alice Paul, Elizabeth Cady Stanton, Harriet Beecher Stowe, Dorothy Day, Mother Seton, Carrie Nation, Margaret Sanger, Lucretia Mott, Mary Lasker, and on and on. It's the only one of three sectors that at least has begun to tap the full spectrum of the nation's talent.

It's easy for the individual to think that he or she can't make much of a difference, but in a democracy which encourages diversity, innovation, and criticism, it is often an individual or a small group that starts a cause and even a crusade. It has become almost trite to quote Edward Everett Hale:

> I am only one,
> But still I am one,
> I cannot do everything,
> But still I can do something;
> And because I cannot do everything
> I will not refuse to do the something
> that I can do.

Not long ago, I was fascinated to come across an essay from McGuffey's Reader written in 1844. It is entitled "True and False Philanthropy" and offers one of the most succinct lessons about why people must care about their neighbors and others.

The essay starts with Mr. Fantom talking about global designs for doing good while Mr. Goodman is trying to get him to focus on needs closer to home. Mr. Fantom says, "I despise a narrow field. Oh, for the reign of universal benevolence! I want to make all mankind good and happy." Mr. Goodman responds, "Dear me! Sure that must be a wholesome sort of a job: Had you not better try your hand at a *town* or a *neighborhood* first?"

With disdain Mr. Fantom retorts, "Sir, I have a plan in my head for relieving the miseries of the *whole world*. Everything is bad as it now stands. I would alter all the laws, and put an end to all the wars of the world. *This* is what I call doing things on a grand scale."

Mr. Goodman brings up a great many local needs and Mr. Fantom disparages the attention that each would take away from global solutions. Finally, Mr. Fantom says, "I despise the man whose benevolence is swallowed up in the narrow concerns of his own family, or village, or country." The lesson ends with this exchange:

> **Mr. Goodman:** "But one must begin to love somewhere; and I think it is as natural to love one's own family, and to do good in one's own neighborhood, as to anybody else, and if every man in every family, village, and country did the same, why then all the schemes would be met, and the end of one village or town where I was doing good, would be the beginning of another village where somebody else was doing good; so my schemes would jut into my neighbor's; his projects would unite with those of some other local reformer; and all would fit with a sort of dovetail exactness."
>
> **Mr. Fantom** snorts: "Sir, a man of large views will be on the watch for great occasions to prove his benevolence."
>
> **Mr. Goodman** concludes: "Yes, sir; but if they are so distant that he cannot reach them, or so vast that he cannot grasp them, he may let a thousand little, snug, kind, good actions slip through his fingers in the meantime; and so, between the great things that he *cannot* do, and the little ones that he *will not* do, life passes, and *nothing* will be done."

Whether the cause involves handicapped children, the terminally ill, reforestation, voter registration, day care, modern art, ballet, international exchange, or whatever, it is part of the mosaic that gives Americans an opportunity for options, experimentation, recreation, criticism, and, where necessary, reform. In the composite, the volunteering creates a national character in which the community and the nation take on a *spirit* of compassion, comradeship, and confidence.

3

Today's Volunteers: Who Volunteers and For What Causes?

AT TIMES, just about every volunteer reaches the point of wondering, "Why me?" or even, "Why does it always have to be me?" And occasionally, "Why me, Oh Lord—Why me?"

Sometimes we seem to be the only ones ever asked to volunteer—and at that point we damn the askers. Sometimes we seem to be the only ones who say yes—and at that point we damn ourselves and wonder if we should have our heads examined.

It may be helpful to your sanity—and to your spirit—to know that recent polls indicate that 47 percent of American adults are regular volunteers; 31 percent give at least two hours each week, and one out of every ten devotes at least seven hours every week to volunteer assignments.

The basic participation is also widening. More young people, more men, and more elderly people are volunteering. Every economic group is involved. To the surprise of all who have matter-of-factly assumed that with so many women now in the workforce it's harder to find female volunteers, the happy reality is that there are more women serving as volunteers. Indeed, recent surveys inform us that the woman who works is more likely to volunteer than the woman who does not.

Some other figures are also encouraging:

- The 25 to 44 age group is most active, with 59 percent serving as volunteers; but the other age groups are not far behind: 45–54 years (55 percent), 18–24 (54 percent), 14–17 (53 percent), 55–64 (45 percent), and 65+ (37 percent).

- The volunteer ranks include 46 percent of all women and 47 percent of all men.

- Single and married people are about as likely to volunteer (56 percent and 58 percent, respectively).

- If you live in the West, you are more likely to volunteer (57 percent of the population) than if you live in the South (48 percent). In the East it's 51 percent and in the Midwest it's 54 percent.

- People in smaller and mid-size communities are more likely to be volunteers (55 percent), but even in the large metropolitan areas the figure is an encouraging 46 percent.

- The largest percentage of volunteers (44 percent) first became involved because someone asked them to help. Other important reasons for becoming involved included having a family member or a friend involved in the activity (29 percent) and through participation in a group or organization (31 percent).

From another angle, the volunteers surveyed said that these were the reasons they were volunteers:

- Thought they would enjoy the work, feel needed.   29%
- Wanted to be useful, help others, do good deeds.   45%
- Wanted to learn and get experience, help get a job.   11%
- Child, relatives, or friends in program.   23%
- Religious concerns.   21%
- Had a lot of free time.   6%
- Had an interest in activity or work.   35%
- Thought it would keep taxes down.   5%

The obvious question is what do these volunteers do? For what causes do they volunteer? Drawing on the Gallup Surveys, the general categories are these:

- Religion   19%
- Health   12%
- Education   12%
- Recreation   7%
- Community Action   6%
- Citizenship   6%
- General Fundraising   6%
- Political   6%
- Social Welfare   5%
- Arts and Culture   3%
- Other   18%

There have been several important changes in patterns of volunteering in the past several years. People are more likely to be involved in more than one cause. They are more likely to spread their volunteering over several different causes. They are also more likely to be interested in advocacy and activism. While people are still willing to be involved in what might be described as service volunteering, they also want to make a difference through petitions, studies, testimony, and other forms of active citizen participation. Another difference involves the number of women who work. Although they are still likely to be volunteers, they rarely can give that full day or several evenings to the church or hospital.

With these changes in the patterns of volunteering and volunteers, the situation facing the volunteer recruiter is either very bad news or very good news. For the organization that is still trying to get large amounts of time from a relatively few middle-class and upper-class women in the immediate neighborhood, the picture is discouraging. For the recruiter willing to include a broader spectrum of geography, gender, age, and economic group, and willing to break the assignments down into more reasonable sizes, the news is very good. In addition, this broader outreach can spread news of the institution and its program activities and can increase its influence and impact.

It is important to add one more thought on this matter of advocacy and service. For a while, some of the women's organizations characterized volunteering as demeaning to women. They characterized volunteers and voluntary organizations as "do gooderism" in the most negative sense. I always point out that the women's movement and activist women's organizations are among the most encouraging examples of voluntary initiative, adding that the most significant contribution of volunteers and voluntary organizations has been in the great crusades involving human rights. However, if some people choose also to be involved in direct service to help others, this, too, is an important way to make a difference. It helps causes and people. It humanizes an organization's approach to its job, and it provides a degree of citizen education that often leads to the most effective advocacy.

One aspect of personal service relates to the burgeoning growth of what we call the self-help movement but for which the British have the much better term "mutual aid." The mutual help movement is the fastest growing side of the voluntary sector. For almost every problem, there is now a group of people who have weathered the storm and are reaching out to help others newly faced with depression, alcoholism, divorce, physical abuse, heart surgery, or almost any imaginable vulnerability.

Some people look at all these advocacy and mutual help activities and suggest that this is not volunteering, "at least in the old or real sense." I often hear people say that volunteering should describe only the act of helping others who are less fortunate. These same people almost always use the barn-raising as their quintessential example. I believe as passionately as they that one of the best motivations and forms of volunteering is embodied in the religious teachings involving charity to others. But we can't ascribe our tradition of voluntary action solely to these lessons and examples of goodness. The matter of pure need and mutual assistance cannot be overlooked. The minutemen and the frontier families who built one another's barns practiced pretty basic forms of enlightened self-interest. To portray our history of volunteering as relating solely to goodness may describe the best of our forebears, but it ignores the widespread tradition of organized neighborliness which hardship dictated and goodness tempered.

The important thing is that more people are involved in all kinds of causes today and have more opportunities to influence their lives and to be of service to others. Happily, we have moved by stages from the exclusive level of Lord and Lady Bountiful, through the period of the elite "400" and the years of the concentrated power structure, and are now beginning to recognize that participatory democracy is everybody's business. We owe a debt of gratitude to Dorothea Dix and her kind and to the community fathers who served so many causes; but the grandest huzzahs should be reserved for the here and now when democracy has truly come alive with all parts of the population joining in the traditions of service and reform. Today, anyone who cares and who is prepared to do something about the caring can make a difference.

We usher, collect, inform, protest, assist, teach, heal, contribute, build, advocate, comfort, testify, support, solicit, canvas, demonstrate, guide, criticize, organize, appeal, and—in a hundred other ways—serve people and causes.

Many people don't understand how much volunteering means to our society, or even have a grasp of the dimensions of it, because this is an aspect of our national life that we take for granted and have never really felt a need to study. Now that there seems to be a growing realization that citizen participation is a vital part of our national character, there is a greater interest in having a clearer grasp of the facts, trends, and impact.

Misunderstanding exists on the giving side also. Most people assume that foundations and corporations represent a very large proportion of giving in America. As important as their dollars are, the two combined represent only 10 percent of all that is given. Ninety percent comes from individuals.

Most people assume that wealthy individuals represent the bulk of personal giving, but in fact just about half of all charitable dollars comes from families with incomes under $25,000.

Also, people with incomes under $10,000 contribute proportionately about three times more of their income than do people with incomes of $50,000 to $100,000. In 1982 the figure was 3.85 percent compared with 1.35 percent. Even in families with incomes of $5,000 or less, the average amount given in 1982 was almost $300, which was about 5 percent of their income.

A 1981 Gallup Poll devoted to giving pointed out that approximately 90 percent of all American adults make contributions to the causes of their choice.

According to *Giving U.S.A.*, published by the American Association of Fund-Raising Counsel, these are the general areas to which we give our contributions:

- Religion   46.5%
- Education   14.5%
- Health and Hospitals   13.9%
- Social Welfare   10.5%
- Arts and Humanities   8.2%
- Civic and Public   2.8%
- Other   3.9%

These general causes or categories are represented by at least one million specific voluntary organizations to which we give our time and money. Were there an accurate count of churches or of local units of national organizations, or of the thousands of organizations that do not have to apply for tax-exempt status, we would be dealing with several million organizations in the independent sector.

Not surprisingly, the persons who volunteer are much more likely to contribute dollars, too, and give not just to the voluntary organizations with which they work, but to charity in general. Ninety-one percent of all volunteers make charitable contributions, compared with 66 percent among nonvolunteers.

John W. Gardner has noted that:

The sector encompasses a remarkable array of American institutions—libraries, museums, religious organizations, schools and colleges, organizations concerned with health and welfare, citizen action groups, neighborhood organizations and countless other groups such as Alcoholics Anonymous, The Urban League, the 4-H Clubs, the Women's Political Caucus, the Salvation Army and the United Way.

Americans have always believed in pluralism—the idea that a free nation should be hospitable to many sources of initiative, many kinds of institutions, many conflicting beliefs and many competing economic units. Our pluralism allows individuals and groups to pursue goals that they themselves formulate, and out of that pluralism has come virtually all of our creativity.

Beyond the urgent causes and crusades, the independent sector simply provides people with a chance to do their own thing—to be different—to be free—to be unique. In *The Endangered Sector*, Waldemar Nielsen summarizes the variety of interests that Americans freely pursue through their voluntary organizations:

> If your interest is people, you can help the elderly by a contribution to the Grey Panthers; or teenagers through the Jean Teen Scene of Chicago; or young children through your local nursery school; or everyone by giving to the Rock of All Ages in Philadelphia.

> If your interest is animals, there is the ASPCA and Adopt-A-Pet; if fishes, the Isaac Walton League; if birds, the American Homing Pigeon Institute or the Easter Bird Banding Association.

> If you are a WASP, there is the English Speaking Union and the Mayflower Descendants Association; if you have a still older association with the country, there is the Redcliff Chippewa Fund or the Museum of the American Indian.

> If your vision is local, there is the Cook County Special Bail Project and Clean Up the Ghetto in Philadelphia; if national, there is America the Beautiful; if global, there is the United Nations Association; if celestial, there are the Sidewalk Astronomers of San Francisco.

> If you are interested in tradition and social continuity, there is the society for the Preservation of Historic Landmarks and the Portland Friends of Cast Iron Architecture; if social change is your passion there is Common Cause; and, if that seems too sober for you, there is the Union of Radical Political Revolutionary Satire in New York.

> If your pleasure is music, there is a supermarket of choices—from Vocal Jazz to the Philharmonic Society to the American Guild of English Hand Bellringers.

If you don't know quite what you want, there is Get Your Head Together, Inc. of Glen Ridge, New Jersey. If your interests are contradictory, there is the Great Silence Broadcasting Foundation of California. If they are ambiguous, there is the Tombstone Health Service of Arizona.

John W. Gardner has added, "If you can't find a nonprofit institution that you can honestly disrespect, then something has gone wrong with our pluralism."

All this voluntary effort and the giving that supports it enable us to be unique as individuals and as a society. Through our voluntary initiative and independent institutions, ever more Americans worship freely, study quietly, are cared for compassionately, experiment creatively, serve effectively, advocate aggressively, and contribute generously. These national traits are constantly beautiful and, we hope, will remain beautifully constant.

Part II

Making a Difference:
The Role of the Board

4

The Role of the Board
and Board Members

AN INTERESTING LIST of objectives for the ideal board member, attributed to Michael Davis of the Rosenwald Fund, has endured for about fifty years. Here are five of his best:

> Know why the organization exists, and annually review why it should.

> Give money, or help get it, or both.

> Face budgets with courage, endowments with doubt, deficits with dismay and recover quickly from the surplus.

> Interpret the organization's work to the public in words of two syllables.

> Combine a New England sense of obligation with an Irish sense of humor.

Boards of directors differ according to the organization's size and age; if it functions as a federation or a single institution; if it has a staff; and whether it is a service organization with the board having ultimate authority or a cause-oriented association where the membership body shares responsibility.

There are some universal truths applicable to every nonprofit organization, beginning with legal responsibility. Whether as board members you are called

19

trustees, directors, governors, or something else, you are in essence the trustees in the literal and legal sense of the term. No matter how the organization is structured or the degree of authority delegated to staff, committees, or affiliates, the board and therefore the trustees are ultimately accountable.

In the 1984 court action in New Jersey involving an organization called "Friends of Clinton Hill," a sympathetic judge listened to the board members' reasons for not knowing that their association had failed to pay the government for income taxes withheld or for social security taxes. He described these volunteers with such terms as selfless, dedicated, and compassionate but said nevertheless that the law left him no alternative but to hold them accountable for all such taxes and stiff interest penalties.

Whether it is a service agency or a cause-oriented membership association, the board has the principal responsibility for fulfillment of the organization's mission and the legal accountability for its operations. Usually the bylaws stipulate something like "the affairs of the corporation are vested with the board." There have been several legal cases where board members were held legally accountable, largely because they had failed to exercise reasonable oversight and objectivity. When those cases are reported in the papers, the trustees are often quoted as "not having seen financial reports," "not having known," or "not aware that the organization had contracted with a firm owned by one of the staff or board members"—or in other ways making clear that the trustees had not taken responsibility for knowing what was going on.

The law, however, is fair as long as the trustees' attention to responsibility is reasonable. Joseph Weber, former head of the Greater New York Fund, pointed out in "Managing the Board of Directors" that "this does not mean that a director needs to fear liability for every corporate loss or mishap that may occur. On the contrary, a Director is generally protected from liability for errors of judgment as long as he or she acts responsibly and in good faith, and with the basic interests of the corporation as the foremost objective."

Although the legal responsibility is real and some boards and agencies are highly complex, the role of the board should still be seen in the fairly simple framework of, "What have we trustees agreed to be accountable for?"

I have been through hundreds of books, pamphlets and training manuals relating to boards of directors and find that most of them try to deal with bylaws, policies, committees, recognition, and other specifics before or even in lieu of dealing with the basic question of what they are accountable for. I find it helpful to start with the standards of performance by which organizations are held accountable and then work backward to see how the board can be sure that the organization passes those tests.

Two groups that have worked for years to develop and summarize the basic standards for voluntary organizations are the National Charities Information Bureau (NCIB) and the Philanthropic Advisory Service of the Council of Better Business Bureaus (CBBB).

In 1984, NCIB outlined these basic standards:

Philanthropic organizations have a high degree of responsibility because of the public trusteeship involved. Compliance with the following standards, with reasonable evidence supplied on request, is considered essential for approval by the NCIB.

1. Board—An active and responsible governing body, holding regular meetings, whose members have no material conflict of interest and serve without compensation.

2. Purpose—A clear statement of purpose in the public interest.

3. Program—A program consistent with the organization's stated purpose and its personnel and financial resources, and involving inter-agency cooperation to avoid duplication of work.

4. Expenses—Reasonable program, management and fund-raising expenses.

5. Promotion—Ethical publicity and promotion excluding exaggerated or misleading claims.

6. Fundraising—Solicitation of contributions without payment of commissions or undue pressure, such as mailing unordered tickets or merchandise, general telephone solicitation and use of identified government employees as solicitors.

7. Accountability—An annual report available on request that describes program activities and supporting services in relation to expenses and that contains financial statements comprising a balance sheet, a statement of support/revenue and expenses and changes in fund balances, a statement of functional expenses, and notes to financial statements that are accompanied by the report of an independent public accountant. National organizations operating with affiliates should provide combined or acceptably compiled financial statements prepared in the foregoing manner. For its analysis NCIB may request disclosure of accounting treatment of various items included in the financial statements.

8. Budget—Detailed annual budget approved by the governing body in a form consistent with annual financial statements.*

---

* Reprinted from "Standards for Voluntary Organizations" with permission from the National Charities Information Bureau.

The Council of Better Business Bureau's list is called "Standards for Charitable Solicitation." Because they relate substantially to fundraising practices, they are fairly extensive. Some of them are covered in the chapter on fundraising. Those most relevant to the board's role and performance are listed below.

Governance

1. Soliciting organizations shall have an adequate governing structure.

2. Soliciting organizations shall have an active governing body.

3. Soliciting organizations shall have an independent governing body.

Use of Funds

1. A reasonable percentage of income from all sources shall be applied to programs and activities directly related to the purposes for which the organization exists.

2. A reasonable percentage of public contributions shall be applied to programs and activities described in solicitations, in accordance with donor expectations.

3. Fundraising costs shall be reasonable.

4. Total fundraising and administrative costs shall be reasonable.

5. Soliciting organizations shall substantiate on request their application of funds in accordance with donor expectations, to the programs and activities described in solicitation.

6. Soliciting organizations shall establish and exercise adequate controls over disbursements.

Public Accountability

1. Soliciting organizations shall provide on request an annual report.

2. Soliciting organizations shall provide on request complete annual financial statements.

3. Soliciting organizations' financial statements shall present adequate information to serve as a basis for informed decisions.

4. Organizations receiving a substantial portion of their income through the fundraising activities of controlled or affiliated entities shall provide or request an accounting of all income received by and fundraising costs incurred by such entities.*

---

* Reprinted from "Standards for Charitable Solicitation" with permission from the Council of Better Business Bureaus.

It's revealing that both standard-setting bodies emphasize the role of the board itself. Although it may seem simplistic to say that the first role of the board is to be sure that the board is fulfilling its role, that's often the last place where accountability is exercised. Board members blame staff, committees, the fundraising chairman, the treasurer, and everyone else for failures in the operation, but rarely take a look at whether the board itself meets the kind of standards laid down for boards by NCIB and CBBB.

In "Major Challenges to Philanthropy," a paper commissioned by INDE-PENDENT SECTOR, Robert L. Payton, President of the Exxon Education Foundation, put it on the line:

> As a group, it is the trustees who are most important in protecting the standards of philanthropy. If you smile at that, knowing from your own experience of trustees whose ignorance or single-mindedness made them part of the problem rather than part of the solution, I also smile—but in pained discomfort. Like it or not, the trustees are the structural bulwark defending the public interest in philanthropy. And if I'm right about that, then the education of trustees claims a very high priority on our collective agenda.

Their standards affect other fundamental ways by which the organization fulfills its accountability, such as financial reporting and evaluation. Several of the chapters in this book attempt to deal with those subjects. I want to deal here with some of the unique aspects of the *board's* responsibility to be sure that these functions are fulfilled.

At its core, the board's job is to be sure that the organization measures up to the standards, not just as an evaluator but as *the* sole group responsible for seeing that the organization develops the capacity to meet the standards. Trustees can't sit back and be the high court or critic; likewise, trustees can't hide behind the myth that it is the board's responsibility to make policy and the staff's responsibility to carry it out.

For a moment, it is useful to imagine the board's role if the organization did not have a staff. If an association were run entirely by volunteers, the accountability would be much clearer. One can't just make decisions and then walk away without being sure those decisions are translated into practice and results.

In a very helpful publication, "Trustee Responsibilities," published by the Association of Governing Boards, John W. Nason lists twelve functions. They are written for educational institutions, but are applicable to almost all nonprofit organizations. To that end, I've substituted the title of chief staff officer for president.

Appointing the chief staff officer.

Supporting the chief staff officer.

Monitoring the chief staff officer's performance.

Clarifying the institution's mission.

Approving long-range plans.

Overseeing the educational program.

Insuring financial solvency.

Preserving institutional independence.

Enhancing the public image.

Interpreting the community to the organization.

Serving as a court of appeal.

Assessing board performance.

These functions are similar to any description of the board of directors of a business corporation, but in many ways the nonprofit organization depends far more on its board for fulfillment of the organization's goals. Indeed, the smaller the organization, the greater is the dependence on volunteer performance.

Kenneth N. Dayton, former chief executive officer of Dayton Hudson, serves on many corporate, foundation and large and small voluntary agency boards and has this to say about the similarities and differences in the boards' responsibilities:

> It is my experience that a board's role in the governance of nonprofit organizations—both philanthropic and voluntary—is exactly the same as it is in for-profit corporations.
>
> This covers moral and legal responsibility, strategy determination, allocation of resources, goal setting, evaluation of performance, rewarding and motivating management, making the tough decisions on top personnel, and being willing and available to assist in the areas of special experience. (It also involves strengthening the Board itself—determining criteria for membership and setting policies for tenure and rotation.)
>
> Those board roles are absolutely essential to the effectiveness of all public corporations—profit and nonprofit. Contrary to popular notion, I've found that it is often on the nonprofit side that boards take those responsibilities most seriously.

Dayton's last point about the degree of responsibility exercised by volunteer trustees contradicts other perceptions, but if one thinks about it, although the businessperson serving as an outside director of a corporation might take that responsibility seriously in terms of prestige, attendance, and legal liability, he or she really knows that the trustee's role means far more to the success of the institution in the voluntary world. A business corporation obviously needs its board for legal and practical reasons, but it isn't nearly so dependent on those *individuals* for its income and community outreach. Nor is it likely that corporate board members serve on the sales, marketing and manufacturing committees as they do on the nonprofit organization's rehabilitation, fundraising and public relations committees.

Perhaps even more important is the degree to which voluntary organizations look to individual trustees for leadership. Beyond all the essential procedures and participation to assure accountability, the board of the nonprofit organization has a substantial but rarely defined responsibility and opportunity for leadership.

The National Charities Information Bureau has an extensive checklist under the heading "What a Good Board Member Does"; it's significant that the first point is "inspires and leads."

Usually when we think of leaders and leadership, we envision the towering giant who can do anything or the charismatic magician who can get the rest of us to do anything. In "A Guide For New Trustees," Nancy Axelrod of the Association of Governing Boards quoted a *Wall Street Journal* article which described the ideal board member as "a man or woman with the versatility of Leonardo da Vinci, the financial acumen of Bernard Baruch, and the scholarly bent of Erasmus."

Most leadership actually comes from ordinary people who have it in them to rise to responsibility. These people are all around us leading thousands of community and national institutions through conviction, hard work, and quiet ability to help individuals and organizations see their own roles and worth.

In all of the resource materials I've been reviewing, most of the experts enumerate the kinds of professional experience an organization will need on the board and pay no attention to personal qualities. But when I look at what makes a board tick, it's often the ability to work together that counts and this depends on qualities that lend themselves to team work. Cyril O. Houle, in *The Effective Board*, says, "Organization is merely the way by which people relate themselves to one another so as to achieve their common purposes."

Because I've learned this lesson so totally and am so pained to see others preoccupied with the buzz word "expertise," I want to dwell a bit to try to communicate what I mean and how much I mean it. For years I have been watching boards and making mental notes of the personal qualities of people who become the formal or informal leaders. If I were restricted to one quality, I would single out the ability to start and end every analysis and evaluation with the standard of what is right. As simple as that may seem, it is too rarely in evidence. Determining what is right becomes obscured in a multiplicity of other considerations which so confuse the analysis that decisions are far too often made without primary consideration of what, in fact, is right. One of the most significant lessons I've learned is that when I let other factors intervene, such as timidity, ambition, wanting to please, and all the other things that come to the fore when we're asked to speak our minds, I generally end up using poor judgment. On the positive side, there have been times when, for one persuasive reason or another, I did not want to take on a hassle or be in the minority, but I persisted and subsequently learned that by following the rule of doing what was right, my point was won or at least respected, and to have done otherwise would have been wrong in every respect.

As hard as it often is to figure out what is right, that approach frequently makes even complex matters surprisingly clear and their solutions fairly obvious. I've seen boards struggle interminably with decisions, only to have someone bring them gently back to the starting place by pointing out that they first have to articulate what is right and then concentrate on how to achieve it. Often groups prefer not to struggle with this primary consideration or want to bound off under the false assumption that there is a common grasp of the issue. Just as often, the board will erroneously assume that what is right is unachievable and will proceed from there without really shaking the hell out of that assumption.

It's important not to be among those who feel they must stand up and be counted on every issue. Those kinds are pains in the neck and usually confuse personal privilege with principle. As a private habit, though, it's important to begin each analysis with the standard of "what is right" foremost in mind before moving on to the "what ifs" and "so whats." By starting there and ending there we at least know what the basic issue is. That's a comfort in itself, and in addition, the exercise of the standard provides a healthy discipline.

The second most important quality of a leader I've observed is fairness. This, too, is simple in concept but difficult in application. It's obviously related to any determination of what is right, but it is important in itself. For one thing, it lends to leadership an important and attractive kindness.

Sometimes what is fair to some people is in conflict with what is right. What's right may have long-range considerations but might not be fair to people caught in the short-term consequences. At least by determining what is right and what is fair, we have a better grasp of all considerations and may be able to minimize the consequences or provide compensation to those unfairly affected.

Fairness also involves giving credit to others for their contributions. Not only is this an important attribute, but it's amazing how much mileage it gains an individual. It is rarely done, at least with grace and sincerity.

Toughness and sensitivity are a necessary combination of characteristics for good leadership. It's a beautiful thing to see the individual who sticks tenaciously to a plan or a goal yet can still remain attuned to the human side of the enterprise. Successful leaders often handle themselves so badly that we marvel that they ever could have become successful. The answer is that they've forgotten or underestimated how much a part of their success involved alertness to moods, feelings and needs. It's almost an axiom of success that fairly quickly the toughness survives and the sensitivity subsides. The leader who can go the long haul is one who can somehow manage to keep these two qualities in balance.

I'm at a level of activity where I can see some of the former young superstars beginning to be passed over because, while they are still spectacular individual doers, they haven't the patience or reasonable team play necessary to pull together a really large operation.

In the reverse, it's fascinating to see some of the sleepers coming to the fore. Supported by their peers, they've grown quietly and steadily in organizing opportunities and abilities.

Jesse Jackson says there are two kinds of bright young leaders, the "stars" and the "satellites." "Satellites burn very bright in the sky," he says. "They outshine the stars for awhile, but they burn themselves out and they just disappear. But the stars come out every night. They have pace."

Related to pace and peer support, but deserving separate mention, is reliability. There's no need to dwell on it, but suffice it to say that depending on people who aren't reliable is a nightmare and working with people who are is a delight.

The next quality involves contradictory characteristics. It's controlled ambition. Ambition is a healthy trait, but when it's out of control there's nothing less appealing. I delight in watching a person who is able and ambitious but who has learned that the way to achieve important goals is to subordinate the ambition to fairness with a dash of humility blended in.

There is an apt Chinese proverb that says, "Those who lead well will know that their followers might say that they led themselves."

Given the above difficult combinations of attractive qualities, it's probably not surprising that the next characteristic of the best board members and leaders is flexibility. Maybe it's assumed that anyone who possesses the qualities mentioned would have to be flexible, but I've seen many people who seem to have everything going for them still miss the mark, and the problem invariably comes down to inflexibility. People who are capable often learn early in life that they are special, and this unfortunately leads to excessive confidence in their own judgment and capacities. Gradually doubt recedes, humor gets pushed into the background, and temper shows more often. The person who knows what is right, is tough, efficient, and ambitious, and has had success and recognition tends to become impressed with himself or herself, and begins not to look at each new situation in its own right. Adding flexibility to the blend of fairness, sensitivity, and imagination helps the product to rise.

I can't leave out enthusiasm either. I can hope that people will have a strong sense of humor, but I can survive, for the short run, if they don't. But lack of enthusiasm I can't quite survive. Thornton Wilder provided this counsel:

It's your business not to be eager about the thousand and one things in the night-sky of knowledge, but to be enthusiastic about the one or two constellations that you have marked down for your own . . . Count that month lost in which you have not been swept up in an enthusiasm.

Ralph Waldo Emerson put it even more definitely. He said, "Nothing was ever accomplished without enthusiasm."

Although I obviously believe that these personal qualities are even more important than specific skills, I realize that they don't satisfy the usual questions about specific responsibilities. I've also learned that it's not sufficient to give the simple reply that each trustee is responsible for assuring that the board as a whole is fulfilling its accountability through planning, execution, and evaluation, although that is still the best answer.

In *The Volunteer Board Member In Philanthropy*, the National Charities Information Bureau lists the qualities of good board members. They:

1. Are dedicated to helping others and modest in the light of their responsibilities as board members.

2. Approach their responsibilities in the spirit of a trustee on behalf of contributors, their intended beneficiaries, and the public at large.

3. Stand up for their convictions, even at the cost of misunderstanding or disapproval in business or social life.

4. Back up other board members and staff, rising to their defense when they are unjustly criticized or attacked.

5. Treat staff as a partner in a high calling, maintaining overall supervision and control but not interfering with day-to-day administration.

6. Avoid being overawed by others on the board, whether they be executive staff; tycoons of business, labor or society; professionals in social work, education, medicine, etc.

7. Welcome information and the best available advice, but reserve the right to arrive at decisions on the basis of their own judgment.

8. Respect the right of other board members and of staff to disagree with them and to have a fair hearing of their points of view.

9. Accept as routine that decisions must be made by majority vote and will at times go against one or more members.

10. Criticize, when necessary, in a constructive way, if possible suggesting an alternative course.

11. Recognize that time and energy are limited and that over-commitment may prove self-defeating.

12. Endeavor to keep disagreements and controversies impersonal and to promote unity.

13. Maintain loyalty to their agency, within a higher loyalty to the welfare of the community and humanity as a whole.*

---

* Reprinted with permission from The National Charities Information Bureau.

I've been through enough board orientation and training sessions to know that many of you newer board members are frustrated and maybe even exasperated and want to shout, "But you still haven't told me what I'm supposed to do!"

On the most basic level, you, as a board member, should understand the mission of the organization, attend board meetings, serve actively on at least one committee, be certain that you and the board as a whole are in control of planning and evaluation, contribute to a sense of camaraderie and teamwork, and ask questions.

At least half of those board members who wanted me to say *exactly* what they should do are now exclaiming, "That doesn't seem enough!" If it's any help, I can pretty much guarantee that if you'll do those things the rest will become obvious.

Most lists of fundamentals refer to the trustee's role in raising money. The veteran fundraiser Harold Seymour used to put it bluntly: "Contribute wealth, wisdom and work." Today, in our efforts to be more representative, it's not fair to put the arm on everybody for $10,000 or even $500. On the other hand, I think it is fair to ask all board members, within their means and spheres of contacts, to contribute as much as they can and to help raise money. Asking for this help should be the responsibility of other volunteers and not the staff, and no board member should feel above these obligations.

Just a word on another basic responsibility involving the importance of asking questions. If you don't understand the financial statements or the budget or the issue being voted on, ask questions. Sometimes these are better asked ahead of time or during the break so that you are not taking up too much time, and you can use these opportunities to get a bit of tutoring in areas where you are not as knowledgeable as others. However, the ultimate and necessary task is to understand what you are voting on. I can guarantee that other trustees will be grateful that someone else admits confusion, which will lead to a broader sense of comfort in asking even more questions. If you are accountable and don't understand it, where does that leave you and the organization?

There is a balance between not being intimidated into inactivity and at the same time not feeling guilty if you don't understand everything. Pick the areas that really seem important and on which others don't seem to be coming forward. Don't be critical of yourself or others because you or they don't seem to understand or don't have an interest in everything. It's not realistic to expect that all board members will have an interest in or a grasp of all the things the organization is doing. My experience is that voluntary agency boards of any size are rarely composed of individuals who have across-the-board interest or knowledge. I find that if a board is effectively organized, some people participating will have an intense interest in certain topics and others will have a like interest in other issues and that, in toto, the group will provide an effective screen for all the issues and reasonable discussion of them.

Boards tend to build and perpetuate more structure than is necessary and thus obscure comprehension and accountability. You don't have to reach the extreme point of needing a committee on committees to know that too much time is going into organization. It's amazing how quickly organizations become occupied with committee structure and with involved procedures and complicated lines of authority to the point where the organization ends up serving its structure and not its mission.

The structure of a service agency can be a good deal simpler than that of a federation or cause-oriented association that has a large voting membership and many affiliates. The latter may need a far larger board that is more representative of many constituencies, and the board will need to be extremely careful in the division of activities and power with the voting membership, delegate assembly or whatever the larger group is called. On the other hand, the smaller board related to the service organization will have the disadvantage of not having the fuller groups to draw on for proven leadership. It will have the advantage of simpler structure and lines of authority, but will pay a price in limited outreach. Thus, the board members for the service organization must be chosen very carefully to compensate for the shortcomings in outreach, experience, representation, and proven commitment. The importance of this factor is compounded by the small size of the board, which makes each place count all the more.

Because of size and fewer opportunities to come up through the ranks of the organization, attendance at board meetings is all the more important in the service operation. That's also necessary in order to build a sense of responsibility. People will come into the organization without much prior exposure or sense of continuity and will be inclined to be passive and a bit too respectful of the leadership. It's helpful to realize that on the surface the board will seem less important because the staff is so much in charge, but you will need to overcome the disadvantage of that and work all the harder at building a sense of responsibility and participation.

Whatever the kind of board, don't be afraid of healthy give and take. Among other things, it builds a sense of family. Board meetings should be viewed as healthy arenas for controversy. If the issues are laid out in advance, well formulated and clearly presented, and if sufficient time is available for debate, then it is healthy and constructive for all board members to question, debate and disagree.

One of the faults of nonprofit organizations is that the leaders strive for compromise and for unanimous votes. My experience has been that if you are dealing with real issues, striving too hard for compromise and unity may mean that you are not facing squarely the issues themselves, you don't have the right mix of people, or you've watered down the issues until they're harmless and impotent. It's far healthier to have a split vote as long as the issues are on the table, the debate is fair and there has been sufficient time for consideration.

Providing for fair and objective consideration is easier said than done. Those in charge of the meeting often have strong feelings about the issues, meetings are usually too short for any real discussion; and there is too little advance dissemination of the facts to prepare people for adequate debate and vote.

If there is significant controversy, the organization must take the time to present the issues before the board so that the matter can be decided without feeling that something has been put over on people. There will always be the temptation to slip a touchy matter through to avoid hurt feelings or ill will, or to let the executive committee handle a matter simply because it is potentially upsetting. Don't tolerate any of it. Be certain that a proper process is available and that this process is objectively and fairly followed to the letter.

It is far better to lose even on critical issues as long as the organization comes out of the battle with greater confidence in the integrity of the process. It's also better to take additional time for debate and decision on major items than to put them behind you. For instance, on a major issue I always suggest that the matter should come up initially for reaction and discussion without a vote, even though this means postponement. It is more conducive to correct decision-making and to confidence in the system to take extra time for consideration and review. Even on lesser matters, I generally favor having the board consider issues at one board meeting for vote at the next. Committee chairpersons and staff members are almost always dismayed when I recommend this process. Usually they have worked hard on a project, on guidelines, or on a position statement, and they feel it's imperative that the vote be taken as soon as possible. My approach is that if the matter is so important, it's worth being sure that the people know the issues. I also believe that with this course there is more likely to be followership once the vote is taken.

The posture of the leader should be one of patience, tolerance and flexibility. I include flexibility because leaders will often have their own biases, and yet they especially must be willing to seek out and hear new facts and different opinions. The more important the issue, the more intense the feelings and debate are apt to be. You will find some people dig in their heels very early and are adamant about a given position. You will also find that people tend to describe the issues as a matter of principle or moral right. Generally, if you look closer, you will find they have confused policies with principles, or rules and regulations with philosophy. It's helpful to delineate the important distinctions between philosophy, principles, policies, procedures, rules and regulations. It's easier to take something lower in the order too seriously simply by confusing it with a higher value.

Although this will not apply to the majority of readers, it is important to say something about the national board of an association with local chapters. It doesn't matter whether the national operation is organized as a corporate headquarters or the hub of a federation; it will still be the central entity and as such must provide dynamic leadership for the total organization. This includes responsibility for the organization's spirit, direction, thrust, policies and guidelines.

One basic way to reduce built-in tensions and to keep the national level attuned to local needs is to be sure that the national board of directors is composed overwhelmingly of people who come from the affiliates. Even if your organization operates as a tight national corporation, there can't be correct decision-making and follow through without local volunteers having a substantial part in making the decisions. On the national level, the organization should be very largely peopled and run by individuals who have current or at least recent experience on the firing line. The local affiliates must feel it's *their* national association or, regardless of how dynamic the leadership, there won't be followership.

Even if you achieve the ultimate in representation, don't expect that harmony will automatically follow. You will still have to work hard at it. Remember Pogo's discovery: "We have met the enemy and he is us."

The object of all the lessons to minimize friction and create unity is to use the wonderful volunteer energy and time to fight for the cause and not against one another.

That's a pretty good rule for the role of all boards and board members.

5

The Role of the President

Many presidents of voluntary organizations confide that they're well into the job before they really understand what it's all about. This is a sorry state of affairs, particularly because much of what the president's term will mean can be represented by what is accomplished during the first months on the job. The planning, recruiting, orienting, training, and other essential leadership functions have to be accomplished, and accomplished very early, if the operation is to have sensible direction and exciting thrust. It's toward the goal of early preparation that the following urgent suggestions are made.

Mr. or Mme. President, you are the person morally responsible for your public agency. No matter how inadequate you may feel on the job, or even if you have people to whom you can delegate, you are the person who is accountable to your fellow citizens for the expenditure of their dollars contributed to help your agency pursue its service to society.

One of the biggest problems for voluntary agencies, particularly those large enough to have a staff, is that the presidents do not really perform as presidents, usually because they exaggerate the role of the staff. Because this is such a significant failing of voluntary agencies, and because the effective fulfillment of the role of president makes such a fantastic difference in the thrust of an agency, I have separated my comments concerning the presidential role from discussion of relative roles of staff and volunteers. The next chapter will deal with that topic, but now I want to try as hard as I possibly can to help presidents grasp how important they are.

Even if the organization has a staff, a president should step back and view the job from the perspective of an agency with no staff. It may assist you to understand your presidential identity and responsibility if you imagine, at least at an early stage and perhaps periodically during your term, what your task would be like if you did not have staff backup. In an unstaffed Parent-Teachers Association, for example, the president is responsible for the recruitment, orientation, stimulation, and follow-up of all committee chairpersons; and unless the president functions, the organization doesn't go anywhere.

Look at your own table of organization—you probably won't see staff members on it. Such organizational charts usually include the board of directors, executive committee, president, and committee chairpersons, and that's the way you should see your job. You are the president, and you've got to go through the basic steps required of the chief of any operation. You are the person most essential to the agency's performance and, as such, the basic leadership responsibilities rest with you. These responsibilities include planning, recruiting, motivating, coordinating, and evaluating.

One of the problems of large voluntary operations is that planning becomes a staff responsibility. Thus, the volunteers themselves aren't really deciding where the organization should be going, and as a consequence the volunteers don't feel the vital commitment necessary to fulfill ambitious plans. You, as president, have to bring planning back to the volunteer side. And believe me, this is tough to do. Even the aspirations you have, and indeed may have voiced in your inaugural speech, are easily suffocated in the day-to-day crises and tasks that so easily absorb the time you give. As a result of lack of planning, you, the president, become absorbed with what the organization serves up rather than exercising your real opportunity to accomplish the things you set out to achieve.

To remedy this, I sit down as early as possible with my incoming president, and I urge him or her to decide on the one, two, or—at the most—three things that he or she wants most to have accomplished when the term is finished. Most presidents make the mistake of starting out with too many aspirations, hoping that somehow they can achieve all those exciting goals. Unfortunately, they don't really pin down what it will take to accomplish the goals. Then, because of a lack of focus or the press of immediate problems, the goals never get identified firmly in the organization's mind and rarely are accomplished. Many presidents look back with regret that they never really got their teeth into some of the things that seemed so important to them at the beginning.

You, as president, should think hard and early about the things you really want to accomplish during your term. If the goals are realistic, then, despite all the other responsibilities that hit you, somehow you will reserve a portion of your energy and resources to move ahead on your special projects. But you have to plan. You have to decide now what it is you want your organization to have achieved one or two years from now. You've got to involve the board of directors in a shared commitment to those goals and help the organization accomplish them.

It's important not to seek too much change. An organization can sustain or survive only so much upset. Often a president wants to change too many things, with the result that the upset is destructive. In some cases total reorganization may be indicated, and this should be frankly reviewed with the board so that a basic decision can be made. If that's not the problem, then choose your areas carefully and concentrate on them. Thus, you won't be creating additional problems of morale, suspicion, or anger that would only stand in the way of accomplishing your goals. Another aspect of planning involves your own schedule. Be sure that you have cleared your docket to give the job the time and devotion it needs, and be sure that your family and associates are aware of the commitment and what it entails.

Involve the full board in deciding attainable goals and the best methods for achieving them. The basic rule is to involve the group in identifying attainable goals and agreeing to stick to them tenaciously. You'll find that at different stages your people will want to change strategy, expand unrealistically, or even retreat prematurely. Decide *together* what it is that needs to be done and how to go about it, and then tear into that effort with absolute conviction and resolve.

Keep in mind that you're probably a unique individual and probably a strong one. You have to be careful that your leadership does not dominate. Give others a chance to participate or they won't feel any ownership in the plan. Keep very much in mind that if it is an important cause, you can't do it alone and you will drive others away if you're too overbearing. One of the frustrations that you'll face is that it will probably be important to take some steps backward before moving forward. For instance, you may have been involved in the organization much longer than the others, or at least have a good deal more experience with some of the projects at hand, and you will assume that the group understands and accepts the facts as you see them and is ready to move forward. That's not very likely. The other trustees will probably have to cover some of that same ground for themselves. People have got to feel that they personally have gained a grasp of the facts and have a chance to sift through them before they develop a commitment to the course of action.

Often the president leaves the critical task of recruitment to the staff. This doesn't do the job. You, as president, have to decide who it is you really want to assist you in accomplishing the things you want to do, manage the ongoing activities, and deal effectively with the crises which are the day-to-day fare of a vibrant voluntary agency.

Don't take the easy way out by simply letting Joe have a fourth term, even though he hasn't been a very good chairman up to now. Don't just hope that Harry will be better in his second year than he was in his first. And don't let the fear of relationship problems stand in the way of doing what's right. These are things that an effective president of any good operation has to face up to, and unless you're willing to conscientiously undertake the job of recruitment of able people, the organization won't aggressively move forward to fulfill your aspirations or even perform its public mission.

Carefully analyze the jobs to be done and then spend a lot of time identifying the people qualified for them. This is worth a good deal of your time early on or even in advance of your administration. It will not only save time later but will make the difference in how much progress is made.

One mistake organizations make is to automatically recruit as leader the expert on the subject without regard to his or her organizing skills. We eagerly recruit people to do organizing jobs for which they may be utterly incapable. If we want to organize a community program to reduce the incidence of stroke, we tend to seek out the cardiologist most experienced with vascular accidents. If we want to organize an advisory board to a community mental health center, we look for psychiatrists and clinical psychologists. If we want to organize a local chapter of the American Cancer Society, we look for a radiologist. Experience instinctively leads me away from such experts as committee heads and toward people with organizing skills. While experts should be an important part of the committee, they are not likely to have the necessary organizational skills. Also, they may intimidate or otherwise turn off the very group of people whose enthusiasm and activity they should be building.

When setting out to recruit people, the approach is generally characterized by "get as many as you can—the more the better." The unfortunate result of all this enthusiastic freewheeling is that the recruiters almost always are overly optimistic, and when their accomplishments begin to fall short of aspirations, the whole effort tends to crumble. Instead, figure out how many people are needed and cautiously predict how many of this number can be recruited in the first six months or even the first year. Do it *realistically*. Set *attainable* targets. Divide the workload so that no one person is given an assignment in which failure is almost inevitable. Beware of the individual who wants to impress the group with how much he or she is going to do or how many cards she's going to take or how many friends he's going to sign up. A group that goes at building in a deliberate, realistic way (and this doesn't preclude fervor and determination) will be a lot farther ahead at the end of a year than the group put together by optimists who assume that their enthusiasm will carry the day.

Numbers are important, but so are the right people. Identify whom you need on your side to put together the facts or the strategy and who will have the capacity to put that strategy to work. There will be times when you won't want people who already occupy seats in the power structure because they represent the status quo and that's what you want to change. Do not asume that you can't get somebody and move ahead to form a committee of lesser impact. Identify the people, or at least the types of positions you need, and launch an effort to get the right persons to join you. You will be surprised how often they will say yes or lead you to other good people.

Effective people turn down appointments not because they are uninterested, but because the assignments are put to them in such a vague way that saying yes could lead into a bottomless pit of responsibility. Often we ask a person to come aboard without making clear exactly why we want him or her and without breaking the task down into reasonable proportions. If you want a member of the school board to join a committee looking at special education, ask him or her to sit in on those committee meetings that will include the topic. We make a mistake in assuming that in order to be effective someone has to join the committee or board, when we are likely to enlist more of the right people by involving them only in the bite-size ad hoc assignments for which they really are needed.

Break the job down into bite sizes and specific assignments so the individuals can grasp exactly what you want and will not be frightened by the implications of the commitment. Let them know you will be around to help. There is nothing worse than coming out of a hard sell only to wake up and find the leader acting as if he or she has got the sucker and is off to other victories. You have a responsibility to assist this individual in doing the very things you have been struggling with in your own assignment, including deciding what's needed, identifying the sources of help, and recruiting people.

The greatest temptation in recruiting volunteers is to make the job sound easy. It's natural to be eager to get a yes, but in the long run this deception will catch up with you. It is better to give the individual a clear picture of the assignment, so that when you get a yes, you will know you've got someone who is committed to getting the job done. It's better to get a few no's, than to end up with someone who isn't likely to produce or who can't be held accountable because there is no mutual understanding of what is to be done. Keep in mind that you want to come out of your recruiting effort with an individual who knows what is expected and is eagerly looking forward to getting it done.

Recruiting does involve enthusiasm. People have to know by your approach that this is something you believe in and that it merits their time and attention. People want a cause—even busy people are willing to be further involved, if they feel their service will make a difference. Don't assume that people already know about the cause. This applies even to persons who have been serving on committees or as board members. When you recruit someone for a key job, take the time to be sure that he or she knows the cause. This is likely to build a more positive frame of reference and a feeling of being part of something worthwhile.

Orientation begins during the recruitment process. This includes orientation to the cause, to the organization, and to the individual's job. Each person needs special attention, and the effectiveness of these efforts will often determine whether or not the individual in fact succeeds. Orientation is often dismissed by giving the poor individual an unbelievable amount of material that won't be read or understood. Think carefully about the persons your recruit should meet if he or she is to gain greater knowledge or enthusiasm about the cause and set up these appointments either on a one-to-one basis or in small groups. Put yourself in the place of the new person and figure out what he or she really needs to know in order to increase interest and enthusiasm and to effectively fulfill the assignment.

In addition to initial orientation to the cause and the agency, most volunteers should receive continuing orientation so that they will feel abreast of the agency's impact on the cause. Often orientation, if done at all, is limited to the first few weeks; then we assume individuals learn all they need to know from occasional contacts with the organization.

Every committee meeting and many board meetings should begin with an orientation segment that provides members with knowledge of major thrusts and activities of the organization. We often forget that a committee member has little knowledge of the organization beyond his or her own assignment. From this limited vantage point, he or she can hardly serve as an enthusiastic communicator to the outside world. The president or committee leader should use every communication channel possible to give the volunteers a continuing sense of the mission and activities of the operation. This is essential if the committee members are to know that their efforts make a difference. People want to feel part of an exciting cause but they won't get that feeling about your organization unless you, as the leader, take time to think through what they must know in order to carry out their jobs effectively, and what they would like to know in order to feel part of an exciting endeavor.

People will stay with your effort if they feel useful—that they are doing some good and that the agency represents a cause worth devoting their energy to. These factors, in turn, relate to the leader's responsibility (1) to give people jobs that are accomplishable, (2) to give them an awareness of the effectiveness of the good work the organization is doing, and (3) to offer every possible opportunity to learn that they are making a difference. Giving people responsibility commensurate with their abilities and levels of interest is also a key to retention. People are just as apt to walk away if they feel they are being underused as if they are being overused.

Most important causes require sustained effort and depend upon a great many volunteers working together in a systematic way. When a good-sized army is needed, a conscious effort must be devoted to building the organization. Many organizations gravely underestimate this and their voluntary operations are disastrous. Building an organization begins with training the current leaders to recognize the need to devote time and resources toward increasing the capacity of the operation. This may seem easily done, but it's usually not done at all. The leaders are so impatient to be on with the crusade that they assume that everybody feels the same fervor and knows what to do instinctively. An organization's leaders must be shown the necessity of building the organization to match the goals and they must have help in learning how to do it.

In training sessions for volunteer and staff leaders, I use a two-part presentation entitled "Achievements Worth Building For" and "Building for Greater Achievement." This provides an opportunity to present the accomplishments we can achieve, while at the same time making clear that the achievements will be realized only if we build an effective organization capable of such fulfillment.

Even after presidents have given realistic attention to planning, recruiting, and orientation, they usually leave the rest to staff or to chance. Staff members can carry a good share of the load of volunteer training and development, but your presence must still be felt. Your efforts in effectively involving your key subordinates in major activities and decision-making are essential. Keep in mind that these are your people. Committee heads, project chairpersons, and other officers are *your* subordinates. They want to know what *you* think; they want to know where *you* are going, they want to know how *you* perceive the organization, and they want to know what *you* consider important to be done.

Most presidents assume that this kind of thing just happens; that the executive has somehow communicated all these things; or that a past chairperson has oriented a successor; or even that a person, simply by having been a member of the board, has a grasp of the new and larger responsibility. There can't be cohesion in the organization without your involvement in orientation and training and without your giving a great deal of thought as to how to effectively motivate, inspire, and stimulate persons who will be carrying the major part of the load. The organization can't move as a unified phalanx toward the goals set by you and the board unless your key subordinates have participated with you in deciding where the organization is going and feel they are really an integral part of the operation.

You also must function as the motivator, encourager, and prodder. It's not sufficient to merely involve your subordinates in planning and assist in their orientation and training; you've got to provide regular opportunities for discussion of progress and problems. It's important to be on that phone five or six times during the year just to say, "Mary, how's it going? I heard about your meeting last week. I am sorry I couldn't get there, but I am delighted with what I hear about it. Is there anything I can do? We're putting you on the agenda of the board meeting and we're really looking forward to that report. I hope we'll get the material well in advance, so everybody can enjoy it and act intelligently on it."

Don't asume that if you're regularly communicating with the executive director, you're really touching base with your own subordinates. They are human beings, and an organization will respond far better if you, as the leader, are in touch with your subordinates in a human way. If they feel you're really interested, they'll respond; they'll perform similarly with the people responsible to them, and the total operation will be many times stronger. Obviously, it's important not to overlook the need of people to have their backs patted and, in some cases, their bottoms spanked—and only the president can perform these functions.

It's your responsibility to see that the activities which the officers, board of directors, and committee heads set out to do are being carried out. One of the basic approaches is to have certain checkpoints during the year. At these times, provide project and committee chairpersons with an opportunity to report at meetings of the executive committee and board of directors. It will also be important for you to stay close enough to be able to judge the progress or lack of it and to sit down with the chairpersons to discuss any impediments.

If a key subordinate is letting you down, face up to the task of replacement. Usually the individual will be relieved to be out from under the responsibility. But even if he or she is unhappy with your action, your larger responsibility is to the contributors of public money and to your community.

To have time for basic management responsibilities, it will be essential for you to avoid being directly responsible for immediate projects. Find people who can carry these projects for you. Your function and goal is to see that the volunteer talent of the organization is being developed. To the extent that you get trapped into assuming responsibility for individual projects and issues, you will not be using your limited time to expand the capacity of the organization to deal with an increasing number of projects and issues.

Be fully conditioned to the human relationship aspects of the role of president. Be prepared and leave time for dealing with many different personalities, most of whom at some point will need soothing, stroking, and encouragement.

Your success will be measured in three important ways: (1) the achievement of the things you set out to accomplish; (2) the fulfillment of the organization's other major projects and its response to the unexpected crises and opportunities; and (3) the increase in volunteer involvement, leadership, and responsibility that has been generated during your term.

Develop a checklist to gauge progress on the specific tasks set out at the beginning of the year and to measure increased volunteer activity. At mid-year sit down with some objective persons you can trust and take a hard look at the progress or lack of it. If you know that you're going to be doing this at various checkpoints, it will increase your determination to come off with good scores.

Over the years I've developed a list of "musts" for presidents. Individual situations vary, and perhaps not all of these will fit your circumstances, but my observation is that the president who rates well on this checklist will be running an exciting operation. On the other side, in the breakdowns I've seen of presidential leadership in nonprofit organizations, the failures can usually be traced to ignoring some of these musts:

- Decide in advance that your largest goal for the year will be to increase the degree of volunteer leadership within the organization.

- Be the president. This leadership role cannot be delegated to the staff, and to the extent that you are confused about your leadership responsibility or that you turn over this role to staff, your success will be compromised.

- Involve your key officers and other colleagues, including staff, in a planning session to effectively determine where you as a team want to be at the end of your term. Be sure that these plans are realistic and attainable. Be sure that the board of directors has the final opportunity to approve them.

- Approve all board of directors and executive committee meeting agendas and make certain that these are sent out at least ten days in advance of the meetings. Much of what you will be trying to do as the leader of the organization will be lost unless these meetings are *your* meetings and represent *your* checkpoints for progress toward the year's goals. It is essential that the agendas be sent in advance so thoughtful people can give thorough consideration to the issues.

- Involve your key subordinates and keep in regular personal touch with them.

- Appoint, orient, encourage, and follow up on your project and committee chairpersons. If you leave it to the staff, it may be done but it won't be accomplished with the same degree of warmth that your personal contact supplies.

- Plan regular meetings with your executive director, setting aside ample time so that the two of you can get into some of the current issues and have enough time left over to check on progress or lack of it on the year's goals.

- Plan for the annual evaluation of the executive director. Even if he or she is tops, small problems can compound into larger ones if there is not some process by which the volunteers can make observations and suggestions. Build it into the system that the executive committee or board of directors should do the annual evaluation and then set aside time for it.

- Build positive relationships within the total organization. If your group is part of a larger organization, develop personal relationships with the volunteer leaders at the other levels. Try to do everything possible to minimize friction and to promote effective relationships.

- Make it exciting and worthwhile. Keep in mind your unique position and opportunity to know what's going on in the organization. Provide regular occasions through board meetings, newsletters, personal communications, and every other possible way in order that your fellow volunteers can enjoy the fun of being part of an organization that *is* making a difference.

- Realize that *you* are responsible, and if you leave a void, it will be filled of necessity by the executive director, who thereby will become too influential and too preoccupied with doing your job to help expand volunteer involvement and impact. Don't worry about making the staff director too important. The greater danger occurs when you let the staff become too important at the expense of building volunteer responsibility.

This chapter has sought to give you a clear perception of your identity and responsibility as president. If you have a staff, your role is still the same—your goals will still be the same—but you will have skilled hands to help you fulfill your functions. The next chapter is intended to give you and other board members a fuller grasp of the relative roles of volunteers and staff.

6

Board and Staff: Who Does What?

In reviewing the role of the president, it was useful to try to see the president's job in the context of an agency without a staff. It might be similarly useful here to take a look at a volunteer organization that has come to the point of needing and being able to afford a staff.

In most of this section, I will speak about the cause-oriented membership association, rather than the agency providing direct professional services. However, many of these lessons apply to the organization in which professionals provide one-to-one services. Later in the chapter, I'll come back to some of the distinctions in board/staff roles in the service operations.

I've observed that most organizations go into a temporary downturn when staff is first hired. The pattern is fairly typical. A wonderful group of dedicated volunteers, through their own individual efforts and without staff backup, have scrambled, kicked, and scratched their way to having a significant program and are now at the point where they need and can afford some staff assistance. They hire a person and immediately the volunteers relax, turning much of the work over to the staff director. The volunteers assume that the agency will not only carry on the existing activities, but will now be able to spurt forward.

In about one year, however, or at the most two, the volunteers begin to view the scene with bewilderment. They find that the agency is doing less than it was before they hired staff and has lost much of its visibility and vitality. Volunteers will tend to conclude that obviously the wrong staff was hired because more was being accomplished when the volunteers were doing it by themselves. Before the downturn and the discouragement become irreversible, the group's members may finally realize that they had turned over far too much of the job to the staff and retreated to occasional approvals of what the staff did, along with some irregular assistance to the poor bloke who is president, but who has begun feeling less and less responsible for the operation.

The worst illusion ever perpetrated in the nonprofit field is that the board of directors makes policy and the staff carries it out. This is just not so. The board, with the help of the staff, makes policy and the board, with the help of the staff, carries it out. Unless volunteers are committed and involved in the action phase of the organization, the agency cannot develop and, in fact, should not be characterized as a voluntary organization. Also, it is naïve to assume that the staff doesn't have considerable influence—usually too much—on policy formulation.

The staff exists to help the volunteers do the work of the organization. Staff members should not be expected or allowed to do the job directly. The greatest sinner is often the president who far too often gives over his or her responsibility to the executive director.

Most presidents and boards are not certain about the appropriate and relative roles of volunteers and staff in a voluntary agency. Whenever I counsel a president or a board, I find it useful to bring them back to the exercise of viewing the organization without staff members so that all the volunteer responsibilities and functions can be clearly identified. Only after that's done do I reintroduce the availability of staff, making it clear that the staff is hired to assist the volunteers to do their citizen jobs in fulfillment of the voluntary agency's mission.

There are two extreme views of the concept of the staff's role in voluntary organizations. The first identifies the staff person as the expert who acts principally in an advisory capacity to the interested volunteers. This interpretation is typified by the fundraising consultant who is hired by a church or a hospital to show the volunteers how they themselves can raise a stipulated sum of money. The second identifies the staff person as simply the individual who carries out the clerical details of the agency's function. This interpretation is typified by the part-time executive secretary hired by a service club to arrange details of meetings and handle routine correspondence. In vibrant citizen organizations, the correct role rests squarely between these two. The professional staff person is no less an expert in the specialty than the church's fundraising consultant; neither are the staff functions different from the everyday activities of the service club secretary in handling the routine business that volunteers do not have time to process.

The reason most staff people must be experts and detail people at the same time stems from the nature and magnitude of their organization's mission. Because they are probably working with staggering community or national problems, even the details of working out a program and launching it require the daily attention of a skilled community organization specialist. On the other hand, the staff member must be a detail person because he or she is dealing with a problem so comprehensive that no one expert could possibly cope with it alone. An intelligent attack requires the concerted action of many different specialists and community representatives who volunteer their time to determine and pursue solutions.

Voluntary organizations are fortunate in being able to bring the thinking of many specialists to bear on the problems; but in doing so, citizen volunteers must be served with facts, with legwork, and with all the other details that go into making volunteer time pay off. To illustrate how this works in daily operation, we may take the example of a staff person working in the area of rehabilitation for the American Heart Association. Basically, this person must be knowledgeable about the process of rehabilitation. He or she must know what has been and is being done in rehabilitation in the community and in the association, as well as what specialties are needed to properly attack the problem at hand. At this point, the job becomes a matter of feeding all necessary facts to the proper individuals so that the right committee is formed, and can as quickly and efficiently as possible devise the right programs to meet the principal needs with which it is concerned. In a sense, the organization and the staff person are picking the brains of these volunteer experts, translating their thinking into a program plan that utilizes existing knowledge and services, working with the committee to modify that plan, and helping the committee launch a program in the community.

In every sense, the rehabilitation staff person is servicing the committee with the facts, legwork, knowledge of the agency, knowledge of the community, and an ability t translate the intentions of the volunteers into a plan and, in turn, into the kind of program which the thinkers themselves would inaugurate if the agency could ever afford such a full-time team. Having a staff means that the committee can be utilized to its maximum because the volunteers are not continually bogged down with details or lack of information. In an agency where volunteer leaders can give only limited time, the business of processing details and gathering facts would mean indefinite delays if someone was not available to do this for the committee. With staff, the rehabilitation committee, instead of taking two years to develop and effect one program, can actually develop and undertake many programs in the same time span. The basic concept of staff assistance is to leave the *big* people free to think about the *big* things and then give them sufficient assistance to translate their thoughts into *big* results. With this interpretation of the role of the staff, the American Heart Association is able to attract the important volunteers to the organization who will serve as the program force of the agency; in this way the organization is making the most of the time they give.

A few years ago I collaborated with Geri Joseph, then national president of the Mental Health Association, to put together a summary of what we, as the chief volunteer and staff officers, jointly considered the essential functions of staff. This is the way we framed the job:

The role of staff in a voluntary agency is simple in concept (though certainly not in execution). Your job is to bring about the maximum *volunteer* dedication, *volunteer* involvement and *volunteer* satisfaction.

You must stimulate, educate and service. Everything you do must be directly related to the single underlying concept of voluntary action—the promotion of citizen interest in public affairs.

To the extent you become project oriented and lose sight of your basic role of developing the *volunteer* capacity of your organization, we might just as well declare ourselves a branch of government. Your mission, your project, your goals and your record must be measured in quotients of *volunteer* commitment and *volunteer* results.

We then listed twelve functions staff can perform to make volunteers more responsible and active. These are abbreviated below:

- Set one part of your annual goals not in terms of pursuit or completion of specific projects, but in terms of increased volunteer involvement and commitment.

- Provide all possible assistance to help volunteers understand the problems in the field and the role and work of the organization. Volunteers won't feel comfortable and therefore won't give fully of themselves unless they are well informed and briefed on all relevant matters. That doesn't mean sending reams of material; a key part of your job is to summarize information so that it is understandable to volunteers.

- Provide excellent staff service to the president or to the committee chairpersons who rely on you for staff backup. Nowhere is this more critical than in the executive director's responsibility to the president. While the executive director is many things to many people, he or she is also the executive assistant to the president. See that the president has all the information needed to fulfill the obligation as elected head of the organization. Don't do the president's job, but help him or her understand that job in order to do it well.

- Provide the best possible service to other officers and to the board, committee chairpersons, and committees. If there is one general failing of staff in organizations, it is that the staff somehow assumes that volunteers are mind readers, that they know the issues and facts. How often we go to committee meetings without the agenda and related details having been distributed in advance. And how often we simply listen to a staff member or an uninformed committee chairperson ramble on about some issue we don't understand, but which must be solved at that very meeting. If you care about the involvement of volunteers—quantity and quality—then be certain that every meeting is carefully preceded by a sharing of the agenda and all pertinent information at least a week in advance. Volunteers can then think about the subject and come prepared to offer competent advice. You'll find that people will be more willing to come to meetings, too. If you don't do this, however, many people will feel that the organization is haphazardly run and will not want to be part of hasty decision-making.

- Help identify the points of view and talent needed on the board and on the committees; to the extent necessary, help in the recruitment of such people. Leave as much of the job as possible to the president and committee chairpersons. Once these people are assembled, let them make the decisions. Don't try to have all the bright ideas. Your skills are needed in knowing the type of people who should be brought together and in giving them the right support. If a staff person—or, for that matter, a volunteer—assumes that he or she has talents equal to the composite brains and skills of a board or committee, then the organization either has a genius on its hands or, more likely, is in trouble.

- Know the related activities and facilities in your own area. Only to the extent that you really know what is already available can your volunteers help identify gaps, weaknesses, and needs.

- Be certain that your organization operates a competent information and referral program. This may seem a minor point, but the basic service activity of a voluntary agency is to serve as a channel between those who need help and those who can provide it. Often a voluntary agency tends to wait for the glib, exciting projects when, in fact, its fundamental job is to fulfill the basic roles of gadfly, information and referral source, demonstrator, and so on.

- Make planning a priority. Identify those things that most need doing and then do them well. Despite the many temptations, don't spread yourself so thin that basic obligations and priority projects are not done adequately.

- Stay loose or at least stay flexible. The basic role of a voluntary agency is to see that whatever needs doing is, in fact, accomplished by whomever can do it best. This requires the *habit* of *flexibility*—two seemingly contradictory words—and an ability to move from one challenge to another. The role of staff is obviously to be responsive to the need for change.

- Recognize your role as the basic communication link in the organization. Because you represent continuity of service, you are the source of information on the past. You are also a key source of information about what is happening now in your community and in your organization.

- Keep the dream alive! Don't let yourself be so concerned with the problems you face that you fail to recognize that volunteers look to you to keep the goals in sight. It is up to you to be certain that people are aware of the long-term goals and of the organization's capacity to work effectively toward those goals.

- Provide all possible credit, thanks, and satisfactions for volunteer activity. This will require a good deal of subordination of your own ego, but your goal and your satisfaction must be measured by the degree and kind of volunteer effort achieved.

Of all of those points I'm quite certain that both Geri Joseph and I would give first place to "Keep the dream alive!"

Some of this advice won't apply equally to the service agency, where most of the work is performed on a one-to-one basis by teachers, therapists, or scientists. However, this is often used as an excuse to keep the board at a comfortable distance. "Raise the money and leave us alone" is sometimes the byword.

Obviously, lay board members should not be substitutes for highly skilled specialists, but neither should the specialization of the program obfuscate the board's role and responsibility. Nor should it freeze out the greatest possible utilization of volunteer time and talent.

Recent federal budget cutbacks caused significant income reductions for many nonprofit service organizations, and although this caused serious hardship, there were a few healthy lessons. Most of the service organizations that were impacted were determined to preserve as much of their service as possible. Indeed, in the face of growing client needs, they needed to figure out how to do more with less. In the process, many of the most alert and flexible of these organizations rediscovered the volunteer. They relearned how much talent human beings have and how willing people are to be involved in rewarding assignments.

During this period, I saw a great many sensible, sensitive service groups adjust in such remarkable ways as these:

- **Revitalization of the board.** Board revitalization started because the agency desperately needed money. In the process, the organizations learned how much more the trustees could do in financial planning. Many of them had more experience in dealing with financial crises. They also brought a practical common-sense reality to making some hard decisions.

  Some of the trustees knew how to substitute labor-saving techniques, including automated equipment. Others knew about strategic planning to maximize resources and results. Suddenly it was apparent that these relatively dormant boards had a great deal to offer. In the process of giving, they developed a sense of participation and commitment that resulted in far larger fundraising efforts.

- **Reintroduction of the program volunteer.** Even before the financial crunch there emerged a growing criticism of voluntary organizations: the staffs were becoming overprofessionalized. In the name of standards and professional ethics, but with a counterpart of competition among the professions, many organizations had frozen out the volunteers who had once provided much of the program service. Suddenly, in the face of needing to do more with less and with the help of experienced trustees, these organizations approached it from the other side and began to examine how much of the program could be undertaken by the least professionally trained individuals. Not surprisingly, they discovered that many of the tasks did not require the complete specialist; they also learned how much ability other individuals have and how much these people can grow with increased responsibility. They began to be more flexible in their hiring practices to involve part-time professionals where the skills were necessary. Throughout this process, there was increased reinvolvement of the volunteer through the whole spectrum of program delivery.

  As stated in earlier chapters, this involvement has benefits far beyond the element of service delivery. These volunteers provide additional sensitivity and caring, they tell the agency's story to hundreds if not thousands of people in the community, and they become loyal advocates.

- **Greater reliance on consumers and community.** In the same spirit of doing more with less, these organizations began looking at other community resources with which they could link for more efficient case finding or therapy. They turned to schools, unions, service clubs, clinics, and other agencies to provide better services at less cost. They also discovered how much the consumers of the services and their families could be involved to extend and improve the services. Just as with the involvement of volunteers, they began to realize how much caring and ability there is in the average human being, how much more the specialist can accomplish by taking time to think about the tasks at hand and who is available to share the load.

If a service agency wants to remain essentially a voluntary organization, these lessons must be carried over to noncrisis times. Otherwise, if a board is relatively inactive, and if most of the money comes from and accountability is owed to government and other third-party sources, then the organization is not really functioning as a voluntary institution.

For the service organization that is not funded by government, these lessons have all the more relevance. To the degree that boards feel needed and responsible, they will contribute enormous talent, outreach, and money.

If the underlying attitude is, "We're just lay board members. What do we know about schizophrenia?" or, conversely, "We're skilled archeologists. Who do the trustees think they *are* trying to steer our course?"—in either case and from either direction, the impasse will grow and the organization's characteristics and advantages as a voluntary organization will shrink.

If in the larger society the direction is to help the general public understand our options to, say, control nuclear proliferation or strengthen our public school system, then it should be possible for a group of interested board members to understand your organization's operations, and for all concerned to profit from the composite wisdom and commitment of the total enterprise.

The board will have to be careful not to trespass upon the decisions that require professional judgment—but the number of such decisions should not be exaggerated; when they are necessary, they should be interpreted to the board. Remember that if a *Baltimore Sun* reporter can explain DNA to the public, it is possible for your program specialists to find ways to explain their work to a bright, interested board.

The trustees should not try to decide between treatments A, B, and C or mathematical theories X, Y, and Z, but they may have to decide whether program 1 is given priority over program 2 or whether both are so important that the board will accept a commitment to find funds for each.

Whatever the differences between types of nonprofit organizations, the most important job a board has is to hire the chief staff officer. (Because this is so important, much of Chapter 8 is devoted to it.)

The next most important task is to work with the staff director to be sure that the relative responsibilities of board and staff are understood and fulfilled. For most voluntary organizations, the key issue here is to be sure that the board has the mechanisms by which it can make certain that the staff is not usurping the role of the board—and occasionally vice versa. Maintaining this delicate balance is the most difficult part of board/staff relationships and is usually the source of serious breakdowns in agency operations.

Just as it is essential that the board of directors evaluates its own performance in relation to accountability standards, it is equally essential that trustees annually review the executive director's performance. (This, too, is covered in detail in Chapter 8.)

Although the executive director should have absolute authority over other staff members within the organization, the board of directors will exercise ultimate control by its authority to approve the personnel policies and practices of the organization, including the wage and salary administration program. The board must also have firm authority for the basic table of organization—that is, the executive director should not be free to make significant changes in the deployment of staff without the staff organizational chart being approved by the board. This is a gray area where staff and board often clash. To me, however, it's an inviolate rule that the board must have authority to pass on the staff structure. Because staff organization and job descriptions carry such influence on future directions and activities, the board must have principal responsibility for their determination.

When I began to think about significant reorganization of the American Heart Association staff in Baltimore, I went to the executive committee and outlined the reasons I felt that change was necessary. We had a good deal of discussion as to whether my basic idea had merit, and I was encouraged to develop a more detailed plan. That initial discussion helped clarify and change some of my thinking. I then brought a plan to the executive committee and to the board of directors for their reaction and for discussion. On the basis of those two presentations, I developed a final report which was approved by the executive committee on authority from the board. Once that plan was approved, it was entirely mine to implement with whatever individuals I chose to recruit, assign, or promote. This was my approach also with two reorganizations of the National Mental Health Association staff.

The board should also be heavily involved in development of one-year and five-year plans and in the annual evaluation of the fulfillment of those plans.

An area of frequent difficulty in board and executive director relations involves the degree to which the executive director serves as the spokesperson for the agency. In some agencies the executive director serves in this role; in some, the executive director becomes the public spokesperson by default. In others, the board deliberately wants the executive director to be "Mr. Outside." It is generally consistent with the ideal of promoting citizen responsibility and influence that the executive director should be much more "Mr. Inside," and the public exposure should accentuate the volunteer face of the organization. The president should generally be the spokesperson. If the topic involves a specialized area, then the volunteer covering that area might speak.

It's important, too, that the organization in other ways has a true volunteer characterization. It's a good idea to have volunteers representing the organization whenever possible. Staff members are often tempted and eager to accept assignments which take them away from their own jobs and hide the volunteer face of the agency. Staff people should resist almost every opportunity to represent the agency in the community. Often the executive director, because it's the easiest way or because he or she is fascinated by it, will become the association's representative on the community council and on many other advisory boards. An executive director does not belong on any of those committees unless there is some unique factor calling for staff input. Those responsibilities belong with the volunteers, because without these exposures the agency isn't really functioning as a volunteer organization. If the volunteers aren't getting this kind of experience, they are not gaining the satisfactions, the encouragement, and the insights they need in order to become better leaders of the organization.

During the years I was executive director of the National Mental Health Association, I resisted the most tempting invitations to serve on fascinating national boards and committees and to participate in exciting national and international conferences. I turned them down no matter how tempting and no matter how time-consuming it was to find the right volunteer to replace me. Once volunteers are filling these roles they will derive much greater satisfaction from being part of the organization, and their reports will be much better received because it isn't always the executive director telling the board about this and that.

Often the staff finds itself so burdened with outside assignments that there is no time for the basic inside staff jobs. It's essential that the executive director should not become your "Mr. Mental Health Association" or "Ms. Red Cross." This happens so easily and so quickly that it's necessary to be always on guard against it. This is a fair warning for all volunteers and it is worth repeating: the board should not be too worried about making staff important. The greater danger is in letting staff become too important at the expense of building volunteer responsibility.

The greatest source of friction and breakdown in voluntary organizations of all types, sizes, ages, and relative degrees of sophistication and excellence relates to misunderstandings and differing perceptions between the volunteer president and staff director. I have seen some of the strongest community and national organizations take a sudden tailspin because the individuals, and sometimes the boards, don't agree on the roles of these two leaders.

The problem is seriously exacerbated by the turnover in the chief volunteer officer's position. Whether the tenure is one year, three, or five, new people come with very different understandings of what a chief volunteer officer should be and do. It's also a vulnerable time when a new chief staff officer is hired. The board will assume that the new person has the same grasp of the relative roles and the delicate balance as the predecessor and may be stunned to find a challenge to its cherished authority and prerogatives. In the case of the chief volunteer officer, the board chair may be occupied at one point by the chief executive officer of a very large corporation who overdelegated a large part of his or her responsibility to the chief staff officer; but with new elections that volunteer post is occupied by a person who has made her reputation through leadership of that city's League of Women Voters, which has no staff, and who therefore is ready to take up the reins—and I mean *all* of them. This may be extreme, but it's not far-fetched. By experience, temperament, and style, each chief volunteer officer is going to be different and in the turnover may meet head-on a chief staff officer who has a pretty fixed notion of his or her own responsibilities, prerogatives, and turf.

A source of this growing problem involves the titles themselves. Increasingly, organizations tend to use the term "chief executive officer" to describe the staff director's position. This can lead to an assumption that the board should be relatively passive and the chief volunteer officer should stay in the background. If the chief volunteer officer is the chief executive officer, that leads to an impression that he or she is in charge of everything, including the staff director. Because this is where some of the real trouble starts, I think that title should not apply to nonprofit organizations. Whether the chief volunteer officer is called board chairperson or president, the description should be "chief volunteer officer"; and whether the staff director is called president, executive vice-president, or executive director, the description should be "chief staff officer." Voluntary organizations are very different from both business organizations and governmental agencies, and we only confuse ourselves and our responsibilities by trying to see our roles in contexts that don't altogether apply. Whatever kind of voluntary organization we are dealing with, the role of chief staff officer is unique and is not synonymous with the chairperson and chief executive of a business corporation. Similarly, no matter what the size or nature of a voluntary organization, the job of staff president is not the same as the president and chief executive officer of the business corporation. If we try to make the volunteer the chief executive officer, we overstep the bounds of the staff director, and if we try to do the reverse, we assign to the board and its chairperson far too little role and responsibility.

I acknowledge that the relative roles become harder to describe in large and more specialized organizations. But by starting with these different descriptions, it helps to understand that the two jobs are unique to nonprofit organizations and should be described and addressed as such.

The chief volunteer officer is head of the board in the fulfillment of its accountability functions. That's hardly a passive role; in unstaffed operations, it's one of sweeping proportions.

At its simplest, the chief staff officer is hired to assist the board in its efforts to fulfill its accountability.

As the organization grows in size and complexity, other specific functions may be delegated to the chief staff officer. As this happens, the delegation should be explicit and should be reflected in the job description.

- Do you expect him or her to be the chief program officer?

- Do you expect her to be the chief spokesperson?

- Do you expect him to be responsible for fundraising?

- Do you expect her to be responsible for planning?

The board and the staff need to know whether such functions will be tightly controlled by the board or whether they will be largely delegated.

While it may seem extreme, it gets at the heart of the difficulty for many organizations to ask the questions, "Do you hold the chief staff officer responsible for fundraising or is he or she looking to you for that?" and, "If it's a shared responsibility, who does what?"

A great many of these differences can be anticipated and to some extent reduced if the job descriptions and expectations of both board and staff are clear. The misunderstandings and problems will also be minimized by the annual evaluation of the chief staff officer, which provides opportunities for catching problems early and for making adjustments. Knowing how easily the chief volunteer and staff officers can be in conflict, without any reflection on them as individuals, should create an awareness of how important it is that they work very hard at understanding one another's roles.

In a survey of board chairpersons and presidents, Robert E. Cleary concluded, "How well the chairmen and presidents work together depends less on any characteristic of the institution than on the personal factor, the degree of trust and respect the two feel for each other." He even titled his report "Something Personal About It."

At times, a controversy can divide the chief volunteer and staff officers and if not handled well will lead to an even greater problem than the original controversy. It is hoped that the two will be mature enough to work out their differences or at least be willing to disagree and to have their different points of view presented for consideration and decision. It is especially hoped that maturity will allow each to handle defeat when necessary. I rarely disagree publicly with a chief volunteer officer, but I do make it very clear to each new person in that role that I have a right to do so. It is easily overlooked, particularly in the turnover of chief volunteer officers, that the chief staff officer is hired by the board and is responsible to the full board. This often becomes confused because one of the roles of the staff director is to serve as the executive assistant to the chairperson and this can lead to the misperception that one is the staff subordinate of the other. Although it is slightly presumptuous and sometimes awkward, I sit down with a new chief volunteer officer as soon as he or she is identified and, within many other matters of orientation, review my responsibility to the board. It also helps to avoid later problems if we do find ourselves in disagreement and I think both opinions should be presented to the board.

On those rare occasions when we do disagree and can't work it through, I always suggest that we work together in presenting the whole issue to the board. Fortunately, I have never run into a situation when it was not possible to follow this arrangement. I do know, however, that in several other organizations, even with the most talented and mature chief volunteer and staff officers, there have been occasions when the two found themselves locked in controversy. In such cases it's sensible to have a third party explore the issues and present all the issues to the governing body. This process can be useful if the controversy involves other factions in the organization, and it's particularly valuable if the differences have reached the personality level.

In "Conflict in the Board Room," J. L. Zwingle found that friction between these two positions and between the staff director and the board as a whole is a widespread cause of presidential resignations, but that neither party is likely to seek third-party help. He concluded that they ought to consider such interventions because "experience has demonstrated how even at late stages of controversy, the sense of new perspective or at least a reduction in hostility can be achieved."

The chief staff officer should not try to be in the lead on every issue that comes up. Unfortunately, too many of us tend to emotionally identify ourselves as plaintiff or defendant and are in the middle of issues that don't really require it. As a result, we become more controversial than necessary and tend to get too upset and too scarred. In an organization that truly has the capacity for controversy and dissent, you'll generally find that the staff director has a high tolerance for both and is more involved in maintaining an arena conducive to healthy controversy than in trying to win on every issue. I don't suggest a profile of timidity or passiveness, but I don't think it's healthy for the organization or the individual when the chief staff officer is expected to fight or even stand up and be counted on every issue.

Differences, debate, controversy, and dissent can all be healthy and are a characteristic of vibrant citizen organizations. The organization and its structure must represent a healthy arena for the adversaries. The chief staff officer in particular must have a stomach for difference and an awareness that his or her larger job is to maintain the healthy arena rather than to take on each tiger as it comes along.

It's also important that incoming chief volunteer officers should not come at their jobs with a determination to shake things up and make a great many changes. Volunteer organizations, more than any other kind of institution, get shaken up very easily. Don't start too much controversy and dissent unless the board clearly believes a total shake-up is necessary. Otherwise, pick your spots carefully and move only on those matters most in need of revision.

This chapter began by exploding a myth that boards make policy and the staff carries it out, and it ends by dispelling another myth. People often think of staff salaries as an overhead expense. Even fairly sophisticated boards become concerned if staff salaries begin to represent a high proportion of the budget. Contrary to this view, I frequently counsel boards that unless the staff salaries and other supporting expenses come above 50 percent of the budget, the agency probably is not doing a real job.

The basic program force of most citizen organizations is either (1) the volunteers' time and energy which moves the community toward improved attitudes and practices, or (2) the specialist staff members who provide direct service. The major cost of operating most voluntary agencies is the staff who provide day-to-day service to the volunteers or to the clients. The staff person serving a childhood-mental-illness committee or working to promote jobs for the handicapped or a minority group is just as legitimate a program expense as the nurse in a hospital, teacher in a school, or minister in a church. The staff is not overhead. I certainly agree that overhead should be kept as low as possible, and if the staff is spending most of its time on fundraising or management activities, there is need for concern. But if the staff time is logged on behalf of the mission of the organization, it is program money well spent.

7

Finding, Developing,
and Rewarding
Good Board Members

For the head of the board, having enthusiastic and reliable board members is almost as good as having an enthusiastic spouse and reliable children—and some days, such as just before the annual board meeting, you might trade the kids two for one.

The problem is that most of us wait until those moments of crisis to give adequate consideration to solid board membership. We fail to spend time to find, develop, and reward good board members. It's like trying to build a professional football team without the efforts of scouting, signing, training, and rewarding. Our business is almost entirely people, yet we invest almost nothing in people-building. We get so tied up in today's needs that we don't reserve a realistic part of our resources for developing the talent and dedication necessary to carry and expand the association's efforts tomorrow.

The building begins with the board itself. I wish I could suggest a short cut, but I'm afraid there's no way to avoid beginning with and emphasizing the nominating committee. Businesses have their recruiters and search firms and professional sports have their scouts; for us it's the nominating committee. The difference is that the other groups take it seriously. On the surface, almost all of us would say that the nominating committee is one of our most important committees. But if you look at the number of meetings and hours spent by committee members and staff, I'll bet the contradiction is glaring. Also, we rarely want to use some of our top talent for such a mundane function or, if we assign them to the nominating committee, we don't want to take up much of their time this way. As a result, not much seed corn is sown.

The search begins with a careful analysis of what talent, experience, and representations are needed; this in turn requires a charting of the same characteristics of the existing board. Where do they come from? What and who (gender, age, experience, and so forth) do they represent? The nominating committee should then think hard about the imbalances and determine what skills, experience, and representations are needed to strengthen the board. At this important juncture, their ideas should be presented to the board for discussion and reaction. Often nominating committees operate in secret until their nominees are sprung full-blown on the board or voting membership. Some confidentiality is necessary when the committee reaches the stage of talking about people, particularly current board members who might not be renominated, but this should not preclude an early discussion with the board about the general composition of that body.

Such a frank discussion can ease some hard feelings when favorites of current board members are not selected. Boards often tend to be self-perpetuating, not only with individuals, but also with representation of categories. It's understandable that people tend to nominate others they know, but these people are not likely to be very different in age, geography, and occupation. I can almost guarantee that if you don't think hard about the categories and balances you need, you'll end up taking the easy course of simply choosing from among those names put forward.

Once you are fairly clear about the factors that need consideration, the board and many others can be helpful in identifying candidates who meet those criteria. One small but important point: As you involve the board and others, make it clear that they should not "feel out" whether their people might be willing to serve. This will put you and them in an impossible spot. Interest and availability come later in the process.

When you begin to think about people, look first within the organization. The board members should represent those individuals who, in the significant majority, have proven their interest in the cause and their ability to help pursue it. The heads and members of committees should be the first logical source. If yours is a membership organization, this provides an automatic pool for new board members. There is a great tendency to overleap the people who have proven themselves in hopes of getting bigger names or greater influence. My experience has been that the way you build impact is to build with the people who have proven their interest.

Many boards and nominating committees want to go after the big names and new faces. After all, it makes us feel good to be serving on the board with Mr. or Ms. "Big" and to look down a bit on the organization's *workers*. On the other hand, one of the constant lessons of leadership is that people grow with responsibility and are capable of far more than appears on the surface. Many a leader has been amazed to discover that the people he or she has unfairly pegged at one level of output are capable of much more. An individual who has demonstrated faithful service and effectiveness at one level is the first source of leadership for higher levels of responsibility. This includes precinct captains and task force leaders who have worked faithfully and who often are overlooked for other responsibilities.

Promotion should include some deliberate turnover of top leadership. The emphasis ought to be on the development of an increasing number of persons from the lower levels who are qualified and interested in top leadership posts.

I don't suggest rapid turnover. An organization needs some people who carry forward the history and institutional culture of the organization. One sensible way to capture this is to bring people back onto the board who have served successfully and who have remained active, even when not on the board.

Board terms should be limited. Generally, a three-year term with a chance for one additional term makes sense. After a year off the board, a person can come back on. This recycling should be done with great caution. There is a great temptation on the part of staff and nominating committees to yearn for the good old days and past personal associations, but the larger emphasis should be on seeking new blood.

Persons who cannot be active should be dropped. My approach is to provide a clause in the bylaws which automatically drops persons who have missed a certain number of consecutive meetings, unless the board officially votes forgiveness. Letters should go annually to those board members whose attendance and participation have been irregular, indicating that in the coming year the organization will be depending more than ever on them for active participation and that if the individual board member feels that this level of participation is not possible in the immediate future, he or she can elect to step aside. I often use a sentence such as, "Obviously we very much hope you can be active, but if this is not possible, you may prefer to change your status to voting membership (supporter, inactive, and so forth) that provides continuing identification."

Joseph Reed, former staff director of the Child Welfare League, provided a good description of the qualifications of board members:

> Of greatest importance should be the person's interest in the work of the agency, commitment to its objectives, intelligence, respect in the community, capacity for growth as a board member, capacity to influence favorable public opinion in important areas of the community, ability to work in concert with others, and willingness to ask questions, offer criticism and make suggestions through proper channels.

There will be times when the nominating committee will recognize a particular need which is not yet matched by a person serving anywhere in the organization. In such cases board members must be selected from the community at large. You may know who you want and have access to him or her, know who you want but not have access, or not even know the best people who represent the leadership of that category.

Even where you have ready access, make sure that the invitation is extended in a way that the individual knows that you really mean it. Send an impressive delegation. Remember that these are among the most important investments the organization will make.

Obviously the quality of the approach is even more important when you don't have easy access. With pride in your cause, ask for an appointment and bring a small group who can make it clear how important the work is. You will be amazed how often you'll not only get the appointment but an acceptance, too.

Even where the answer is no, the session can have positive results. In *The Effective Board*, Cyril O. Houle says:

> It will be comforting to realize that at least a constructive piece of community relations has been accomplished. The prospective board member will have been given information about the program, will know that he was wanted and will have sensed that the selecting authority (and probably the Board itself) knows its business. He is probably an influential person (or else he would not have been invited) and it is important to have influential people aware of the work of the agency or the association.

When you don't even know who to ask, go to people who occupy leadership positions and seek their advice. I've often gone absolutely cold to the head of the medical society, current chairperson of the Council of Churches, publisher of the paper, head of the Chamber of Commerce, director of the labor council, and many others who have led me to just the right people. If it's top business leadership you are after, go to the heads of the largest businesses, making clear that you are not asking for anything but their advice. My experience is that unless you know them, you won't even get in the door if you don't offer that assurance. When you see them, present your full story and ask if there is someone in the organization he could help you approach to make your pitch. I know you hope it will be the person with whom you are talking, but that's so unlikely that you should use the door-opening to get his or her help in enlisting someone else. If he or she suggests the executive vice-president or marketing director and helps with the introduction, you will get a doubly loyal individual and will be much further ahead than if you aim unrealistically high.

The Association of Governing Boards of Universities and Colleges has produced an excellent pamphlet, "Building a More Effective Board," based on a presentation by its president, Robert Gale, in which he says:

> Generally speaking, it is not advisable to try to recruit someone who has already reached the top of the career ladder. Even if such a person

accepts the invitation, he or she is likely to be too busy to contribute. It is better to look for persons who are on their way up and who are willing to work. A valuable talent for nominating committee members is the knack of identifying "comers," those who are moving up rapidly. Such persons, committed to the institution before they reach the top, become investments in the future.

Increasingly, businesses want signs that their management people are involved in voluntary endeavors and, as indicated earlier, it's my experience that people want a sense of participation and contribution. Everybody wants the corporate CEO on the board, but there's a wealth of talent and commitment not far below that can be tapped.

Because I know how bewildering it can be if you don't know where or how to turn, I want to elaborate on my reference to making cold contacts. I want to reach out—almost to hold your hand—to say, "Hey, keep the faith, it can happen."

If you are really starting from scratch, I recommend starting with your political representatives. Better than anyone else, they know how the system works and who makes it work, and they usually will feel an obligation to listen and try to help. For example, they are most likely to know, say, who else has a retarded child or is worried about zoning or is concerned with improving the educational system. Also, they are more likely to know who the doers are and to be able to put you in touch with some of them.

The next group I talk to are past officeholders and others who have run for office in the area. Running for and holding office require knowing a lot of people, and that knowledge is what you should quickly tap into. Incidentally, don't be afraid to make a cold approach. These people are political animals, usually easy to approach and surprisingly eager to help a fellow citizen.

My third general circle of contacts involves religious leaders. I've often gone into a community cold and, by visiting a priest, minister, or rabbi, have quickly identified people who share my concerns and people who are real doers. Those contacts serve two purposes—I not only get the names of some likely helpers, but I get automatic entrée. Very few people will not see you if you indicate that, say, Rabbi Bloustein or Father Kelly has referred you. Often the clergyman will make the introductory call. It's amazing how helpful people will be if you dare approach them and ask for help.

The fourth group I contact are the newspapers. Publishers, editors, and reporters know what's happening and while usually not so free with their time as the other groups, they still are approachable and willing to help. This can also lead to an interest in your cause and some helpful coverage.

If your community has a Voluntary Action Center (VAC) or Volunteer Bureau, talk to them. They are a very good source of volunteer leadership.

Whether it's leaders of granges, labor, business groups, media, religion, service clubs, or politics, there are people who know the individual leaders within the categories you need.

Let me repeat that board development has to be *very* high on the current board's agenda, with an awareness of how much has to be invested in it by both the board and the staff. A couple of years ago I was working with a nominating committee that had fine-tuned its analysis to the point that, for the one remaining board vacancy, they knew we needed an individual who would be from the Midwest (preferably Chicago), female, a leader of the performing arts, a volunteer (in contrast to a conductor or ballet director), an individual who had experience and interest beyond the arts, and a person who was immensely capable. That's what we needed, all in one individual! It would have been easy to consider the task impossible and even easier to give up on several of the criteria. For example, in our search we uncovered many men, many professionals, people from other sections of the country, and people from the visual arts. If we had not done our analysis so thoroughly (and there were times during that search when I wished we hadn't!), we would have ended up with another male from New York and have found some way to rationalize that further imbalance. As it was, we found a remarkable individual who fit all those criteria and more.

Some organizations have been so conscientious in attempting to represent the total community that they have found themselves in trouble because they have not also emphasized the need to find people with a commitment to the organization's central purpose. Whether it's representation from business, minorities, women, fundraisers, or other essential categories, the desire for their involvement should not become an end in itself without regard to your central reason for being. During the 1960s and 1970s when I was national staff head of the Mental Health Association, we surpassed all our major quotas for increased involvement of minorities and women on the national board and staff and, with their help, took some giant steps in more humane care for the mentally ill. We improved our work but we did not lose our unique focus. At times it was awkward to have to restate that the basic role of the organization was to improve services for the mentally ill, improve attitudes about mental illness, and work for the prevention of mental illness. In many of those years I was confronted by individuals who argued that, because of past social inequities, the organization should devote all of its attention to the elimination of discrimination.

My position was that we had a moral responsibility to lend our voice to the efforts of those groups organized to deal with the other social ills which tragically befall minorities. For instance, it was incumbent upon the organization to make clear the mental health implications that are so much a part of racism, discrimination, unemployment, and underemployment, but also that it was every bit as important that the Mental Health Association continue its attention to the neglected cause of mental illness, for which we were so uniquely and solely responsible.

As important as it is to be sure that the board is representative of the various constituencies and other factors necessary to the board's work, it is equally important to look for individuals who possess those human qualities that lend themselves to working as a board. I've seen organizations that tend to their needs for professional guidance, geographic and gender balance, age differential, and many other such factors, while the nominating committee does not devote equal time to being sure that many are chosen for the board because they have proven their capacity for judgment, facilitation, respect for institutional process, and just plain kindness.

I was consulted recently by the organizers of a new foundation. They had pretty much identified all of the individuals who would serve on the initial board. When I looked at the list I was dismayed that although they had covered the categories of professional expertness, they had included only individuals noted as much for abrasiveness as accomplishment. When I pointed this out, the founder countered by saying that they were determined to be different, aggressive, and innovative. I tried to make the case that such a board needed a good sprinkling of equally bright people who also had the qualities of judgment, patience, fairness, and conciliation. In all the material I've seen that assesses board make-up in any depth at all, the only points made relate to specific skills and representations without regard to the human qualities that in the end will make the difference in whether it's a board or a barrel of tigers. Maybe that's why so many boards get into such awful trouble. It's another argument for choosing people from within the organization who have not only proven their commitment and ability, but who have demonstrated attractive human qualities.

When the nominating committee's annual work is done and new board members have been elected, the process of their development begins. The orientation phase will obviously have begun with recruitment, but it should now begin to move into high gear. Even though there may be a lapse of several months between their acceptance and election, board nominees should begin to get all the regular board mailings. I also make sure they are signed up as early as possible for an orientation session. These orientation sessions serve many purposes, not the least of which is giving the newcomers a chance to get to know the organization's leadership and to know that the leadership thinks enough of them to take this special time. I try to be sure that the chief volunteer and staff officers conduct the orientation. Often it's delegated to others and that larger value is lost.

Another problem with many orientation sessions is that they try to cram too much information into a session. My solution is to use a good part of the session to acquaint these important individuals with the board manual and to let them become familiar and comfortable with the agenda and attachments for their first board meeting. By focusing on the board manual, they learn what their resources are and where to find them. Thus, they don't have to be told about every program and committee of the organization, but they know where the committee chart and lists are and on what tab they can find a current summary of major program activities. By spending some time on the board meeting agenda, they get a quick grasp of what the current issues are, why they are on the agenda, and what points about them are likely to surface. This gives them a head start and makes them feel less like outsiders when the actual meeting takes place.

The board manual should cover everything from the history of the organization to the policy and procedures of covering expenses for board and committee meetings. In between there should be bylaws, policies and important procedures, organization charts, board list (including, if possible, brief bios and maybe even pictures), committee lists, staff organization chart with a summary of functions, current annual report, summary of major program activities, established dates for board and annual meetings, and the home telephone numbers of the chief volunteer and staff officers. I try to choose loose-leaf notebooks with pockets on the inside of both the front and back covers; these allow the board member to have expansion possibilities for other materials, pamphlets, and reports.

It's important that a member of the nominating committee or another board person be assigned as the host for at least the first board meeting. Some organizations assign a more permanent "buddy." At the very least, the host should call the new board member in advance of the first meeting and arrange to be available for introductions. It's a nice touch to have the host do the introductions at the beginning of the board meeting. Having to prepare for that helps the old-timer focus on the responsibility.

One of the most useful parts of orientation will begin with the new board member's assignments. It's disillusioning to be invited to serve on the board and to come on with great anticipation only to be pretty much ignored. Harold Seymour says in *Designs for Fund Raising* that most people don't drop out from overwork. They drop out from boredom.

Often the conscious phase of board development is limited to the initial orientation. While most of this book is about board development, a few points should be underscored here. Orientation should be aimed at all board members and, to every extent possible, should be a part of each board meeting. We somehow assume that the trustees put together their own overview of what's happening, which isn't likely. It's important to take the time to give them the fun and the value of knowing what's going on.

Board development is achieved in the same way that people are developed in their other roles, such as in their day-to-day work. It's largely a result of their being given the chance to do new tasks along with reasonable amounts of training and on-the-job supervision. In many cases, this involves the board head being available to provide that kind of responsible leadership. Often we throw volunteers into new assignments on a sink-or-swim basis and then wonder why they're not doing well.

If board members are given a role in planning and evaluation, and if board meetings represent a forum for fulfillment of board accountability and leadership, both the new and current members will be growing in responsibility, knowledge, and pride. They will also be developing as a cohesive unit. In *The Effective Board*, Houle says:

> Proper attention to motivation is also essential after people have joined
> the Board—if the Chairman accepts existing motives and acts skillfully

and subtly in terms of them, giving the members a sense of satisfaction about what they do for the agency or association, he can gradually build responsibility on the part of individuals and enthusiasm on the part of the group. The aim should be the strengthening of altruistic motives, for a board never becomes fully mature until its members are bound together by a devotion to some cause outside themselves. This sense of service does not grow automatically. It is created chiefly as people put something of themselves into the work of the board, becoming more and more involved in its activities and seeing the tangible accomplishments which are a definite result.

At another point, he says:

The primary task of the Chairman of the Board is that of helping diverse personalities merge into an effective social whole. In the operation of a board the interaction of the personalities of the members is of the greatest significance. It is the Chairman's task to lead and to restrain, to blend in proper proportion the more capable and vocal members with the less experienced and silent ones. It is his job to foster such a unity of purpose and such a loyalty to objectives that each individual realizes that his own judgment is a part of the collective wisdom of the Board.

Board development also involves weeding out those who aren't performing. This begins with dropping inactive board members, but it also involves dropping heads of committees who aren't doing the job. Some people say "you can't fire a volunteer," but that's not so. People who aren't performing should be given the chance to step aside and, in the extreme, must be asked to make way for someone who is ready to perform. If a bad situation is allowed to linger, it doesn't create a good atmosphere for others in the organization and certainly doesn't encourage up-and-coming volunteers to feel that this is a place they want to make their commitment. It has been my experience that the person who is not performing, and who's had all the proddings and hints you will have given, will be much more relieved than hurt to be taken off the spot.

This brings us to recognition of good board members and other volunteers. Promotion is 50 percent of recognition and reward. More than plaques and pins and pats on the back, people want to know that those they respect think they're ready for bigger things. That's enormously satisfying.

Good leaders don't wait until their best people retire or even until the annual meeting to provide regular encouragement and recognition. Presidents and committee heads should regularly say by phone and note things like, "Just wanted you to know how impressed I was with . . . " or "I know I said it the other day, but I wanted to repeat what an absolutely great job you did. . . . " Find occasions to involve these people in board meetings so that they have the fun and pride of telling the whole board what has been happening and the board can say, "Well done."

The pins and plaques and scrolls are important, too. And don't be afraid to spend some money on them. It appalls me that organizations that receive thousands if not hundreds of thousands of dollars of free time balk at spending more than five dollars for a recognition gift. I'm with volunteers a great deal in their offices and homes and know how much these mementos mean. Despite the warped frames, curled paper, or amateurish calligraphy, the awards remain proudly displayed.

Many organizations such as the Red Cross and Boy Scouts have elaborate systems for keeping service records and providing acknowledgment of years of participation and impact. Some staff members feel that this takes up too much time and isn't really necessary, but they don't know much about human beings. To paraphrase an old saying: "Volunteer recognition is too important to be left to the staff." Periodically, a volunteer task force should look at the recognition program to be sure that it's being observed and updated.

Recognition should include particular attention to the retiring board member. Often he or she is allowed to drift off without true recognition of how much those six years have meant both to the organization and to the individual. When I was with the National Mental Health Association, all board members who had served the maximum of two consecutive terms received a gold key suitable for recasting as a pin, tie-clip, or part of a key chain. It was a tangible way of saying thanks; if they wished, they were also entitled to continue to receive newsletters, annual reports, and notices of annual meetings.

I always suggest to outgoing chief volunteer officers that they provide some memento for the officers and committee heads with whom they've worked. Very often this is small—something like a little paperweight conveying that you were a special team, and you want them to know how much their participation meant.

I don't know exactly what you are already doing, and therefore I'm terribly frustrated that I can't be more specific. But that doesn't stop me from being absolutely definite about the importance of finding every conceivable way of saying "thanks" or "you're great" or "it's been special."

Tangible acknowledgments of participation are an important part of keeping the dream alive, which I maintain is the most important function of both the volunteer and the staff leader in any voluntary enterprise.

8

---

*Recruiting, Encouraging,
and Evaluating
the Executive Director*

Selection of the chief staff officer of a nonprofit organization is clearly the most important decision the board makes. For this reason, and because recruitment is handled inadequately so often, the subject deserves a chapter of its own.

It's my experience, born of many sad lessons, that it takes a unique person to succeed in the staff role in a voluntary agency. Over the years, I've developed a profile that helps me screen persons who are exploring staff possibilities. My current profile of the persons most likely to succeed is as follows:

- **They're committed to public service.** This is more than a generalization. The persons who succeed will face many rocky times. They'll be underpaid for their ability and they'll put up with a great deal of conflict. For these reasons and many more, these persons must have a dedication to public service that will get them over these obstacles and tough times.

- **They like people and get along well with them.** Liking people is often used as the only criterion for selection and therefore can be exaggerated. In carrying responsible positions in voluntary agencies, however, most staff people deal with a wide variety of individuals and must be able to get along with them.

- **They can subordinate their personal needs and preferences to the needs and goals of the volunteers.** This characteristic eliminates the majority of candidates. Most of us cannot consistently subordinate our needs, aspirations, and satisfactions. But the really successful staff persons in the volunteer agency must have this capacity; otherwise competition between staff and volunteers will develop and choke the opportunities for agency fulfillment.

- **They are flexible.** In a voluntary agency there are frequent and discouraging changes of schedules and plans. Staff persons may be ready to accomplish a major task before the end of the week only to find that the responsible volunteer has changed the schedule or is unavailable to carry out his or her part of it. The successful staff person must be able to adjust to and concentrate on those tasks which are attainable.

- **They have a great deal of patience and tolerance.** Staff persons work with a wide variety of volunteers who are often at their most excitable pitch. The more vibrant and active an agency, the more this will hold true. A staff person must be a stable and patient human being or the emotional aspects of working together for significant goals will get out of hand.

- **They are mature.** Psychologists define maturity as the ability to forego short-term satisfactions in favor of long-term goals. This applies to organizations as well as to individuals and particularly to successful staff persons. Most goals are long range and require persistent, dogged pursuit through all kinds of difficulties. The satisfactions are rarely found on a weekly or even monthly basis. It's only as the agency looks back from a fuller perspective that the attainments are visible and the satisfactions present.

- **They're willing to work hard.** Successful people usually work hard, and this is particularly true in the nonprofit field. There is so very much to be done, the dedication of the volunteers is so high, and the number of forces to be dealt with so great that the only way to achieve success is by working awfully hard.

Search committees must recognize the size of the recruiting job. Despite general acknowledgment that recruitment of the staff head is the most important decision the board will make, recruitment is often almost casually approached. As a result, persons who are not really qualified are often selected.

A committee should be appointed by the board of directors. It is essential that a majority of the committee be composed of board members, but it can also include an able staff person or two from other agencies in the community. If there is a parent organization, a key volunteer or staff person from that group should also serve. The first task of the committee is to decide on the skills and attributes necessary. These will constitute a checklist for later interviewing and should immediately be translated into a job description, salary scale, and even advertisements if these are to be used.

In terms of salary scales, helpful information is usually available from the health and welfare council, United Way, the parent organization, or, if necessary, a quick survey that the chairperson of the committee can do on a confidential basis with the presidents of like agencies. Most agencies are willing to cooperate on a volunteer-to-volunteer basis, particularly if they know they will receive a summary of the findings for use in appraising their own salary scales.

Since, as I said, most people would not fit the profile of success, it is extremely difficult to find those people most likely to succeed. I've found that the simplest way to solve this problem is to locate someone who has already demonstrated a capacity to succeed in this unique milieu. For this reason I repeatedly and doggedly advise search committees to look within the nationwide group with which you are affiliated for experienced or promising people. If that doesn't apply in your case, then I advise checking with the directors of major agencies in your area. In other words, do almost anything to find candidates who have already demonstrated a capacity to succeed in this kind of work. Having seen the grief and trouble agencies suffer as a result of hiring the wrong people, I wish I could be sitting across from you right now to make this point so strongly that you would realize how totally I have learned this lesson.

I am often told that it's better to locate a person who knows the local scene. I don't believe it. A bright, effective community organizer is going to see that local scene and develop those contacts in lightning-fast time. Indeed, he or she will not be encumbered by some of the difficulties that the local resident might have. These difficulties involve the set ways in which individuals are already perceived (as being someone's kid sister, being associated with the North Side, having worked for the other newspaper, and so forth).

By the time you've developed your list of skills and attributes, you'll be overwhelmed by your findings that the person you need will have to be very mature, very experienced, and brilliantly able. This, in turn, will suggest an older person. But the experience of many agencies, and certainly the experience of the Peace Corps, VISTA, Office of Economic Opportunity, and other groups, makes clear how fast a young, dedicated person can learn and how much this dedication means in achieving success.

For many years I was involved in developing a trainee program during which we recruited young people who received brief training prior to their first job placement in a voluntary agency setting. These individuals quickly grew to be significant staff leaders, and their youth proved to be an asset rather than a liability. This program allowed us to carefully screen people who had the attributes of success. On-the-job experience provided most of the necessary skills. My strong advice to you is to look for the person who is likely to succeed based on fitting the profile rather than finding someone whose age would seem to be an advantage.

You may find that you want to do some advertising. This can be done through newspapers, organization newsletters, and professional journals. Use newspaper advertising only when you have not been able to generate enough candidates by close examination of personnel rosters in the organization and by talking to other agency executives. When turning to advertising, deliberately slant the ads to attract persons who have had related experience. Write the ads in such a way that you screen out as many unprepared people as possible; otherwise you will be inundated with replies.

At times, professional employment services are helpful. In addition to government and private employment agencies, professional societies often have employment services of their own. My experience has indicated that you need to be adamant about the kind of people you want and the kind of people you don't want. These agencies, particularly the private ones, want to give their current roster of job seekers a feeling of activity and will send all kinds of unqualified candidates. I insist on advance résumés and I *never* accept the employment agency's reference checking as very thorough.

One last word of caution on where to look. Beware of the board member who has a friend. More agencies make bad decisions because the search committees find it awkward to decide against the friend of the president or a person pushed hard by a board member. The smaller the community, the tougher this is. Board members will feel sorry for a woman newly widowed or a county commissioner unfairly defeated, and the search committee will suddenly and totally ignore common sense and/or sound procedures. The result is that the most important decision the board can make ends up by being made badly. This applies, also, to the staff director. He or she should never give in to any pressure to hire a person who doesn't fit the profile needed. This may seem fairly obvious, but many staff people find themselves deciding in favor of friends of board members because it's awkward to ignore the advice. The goal should be to hire the best possible people. The positive result of doing that will outweigh any short-term awkwardness from turning aside the importuning of anyone.

The ideal way to screen candidates is not always available. However, if it is, I urge you to take advantage of it. If you are a part of a larger organization, let the parent organization do the initial screening. Be definite with them in terms of the skills and attributes you want and ask them to provide three or four people whom they view as ready for such an assignment.

If you don't have the luxury of a parent organization to do this and do it well, or if you're combining that process with some other searching, your next steps should be as follows:

- Screen the résumés down to five to seven people and have someone take a personal look at each candidate. If these prospects are in other cities, ask your sister organizations to take a look at the candidates or involve your board people who may travel. Members of your board may have company counterparts in those cities, which at least gives you an opportunity to know whether the person seems to live up to his or her résumé.

- When the group is narrowed down, do some extensive reference checking. I don't put much stock in listed references, although I do contact them and ask pointed questions. I put much more stock in my telephone conversations with past supervisors. I've learned the hard way that most references and supervisors want to be helpful to the candidate, if only to be rid of him or her. Accept that this can be the relationship, and therefore work very hard to get down to facts. It's helpful to explain the importance of the job and the fact that public money will be expended to support it. On this basis, you can make clear how essential it is to get an honest picture of the candidate's qualifications. Make clear how much you are counting on the supervisor's candor. One of the points that I use is that even if the person is hired, I want to know what skills or attributes will need strengthening. This is not only truthful and helpful, it is often the key to opening up discussion of possible weaknesses.

- I'm often on the other side of these reference calls and, with very few exceptions, I am appalled at how cursory the review is. As a consequence, I rarely have to be as candid as I would be if the questioning were sharp. This tells me that most people have made up their minds, but still want to go through the steps of clearance without having their decision shaken. My approach is to shake the daylights out of my judgment. I'd rather face the error at that stage than when the person is on the job. The two things, then, that you have going for you in getting a candid appraisal are (1) the opportunity to make clear how concerned you are about spending public money well, and (2) your desire to check the supervisor rather closely on the grounds that even if a favorable decision is made, you want to know what skills and attributes you can help the candidate develop.

- Do a thorough credit check on your finalist(s). Often the current supervisor won't know a person's credit problems. The last thing you want is to bring a poor credit risk into your job and town. I've known of several public scandals which shook association reputations that could have been avoided by a simple credit check.

- Some candidates stipulate that no checking be done. They make the good case that they are simply looking into a situation and until they are sure they want to apply, they would rather not stir things up. At times you will have to abide by this. Have it understood, however, that if a person does become a finalist, the checking will have to be done before anything is firmed up. This stage is often skipped. You will have screened (except for the reference checking), interviewed, and decided that he or she is the best. There'll be a feeling of euphoria that you've finally located the right person and there's no sense in going through the awkwardness of postponing firming it up when you are so confident that the decision is correct. Resist closure under these circumstances until the reference checking is done. I have learned over the years that the majority of people don't succeed in this field; consequently, there are many inefficient people in it, many of whom contradict their low level of general performance by being superior at selling themselves in job interviews.

- The full search committee should see the candidates, if possible, during the span of the same day, or on successive days. The group should take time to decide how they'll conduct themselves during the interviews. The committee should develop a list of skills and attributes and clear any revisions in the job description and salary scale with the board of directors. It's usually a pretty good idea to check the job description, because there's no better time to change the job description than when the post is vacant.

- Please, please don't play games during the interviews. I've been involved in situations where members of the committee tried to shake up the candidate or tried in other ways to "see what the candidate is really made of." That's a good way of turning off your best candidates. Approach the interview through straightforward, candid discussion of the job and the candidate. The goal is to objectively determine if there is a match or a potential mismatch between the job description and the candidate. It's useful to describe real-life situations in the organization and to ask the candidate almost as though he were an organization consultant to share ideas for dealing with those situations.

- It's important, too, to candidly explain any reservations the committee has about the individual in terms of gaps in experience, possible weak areas, a questionable reference check, and the like. Remember that it's a two-way proposition. Help the candidate to screen himself or herself out. This is hard to do because you want to present a favorable picture. It's human nature to want people to want the job but, on the other hand, it's better to be candid if that helps a candidate recognize that he or she is not matched for what you really want. Better to learn it at this stage than later. If the selection process is strung out at all, keep the candidates posted. This is a courtesy too often overlooked.

- Naturally, the committee's own instincts will play a significant part in the final recommendation. It is advisable, however, to introduce some objective measures in order to check your intuition and to be certain that each candidate is being viewed in light of the same criteria. My suggestion to search committees is that they take the attributes and skills needed and set out a score sheet. I usually suggest a rating of 0 to 5, with 5 being the highest mark. It's a good idea not to use these score sheets during the interview, but, instead, to take a few minutes after each interview for the committee members to mark their score cards. Seeing all candidates on the same day, or on successive days, will bring more uniformity into this process.

- After you've rated all the candidates, the committee will probably be surprised at the scores. I don't suggest that the scores will necessarily contradict instinct, but you will be fascinated by the fact that some candidates who didn't seem very impressive will come up with good scores. This leads to a much more objective discussion of the candidates in relation to the skills and attributes you are really looking for. One individual may not be terribly dynamic but, on scores, comes up pretty solidly right across the board. You may still decide on the individual who has more flair, but, again, you may not. It's the scoring that will lead you to know what you're deciding.

I have had experience enough to predict that when this more orderly method is used, the committee members will end up hiring someone who would not have been their first choice if left to their own instincts. I would further guess that they would agree then and two years later that their instincts, to some extent, had deceived them.

I follow this process in promoting and hiring as well. There have been times when I have known for certain who the right persons were for the given posts, but I still have made myself go through the exercise of trying to objectively identify skills and attributes and to rate the several people. In the end, I have found that my obvious candidates were at least surprisingly well challenged and sometimes overtaken. Good judgment is based on sound analysis, and sound analysis is based on accurate data.

The search committee reports to the board. If it is not possible for the full board to be involved in the decision, the executive committee usually has that authority. Some organizations give the search committee final authority to identify one choice and then refer the candidate to the board of directors or executive committee. I tend to favor the search committee's narrowing the field to two to four people and then having the board or executive committee do the final interviewing. In this case, the board or executive committee should follow the interviewing procedure outlined above. When the process involves the full board or executive committee, the most experienced people in the agency are participating. This also means that the fuller group will have some real commitment to the candidate selected.

If both the search committee and executive committee or board are involved in the interviewing, it can be done in tandem to save time and expense. For example, the search committee can see seven people on Friday and refer three to the board or executive committee on Saturday.

If the position involved is not that of staff director, then the choice should be entirely that of the staff person who will be responsible for the supervision. A staff person may want board members to interview a candidate just to get another perspective, but the board should not have a veto right. Similarly, the board members may be asked to help screen and interview applicants for a department head, but the final decision should rest completely with the executive director.

Follow a strict timetable for selecting an executive director. Prolonged search operations are unhealthy for the organization's morale and are unnecessarily awkward. At the local level the process should not require more than three months, including time to determine attributes and skills, develop the job description and salary scale, and search for and screen applicants.

The appointment should indicate that there is a six-month probation period. This should apply to all professional positions. During the probation period, the new staff person should be entitled to the basic fringe benefits. The letter confirming the appointment should cover all essential understandings, including salary, salary scale, moving costs, and starting date. The candidate should be asked to return a signed copy of the letter for the personnel records.

I am frequently asked if there should be a contract, and I almost always say no. I acknowledge that when I became executive director of the National Mental Health Association, the management consulting firm involved in the search had already written into the procedures that there would be a three-year contract. When that contract expired, I made no move to have it renewed. My own feeling is that a board must be free to change executive directors. If a person goes into a situation hopeful of being able to handle it, that's part of the gamble. I know this doesn't add much to job security, but I don't feel job security is an available luxury in this business. It's important to acknowledge that many experienced people in the field strongly disagree with me on the matter of contracts.

An important consideration is the matter of timing the change. Try to follow the golden rule so that you are not trying to hasten a starting date beyond what you would consider reasonable if you were losing one of your own. I do recommend that people take a good block of time off before starting a new job. This is an important transition with a good deal of emotional and physical stress at both ends. Therefore, if at all possible, there should be at least two months between the agreement and the starting date.

It's usually helpful to have the new staff director make a trip or two to the office before starting. This can involve the person in board meetings or other major events so that, even though he or she will not start for a while, the individual can begin to get a feel for what is going on.

Please do send letters to the references, prior supervisors, and present employers of the person selected. This is a courtesy almost always overlooked and will help your own public relations. The president or the chairperson of the search committee should call the other finalists to thank them for their participation and to outline the final decision. Let the candidates ask questions about the impression they made. This can be useful to them in future situations. Finally, if the new director is from another city, he or she will profit from as much help as you can give in getting settled in and oriented to the new community.

Given the unique profile of a successful staff person and the breadth of activities encompassed by most voluntary organizations, staff turnover is a very costly business. Yet most voluntary agencies still do not approach the important business of retaining good people with anything close to the priority treatment it deserves.

Holding onto good staff is not wholly, nor even largely, a matter of salary and benefits. These people want a sense of purpose, contribution, and fulfillment. In *The Motivation to Work*, Frederick Herzberg found that achievement recognition, work itself, responsibility, and advancement are the primary sources of job satisfaction. This is particularly true of the kind of person who tackles the staff role in a nonprofit agency.

It is essential that there be some regular pattern of training opportunities for refreshment and self-renewal. These jobs grind a person down, and unless there is a means by which a person can be restored and refreshed, zeal and patience are whittled away.

Certainly one can't dismiss the importance of realistic salary scales and fringe benefits. These must be a part of the effort to attract, promote, and retain good people. Fringe benefits should include basic medical, major medical, and retirement coverage, and the program should be transferred automatically if a person moves within a state or national organization. The salary scale should be competitive with other agencies at a level realistic enough that the person is not constantly torn by a failure to provide basic family needs.

Various surveys indicate that salaries run one third to one half of those in comparable jobs in industry. In an important study, "Work and Workforce Characteristics in the Nonprofit Sector," Phillip Mirvis and Edward Hackett reported that "nonprofit jobs provide more challenge, variety, satisfaction and intrinsic rewards than those in private enterprise or government." Their findings indicate that these satisfactions will attract and help retain people as long as the salary differential is not more than one third of what they could make in other sectors.

The board of directors, or at least the executive committee, should annually review an executive director's performance. The review should be based on the job description and on the executive director's role in assisting the board to carry forward the association's work. Most organizations overlook the need for an annual review and in fact no evaluation is done until the point of brinkmanship is reached. The performance of the executive director should be measured in relation to the job description, his or her effectiveness in working with the board to fulfill the annual plan, similar effectiveness in helping the board with its accountability standards, and his or her ability to contribute to expanded volunteer involvement and responsibility. The evaluation should take up a substantial part of the time of an executive committee or board of directors meeting. I don't believe that this critical responsibility should ever be delegated to a personnel committee.

The review should not include evaluation of staff persons other than the executive director. Although the evaluation automatically has to cover staff performance in general, the executive director should be given absolute authority for the annual evaluation of other staff members.

Unless this matter is taken seriously, it will be given only cursory attention. The executive committee or board should take at least an hour because it takes time before the members feel comfortable and will discuss shortcomings. Even if the executive director's performance is tops, it is still important that small problems be caught before they compound into larger problems.

I predict that most evaluations will follow this pattern: For the first few minutes there will be silence. In the next ten minutes there will be laudatory statements. After about twenty minutes someone will finally raise a point, such as, "I know he works hard, but I'm not sure what he does all that time." The session obviously should not be nitpicking, but it should be thorough enough so that, if members have concerns about performance, they will come out and be objectively discussed. At times, this process indirectly solves other relationship problems. A member of the executive committee or board may be laboring under a misconception of the executive director's role or handling of a given situation and once it's brought up the misunderstanding may be dispelled. The president should take time after the meeting to review the report, including items of commendation and areas of improvement. It should be a growth situation for the individual and therefore for the organization.

Throughout this book I've talked about the importance of volunteers and boards and the essentially subordinate role of staff, but none of that is to deny the importance of good staff. Far more of the voluntary organization's planning and resources should go into building and nurturing good staff.

9

Constructive Planning— Even in Voluntary Organizations

A GOOD DESCRIPTION OF PLANNING in voluntary organizations can be summarized as, "We'll do as much good as we possibly can and that's all we can do." There is somehow an assumption that, because the mission is so large and the purposes so desperately important, it is not possible, nor perhaps even humane, to define what is most important, especially if this means conscientiously deciding that certain important goals will not be addressed.

One of the principal results of trying to accomplish more than is attainable is that all accountability is lost. It's not possible to expect or require someone to be finished with a task by next Friday or April 30, if the individual can come back and say that he or she is so swamped with other assigned tasks that there is no way this new task can be done. Presidents and executive directors of organizations start out each year with such sweeping expectations that as the months pass and it becomes obvious that most of these expectations can't be fulfilled, there is a tendency to get discouraged and to begin hoping that next year might be different.

In the absence of more realistic planning, most voluntary agencies are governed, and badly so, by the *bright idea*. A president, committee chairperson, board member, or staff member gets a bright idea about what should be done, and off the agency zags. The organization is almost defenseless against the bright idea because it sounds so good or might help so many people, but there is no mechanism to put it in competition with all the other things that might be done. The board, in particular, may be frustrated because most of its members aren't close enough to really know what's going on, and they can't quite grasp where the agency is and why and what is already being done.

What planning is taking place may be related only to what the staff thinks the agency should be doing. This is another example of the way agency control drifts—or is pulled—in the direction of staff dominance. Many thoughtful volunteers have concluded that planning is always going to be a staff role because only staff members have the necessary continuity, overview, and time to plan. I don't agree. Indeed, I think if the board can't be put in charge of planning, the volunteer character of the organization is considerably weakened.

The board is responsible for planning and must vote on the actual plans. This function can be assigned to a board committee and, in the case of five-year plans, certainly should be. There may be a great deal of delegation to the staff but this should only be to facilitate the board's work. Plans and evaluation of performance in relation to them are what the board is accountable for.

One of the problems of effective board involvement in planning is that people, particularly planners, always make planning seem so complicated. I've consulted with planning officers of large corporations to try to improve my own approach to planning, only to be put off by the jargon and makework of what to me is an unnecessarily complicated process.

It is realistic to engage in an intelligent approach to planning without having the process use up all available time. For several years I've participated in annual "planning retreats" designed to give an organization's officers an opportunity to effectively decide where they want to be a year hence. I've used this process at the local, state, and national levels, and in all cases have found it to have tremendous benefits. The process of an annual planning retreat begins with the president asking board members, committee chairpersons, staff members, and others what they consider to be the most important tasks to accomplish in the current year. These are carefully catalogued for advance study by the officers. The agency's top volunteer and staff leaders then go into a two-day concentrated planning session designed to identify, but not to undertake, the major projects and goals for the year and to determine to whom they will be assigned. The object of the planning retreat is to develop what I call the annual agenda—the organization's carefully planned objectives—for the year ahead. If the agency has had an opportunity to develop its five-year goals, the annual agenda should, of course, relate closely to them.

A typical agenda for an officers' planning retreat should, then, include these topics:

- Review of our mission.

- Review of our current resources.

- What did we get done in the past twelve months?

- What didn't we get done?

- Review of our continuing responsibilities.

- What *has* to be done in the next twelve months?

- Can we get it done?

- What's it going to be like?

- What important projects can't we do next year?

- Can we get the board to agree?

- Who's going to be responsible for what?

If yours is a typical group, this process will represent the first time your leadership group will have gained a common perception of what's most important to do *and* what can't be done.

As a starter, it will be revealing and useful to have each individual privately list the two or three most important things he or she would like to see accomplished in the year ahead. While these are being recorded and tabulated, ask the group to list the assets or strengths of the association. These simple approaches will help set the stage for some very solid planning. The group, as a group, will begin to have a common grasp of where the organization stands and an appreciation of the diverse expectations of its leaders. This should quickly lead to the heart of the session, which is to decide what is *in fact* possible and what is *really* most important.

The process of holding an annual planning retreat has benefits far beyond even the significant advantage of giving a clear idea of where you're going. For instance, the very nature of the session provides the officers with a common grasp of existing commitments and resources. Also, by being involved in the planning, the officers feel a commitment to the goals for the year. These factors increase their capacity for teamwork and reduce the many frictions and breakdowns in communication which could later occur.

One of the most exciting aspects of these planning retreats is the camaraderie which develops. We sometimes forget that the volunteer officers, even if they live in the same neighborhood or city, often don't know one another very well and frequently have quite different perceptions of the organization. By battling out the difficult decisions about how to utilize limited resources, the individuals really come together as a group. The planning retreats are not easy sessions; properly organized, they should be designed to decide what *not* to attempt to accomplish or what should be assigned low priority, which obviously means that some of the individuals will be disappointed. However, through more than fifteen years of this process at the local, state, and national levels, I have never known a case where the end result was not a tightly knit and enthusiastic team.

Still another advantage of the planning retreat is that the individuals in the organization come out of the session and the subsequent board meeting on the offensive—that is, they know where they want to go and they're determined to get there.

One of the real advantages of the resulting annual agenda is that it provides the board and staff with an ability to say no to all the bright ideas that come along during the year. On the other hand, if an idea or project that competes with their carefully determined goals obviously needs to be dealt with, the officers and board can make a conscious decision about it. It's amazing that even after going through this involved process, one of the tough jobs of the organization is to stay on course. If an association is dealing with a critical public problem, there will be many calls for a reappraisal of decisions and many new proposals for priority effort, but at least the process of the planning retreat and the existence of the annual agenda provide ammunition for holding the line.

The existence of an annual agenda makes the whole organization more aware of the need to accomplish the most important tasks. There should be reports to the executive committee and board of directors involving the volunteer leaders responsible for each of the areas of activity, and everyone should know that the progress is being charted.

It's a good idea to print your annual agenda on large posters to be available at board meetings. If your board and committees generally meet in one place, affix a set of these posters to the wall and, if possible, show the degree of fulfillment to date. These devices may sound terribly managerial and, indeed, are foreign to most voluntary agencies, but unless citizen groups learn to identify the most important things to be done and then find ways to lock in resources to accomplish them, they will continue to be characterized as inefficient do-gooders.

During the process of the annual retreat and in the board's consideration of the resulting recommendations for the annual agenda, the following guidelines might be useful.

- **Keep the meeting focused.** The more you search, the larger the focus can become. That's also a way of avoiding saying no. During some of your debates, you and the others won't want to see certain activities voted down, and the temptation will be to say, "Well, that's really a part of D (which, of course, it won't be at all), so let's just make it part of that priority." Don't do it.

- **Keep the plan simple.** For example, don't assume that a new committee or a task force is needed. On many matters your central group should act as a committee of the whole. As the operation grows, decentralization may be necessary, but a good rule is to respond to that only when there is no other alternative.

- **Keep the meeting action-oriented.** Trustees are tired of being involved in organizations which seem to be caught up in maintaining themselves or which are too timid to act. It is hoped that you have enlisted people who want to make a difference in a specific area; if they sense and see that you and the operation are action-oriented, you'll hold the best of them.

- **Involve the group in deciding the attainable goals and the methods for achieving them.** This process requires the genuine involvement of the officers and board members, as well as staff. If this is reduced to a discussion of only specific recommendations served up to the board without their prior participation, you may get approval, but you are not likely to get followership. Two meetings hence, when people propose new program priorities, you'll wonder where they were when the program plan was approved.

- **Make your goals specific.** Goals and strategies for achieving them should be very specific. In your fact-finding stage, pin down exactly what must happen to bring about your desired results and how you can make it happen.

- **Don't assume that your organization has to go it alone.** There may well be other groups who are interested in the same results. Part of your planning should involve the networking necessary to build allies and the specific plans for those negotiations. Decide what your best course of strategy should be. You can picket, boycott, expose, sue, establish, elect, fund, lobby, shame, demonstrate, augment, or whatever else will bring about the change or service you seek. The more specific you can be in defining the problem, goal, and strategy, the more rapidly you'll see results.

- **Condition yourself and the group to keep the faith if it's likely to be a long-term effort.** John W. Gardner has observed that "the first requirement for effective citizen action is stamina." It's almost certainly not going to be easy. For that reason it's essential to latch on to every evidence of progress and to be sure that the board is given full opportunity to know that the effort is getting somewhere, and that they have the right to be encouraged and to rejoice in the evidence of their growing power.

- **Remember that people are very generous toward important public causes.** You have the encouragement of knowing in advance that if you are really willing to work at it, you can raise the money necessary to achieve your goals.

Most of what I've described above represents an effort on the part of the current officers to gain a grasp of where they want to be at the end of their term and to have some means of locking in resources to get there. Several times, however, I've referred to the relationship of this process to the five-year goals of the agency. Here, too, I don't want to scare you off with the complexities of a process, but obviously an agency dealing with a longer-term effort should have an idea where it wants to go in the next five years. This process, too, should involve and emphasize board participation and responsibility. It, too, doesn't have to be terribly complicated; indeed, most things come down to common sense and some rudimentary skills. In the area of five-year planning, a volunteer group should be assigned to take a careful look at the mission of the organization, its current goals, the progress toward those goals, and the available resources. This, in turn, will help the board think about what is most important to be done six and seven years hence. A good deal of time should be allowed for the process so that there can be plenty of give-and-take about what the various elements of the organization believe are important. This process may develop some intense debates and perhaps cause upset; however, in the end, the membership and board will have had an opportunity to think through where they've been, where they are, and where they're going, along with what they consider to be the most promising steps for moving closer to the fulfillment of the agency's mission.

There are, of course, still more sophisticated levels of planning, involving such things as quantification of goals, but my experience has been that professional planners usually scare voluntary agencies away from sensible beginnings by making planning sound more involved than it really needs to be. Obviously, it's wise to take advantage of solid experience in any specialty, including planning. However, carefully select someone who knows your organization and who is realistic. Most planners want to immediately bring the organization to a level of sophistication far beyond the time or resources that can be realistically assigned.

Even as you move into more complex planning, the process and results must never be beyond the board's grasp and control. Be sure that you, as a board member, understand what is behind such terms as "strategic planning," "needs assessment," and "management by objectives." Most of it comes down to common sense approaches to deciding what's most important to be done, what resources are necessary, how to divide up the tasks, and how to evaluate progress. In *Managing for Impact of Nonprofit Organizations: Corporate Planning Techniques and Applications*, James M. Hardy deals with the important technicalities that help a voluntary organization carry on the kind of planning now fairly routine in large business corporations. Much of this is accomplished in four levels.

Hardy points out that initially the board should articulate the "ideal goals." Essentially this is the statement of purpose usually covered in the certificate of incorporation or bylaws. According to him, it is "a description of the ideal or reason for existence of the organization. It frequently defines the organization's ethical tone and basic philosophy, but is never completely attainable. The time span for ideal goals is infinite and consequently they tend to be a relatively fixed organizational anchor point."

His second level involves the "corporate goals," which he says constitute:

> . . . a description of the desired future that is possible and that provides definitive direction for the total organization. These goals are formulated through a process that is directed by the Chief Executive Officer, approved by the Board of Directors and become the "planning umbrella" within which all operating units accomplish their annual planning. The time span for corporate goals is usually five years. Each corporate goal frequently has a related statement of *expected outcomes;* that is, a description of the kinds of conditions that will exist in five years if the corporate goal has been satisfactorily achieved. Essentially, expected outcomes further clarify the goal and provide additional guidance and direction to operating units.

His third level constitutes the ". . . objectives—specifically measurable statements of attainable outcomes within the framework of the corporate goals. Objectives are developed by operating units. The time span for objectives is usually one year."

The fourth level is made up of the ". . . action steps—specific work segments or activities necessary for the achievement of objectives. Time span is usually one to twelve months."

On another level of sophistication, the United Way of America has an ongoing project, *House of Accountability*, which involves a series of publications generally related to planning and evaluation. Included in this series is *Needs Assessment: A Guide For Planners, Managers and Funders of Health and Human Care Services.* Essentially the book is designed to help boards and their planning committees and staff to decide what is most important to accomplish and to begin to break tasks into attainable sizes. For example, they provide "17 Approaches to Needs Assessment," including such steps in the process as general population survey, survey of subpopulation(s), survey of service providers, survey of service recipients, service statistics, social indicators, inventory of resources, and needs identified by other planning systems.

Many other voluntary organizations are moving into strategic planning, including churches, the scouts, museums, orchestras, colleges, and health agencies. The sophistication of their processes and plans is encouraging, but unfortunately some of these agencies give the impression that any organization that hasn't reached their level of planning competence isn't *really* doing strategic planning. That's nonsense. A family that knows its values, decides its priorities, and plots and budgets its income is still one of the best examples of strategic planning. And there's probably a lot less slippage in that unit than in a more sophisticated organization.

Don't be put off but don't put it off. Keep in mind the Peter Principle: "If you don't know where you're going, you'll end up someplace else." I would add to this that, in a voluntary agency, if you don't know where you're going, you'll end up zigzagging in all directions. *But*, if the board has been involved in a common-sense approach to figuring out what the resources are and how best to assign them, you're more likely to end up with a giant step in the direction of the organization's basic purpose.

10

Working with Committees

Be kind to committees. They are our most maligned organizational species. For every person who says with pride, "I got appointed to the committee," there are a thousand who put it, "You won't believe what they've done to me!" The jokes abound:

- An elephant is a horse designed by a committee.

- A committee keeps minutes and wastes hours.

- The best committee has three members—with two always out of town.

- A committee is made up of the unfit trying to lead the unwilling to do the unnecessary.

- A committee is a collection of individuals who separately do nothing and together decide that nothing can be done.

I suppose that raises a question about having committees at all. Committees do serve a purpose, although I will say that I believe in the "principle of least number." The board of directors should handle as many matters as possible. Also, the work of many committees, including such subjects as bylaws, can usually be accommodated by ad hoc assignments as needed. I am a great believer in "ad-hocracy." All committees, except those required and identified in the bylaws, should be ad hoc, including the stipulation that they automatically go out of business at the end of the year unless specifically reconstituted and recharged by the board. Cyril O. Houle, in *The Effective Board*, recalls the quip, "To have one committee is better than to have two, to have two is better than to have three, and so on. It is all too clear what would be better than one committee."

I am also a great user of one-person task forces, or at least few-person task forces, which are asked to do their business in one or two meetings and then automatically to go out of business.

It is standard practice today for all kinds of organizations to go through the exercise of starting with a blank slate. If there were no committees, which ones would you actually recreate, and are there other ways to do the same business?

You may want to write down the functions that must be performed and then decide on the simplest way of carrying out those jobs. Such functions might include bylaws, personnel, finance, annual meeting, fundraising, public relations, awards, nominating, legal, program(s), emergency decisions, and other business between board meetings.

In my current organization, we don't have an executive committee. There was strong feeling on the part of the organizers that executive committees tend to consolidate decision-making among too few people and end up doing the work of the board while leaving out most of the trustees. It's amazing how few matters really can't wait for the next board meeting and how easy it is to fall into the easier pattern of using the smaller group. The classic situation is that the executive committee usually deals with the executive director's evaluation and compensation and the board isn't even told what the staff director is paid.

When emergency matters arise, there usually isn't time for an executive committee meeting, so that, too, is not a terribly valid rationale. We follow the procedure that the chief volunteer officer, chief staff officer, and head of the committee of reference can make a decision on behalf of the organization as long as it does not contradict an existing policy or other decision already passed by the board. I cite this simply as an example of the fact that it is possible to challenge the traditional thinking about committee structure. I realize that for many organizations an executive committee is an important instrument of decision-making. Such committees are usually able to exercise all the powers of the board except changes in the bylaws, which is necessary if the executive committee is to be able to represent the board whenever an emergency develops. This creates the danger of the executive committee functioning in place of the board of directors, but practicalities necessitate that risk. As a matter of fact, executive committees are too often used in place of boards.

The executive committee should be large enough to be representative of the board. It should not be simply the officers and one or two others. Some executive committees include the officers and committee chairpersons. I advise against this, as it puts together a group too easily given to pork-barreling and not equipped to give an objective review of emergency matters coming before it.

Executive committee minutes should be circulated quickly to all board members and each board meeting should include a report of executive committee actions. This all too rarely happens, and the board doesn't have much opportunity to ask why these matters were not postponed until the board meeting. The usual excuse is that the matters were too complex for the full board. Look behind that to see if it really is so, and even when it is, ask why the board didn't at least have a chance to vote on the executive committee's recommendation.

In the name of simplicity, INDEPENDENT SECTOR has a management committee, which consolidates the personnel, finance, audit, equal opportunity, and other management oversight functions. Our nominating and awards functions are also consolidated. Legal issues are handled by the program committee involved or by the management committee. Bylaws revisions are an ad hoc function. On the other hand, fundraising is a very distinct committee function, one that I would never combine with public relations or any other assignment. It's always too easy to get diverted into other less concrete functions and to postpone the urgent task related to the fundraising plan and its implementation.

Having argued for simplification, let me make what could appear to be a contradictory point. When a committee *is* needed, I *don't* argue the "principle of least number." If such a group is in fact needed, then it must include ample involvement from the various forces and interests within the organization and community. If you are convinced the function is necessary, be sure that all who need to be involved in the decision and its implementation are considered for membership. I'm speaking primarily of program and policy issues that have broad implications for your organization and its constituencies.

Except for the nominating committee, the chief volunteer officer should have full authority to appoint chairpersons and committees. Heads of committees should have an opportunity to request a few people they feel are essential to the task, but it is the volunteer president who needs to make all the appointments. This is necessary to be sure that certain individuals are not overused and others underused and to be certain that the organization is reaching out to all the individuals and groups which should be involved. For committees, I don't believe in staggered terms, at least as stipulated by policy or bylaw. This restricts the opportunity of a president to make significant changes when they are needed. The president instead should informally stagger the appointments in order to achieve a balance of experience and new blood.

Unless it doesn't make sense for the task at hand, committees and task forces should include a mix of board members and others. Spread the work and the opportunities; it's a good way to develop future board members and officers.

The chief volunteer officer should serve ex officio as a member of all the committees of which he or she has appointment authority; this should be so for the committee head who appoints subcommittees and task forces. Incidentally, many people assume that the term ex officio means participating but without vote. Actually it means participating by virtue of one's office and that role automatically carries with it a right to vote except where otherwise prohibited.

Every committee, ad hoc committee, and even subcommittee and task force should have a written charge. It's almost always an erroneous assumption that people have a common understanding of the task to be accomplished. At least once a year, the committee should review its charge. I go so far as to put it in the resource materials, which are part of the committee packet sent to the group in advance of *each* meeting. It's amazing how often it is the key to bringing the group back on track.

It will greatly improve attendance and the quality of your discussions and decisions if the agenda and related materials are sent at least ten days in advance of committee meetings. It is important to underscore here that this is rarely done and is a large factor in the inefficiency of so many committees.

It's my standard practice to begin each committee meeting with an overview of activities within the organization. Staff members fight this. Committee heads sometimes feel that it interferes with getting on with the business at hand, but committee members love it. For most of them, it's the only time that they find out how their activities relate to the organization as a whole and what has happened in the fulfillment of the organization's mission. It's a key part of giving meaning to volunteering and keeping the dream alive.

Presidents and boards should not underestimate how much staff time goes into effective service of committees and task forces. Boards, executive committees, and other committees tend to find that an easy way to deal with conflict is to refer the matter to an existing committee or to create a new one. I regularly ask boards whether they are doing this because they really want the matter handled that way, or whether it's an excuse to avoid coming to grips with the situation. Board meetings and annual meetings should provide an arena for reasonable conflict and resolution of differences. It's better to have a matter done with—if this is really the intent—than to prolong the process to be polite or to avert conflict. If people know how much work is entailed in establishing and servicing such unnecessary appendages, or if they recognize that it cuts into the time available to pursue real priorities, they are likely to be more hard-headed and to adopt a more sensible approach. Obviously there are times when the conflict can reach the destructive level, and therefore it's worth the price to keep the subject alive at the committee level. I urge only that you be aware that the price is not small.

The board should be careful to see that committee activity is pointed toward the established *program* priorities and *program* plan of the organization. It's easy to get caught up in *organizational* business. For instance, bylaws committees often take up more time than any other committee. Everyone is interested in bylaws, even when it's difficult to get these same people moving on priority fundraising and program matters. In the matter of committees, I invoke the apt phrase, "Keep your eye upon the donut and not upon the hole."

Committees tend to be better at thinking up activities than pursuing them. It's far more fun to consider what needs to be done than to get on with the decisions already made about what must be done. As a result, committees—and boards, too—tend to be "add-oners" rather than implementers. In one organization with which I worked, this became such a source of frustration and misunderstanding that I went back over the minutes of several committees and pulled out all of the decisions made. Then I matched these against the follow-through achieved and against the staff resources available to the committees. Not surprisingly, there was a startling disparity between expectations and resources, and it became obvious why the committees were upset that so many of their bright ideas had not taken hold. It didn't dawn on them that *they* were equally responsible for implementation. They had had the fun of deciding what should be done but had shirked responsibility for follow-through. We instituted a report, called "Summary of Past Actions," on which each decision of the committee was recorded. The third item of every committee meeting's agenda, immediately following the "Overview of Association Activities" and the minutes, was the "Summary of Past Actions." The committee members had to take a look at what they had already decided should be done and the state of implementation before going on to other business. This automatically led to a focus on things already decided rather than on new ideas.

In terms of structure, it's necessary to deal with the issue of auxiliaries. They can be a wonderful addition to an organization's fundraising and community outreach, but they can take on a life of their own. For example, on the disparity between the resources and expectations, auxiliaries can often make decisions requiring extensive staff time without regard to the organization's other expectations. For this and other reasons, I generally advise against having any part of the structure free from the obligations and constraints faced by the other parts. It comes back to the matter of simplicity. Don't establish any more complexity than is absolutely necessary.

On this point Houle says:

> But the headaches which can be created by a multiple-board system are both numerous and difficult to cure. An auxiliary board may gain a great deal of prominence and prestige, and be confused in the public mind—or, worse, in its own—with the Board where the controlling power lies. An auxiliary board may gradually take on more and more functions until it exactly parallels the Controlling Board; in such a case, there is in effect a two house legislature and every issue must be carried through both boards—to the eventual despair of the Executive. Two boards may crawl, or become deadlocked, or have any other kind of difficulties imaginable, all to the detriment of the service or program they are supposed to guide and aid.

> The basic rule for preventing or curing these difficulties is this: Auxiliary boards should be auxiliary. Only one board can be controlling. The others must have clear-cut functions which they carry out, and these functions should be set down in writing and generally understood.

So much for structure. What comfort and guidance are there should you find yourself not only on the committee, but head of it? For comfort, I can only pass along the advice given to a friend who was active in civil rights efforts back in the sixties, but who, because he came in constant touch with a great many angry people, found himself roundly criticized for what he had not done. He was complaining to a friend that these people didn't seem to appreciate or give him credit for at least being well out in front of most others on these issues. He admitted to being hurt that he was not being embraced for his good works. His friend provided this advice: "Harry, if it's affection you need, get yourself a dog."

Involvement in crucial issues may not bring Harry and you much immediate affection, but you can be sure that someday you will look back on these as among the very best days of your life. It is true, after all, that service is its own reward.

Much of what is true of the role of the president applies to you and your important sphere of activity. You're the one who must encourage, applaud, prod, and even "fire and hire." Although the chief volunteer officer has the ultimate authority for committee appointments, you have every right to ask for a few people whom you know are important to the task and with whom you feel particularly comfortable. Also, you have a right to ask that certain individuals not be appointed or reappointed.

It's your job to see that the committee is as good at implementation as it is at blue-skying. This means giving plenty of time to creativity but at least equal time to hitching the team to those dreams. No matter how much you rely on staff, you're responsible for the committee, including such mundane things as the approval of the agenda and related resource material, and the fact that they are mailed to the committee far enough in advance of meetings for adequate study. You are ultimately responsible for the minutes and for the good of the organization.

Beyond the important mechanics and other details, your basic job is to build a team equal to the task and to give them a sense of being a team. Step back periodically to evaluate your performance, not only in terms of decisions made and their implementation, but whether the group is coming together in a way that will allow for even greater achievement. That includes respect for the group and a willingness to really let them contribute rather than merely respond to your bright ideas or those of staff members. I recall being named to a committee of quite impressive performers who, because of the importance of the task and the quality of persons named, showed up in force at the first meeting. Then, in the form of his opening statement, the chairman threw this bucket of ice water on us, "I do so hope you all agree with me that the course we should follow is. . . ." That was thirty years ago, but I still recall it vividly. On the other hand, I can't recall anything else about it. I never went back.

In "Better Boards and Committees," a pamphlet by the Adult Education Association of the U.S.A., there's a good description of the personal characteristics of the effective committee head:

1. One who has a personal record of being a consistent worker who completed a job;

2. is enthusiastic;

3. has background knowledge of the organization's aims and the Committee's functions;

4. is hard working;

5. is good humored;

6. is quick;

7. is a good executive; and

8. is persuasive.*

In addition, the effective committee head:

1. has confidence in other members;

2. wants to release the potential energy of the group;

3. is willing to give up the Chairman's initial prerogatives, if the job requires it; and

4. is more interested in the Committee's job than in his own feeling of personal importance.*

The pamphlet concludes with: "The good chairman is one who can work with people, who can stimulate them rather than brow beat them and can help the group use all the abilities and experiences its members possess and new ones too that they develop as they work together."

It is important to continually give the group a sense of where they fit in. For example, show them how they fit into the scheme of the organization's overall mission and current priorities and find ways to give them a sense of pride and accomplishment. From time to time ask the chief volunteer officer to come by, if for no other reason than to "show the flag." Take some time at meetings to bring in people who can help provide a broader perspective and some awareness of how their relatively small role relates to the broader roles of, say, building the best museum or finding the answer to heart disease.

---

* Reprinted with permission from Adult Education Association of the U.S.A.

Every now and then, perhaps once a year, provide some social activity. It might help remind you to do this if you think that the committee should have its own annual meeting. On those occasions be sure there's a combination of outside stimulation, review of accomplishments, and socializing. Where it is possible, have a meeting at your home or other private setting. These important gestures add to the evidence that you take seriously both the task and the individuals.

Keep the board informed of committee progress and keep the committee informed of the board's responses. Communicate in personal ways with the committee between meetings. For example, if you've reported to the board, dictate a memo as personal as possible to the group so that they know the results of the presentation, including any action that results. Too often we wait for the next committee meeting, when in fact the really interested members will be wondering, "What in the world happened to our important proposal?"

If there are newspaper stories or other bits of news that relate to the area of your committee's work, send them along with a note, "Thought this might be of interest." It's important to touch base with your own subordinates. What you should be aiming for is that some day, several years hence, you will bump into some of these people, and you want them to say, "You know, looking back on it, we really got some amazing things done. It was one of the most rewarding things I've ever done. And besides—it was fun."

For the committee member to earn a share in that ultimate reward, he or she also has to make an investment.

In the same Adult Education Association pamphlet, there is this very useful "Committee Member Check List":

1. Am I familiar with and sympathetic toward the aims and methods of the parent organization which created the committee?

2. Can I express myself easily and clearly and enjoy the give and take of exchanging ideas with others?

3. Do I have reasonably good focus, a sense of direction and a sense of timing, plus a willingness to stick to the task at hand?

4. Am I receptive, open minded and able to learn and to receive stimulation from others?

5. Do I have vision and perspective which enables me to see the present in terms of the future?

6. Am I fundamentally cooperative in seeking after agreement and unity?

7. Am I able to arrive at decisions and face their implications?*

The summary of specific responsibilities says:

To be effective, committee members should be able to attend meetings regularly. They should seek to understand the Committee assignment and work to complete it. Members should participate in the deliberations and discussions and should share the responsibility of sticking to the subject and trying to understand and use the ideas of other members. They should help in reaching committee decisions, in committee action and in following the final disposition of its work. Committee members should also evaluate their own contributions to the Committee and share the responsibility for evaluating the work of the Committee as a whole.*

If you are a board member serving on a committee with persons who are not on the board, accept responsibility to reach out to these people; they will be sensitive to how you as a board member relate to them. Help them understand the broader work of the organization and develop a sense of shared mission and pride. You can also help them realize the limitations on the organization's resources, but don't constantly remind them that the board has many other priorities. Some board members can be insufferable in the way they exercise their board membership to stifle the initiative and growth of other committee members. Make it a rule to *really* listen to the newcomers. Don't tell them you already covered that ground in 1952. Encourage and nurture them. They are the organization's seed crop. Besides, remember how you felt as a newcomer in some organization and think hard about the people you remember as the best models of kindness and helpfulness. Someone helped bring you along and now it's your turn.

At board meetings when your committee leader reports, be supportive. It's pretty unsettling and even maddening when a person makes a report and the other committee members around the board table hedge their bets waiting to see how the other trustees react. It's your committee, too. Put yourself on the line.

Whether you are on the board or not, find ways to let the committee head know that you are appreciative of his or her leadership. You may not agree with everything being done and may even represent a different point of view on many subjects. But go out of your way to show your objectivity and thoughtfulness in giving thanks where it is due.

Carry your share of the load. That may seem obvious, but it is the source of greatest discouragement in all kinds of organizations. Depending on people who aren't reliable is a nightmare, and working with people who are is a delight.

For all of the frustration and hard work, you will enjoy the satisfactions of the committee's accomplishments and the sense of personal worth. When the work is hard or dull or upsetting, try to remember the largest lesson I've ever learned

---

* Reprinted from "Better Boards and Committees" with permission from Adult Education Association of the U.S.A.

about volunteering, which I tried to summarize in the opening chapter of this book:

> People who get involved with public causes open themselves to frustration and disappointment, but—through it all and after it all—those moments of making change happen for the better are among our lasting joys. There's something wonderfully rewarding in being part of an effort that does make a difference.

You may not feel that way at the end of tomorrow's committee meeting, but I bet you will five years from now.

11

Making the Most Out of Meetings

A SIGNIFICANT PART of the business of voluntary organizations involves meetings and yet, in most organizations, surprisingly little thought is applied to making these meetings productive. It is a fact of life that good meetings create high attendance, improve the quality of decisions, and promote alert follow-through. Bad meetings don't. Thoughtfulness and common sense are the basic ingredients of planning good meetings. These in turn lead to some rules which make up the art of having good meetings. I'll start with some suggestions that apply to both board and committee meetings and then turn to some special features of board and annual meetings.

Give careful attention to the selection, recruitment, and orientation of the group; these are the cornerstones of good meetings. Let me repeat my earlier advice to the presidents that it is important to select as the chairperson an individual who is an effective organizer rather than a person who is an authority on the subject at hand.

The group should have a sense of purpose. Some of this will come with orientation, but it should also be conveyed through the formal committee charge and in the reports from the president, chairperson, and others.

Spread the workload of the board or committee and of the meetings themselves. Try to be certain that several people are responsible for handling individual items on the agenda.

If you don't have topics that really need the group's consideration, cancel the meeting, even though the board or committee may not have missed a monthly meeting in 133 years.

Provide adequate notice and give a reminder call a day or two in advance of the meeting. If it's an ongoing body, have fixed meeting dates such as the first Monday of the month. If that's not possible, then it's generally helpful to have the group set its next meeting date while they are still in session; the day after the meeting a notice should be sent reminding the full group of the next date or dates. It's helpful to enclose a return postal card so that you have an indication of attendance and the members feel they've made a firm commitment.

Submit the agenda and the basic background material to the full group at least a week in advance of the meeting. I am constantly dismayed to find how often the agenda is distributed at the meeting, and even then it often consists of only three or four nondescript items such as "President's Report," "Executive's Report," and "New Business." If the members are worth involving, it's essential that they be served well. The greatest single factor in poor attendance is the failure to provide a good agenda and reference materials well in advance of the meeting. The agenda should state clearly what the group is being asked to consider or decide, and the reference material should prepare the members for intelligent discussion. If the people are committed to attend and if they see that the session is being organized in a businesslike way, they're more likely to be there and at future meetings.

Pay careful attention to the physical arrangements, including location, accessibility, parking, and reasonable meal service. The room itself should be conducive to effective work, including good lighting, heat, and ventilation. If it's at all possible, I try to have a round table or a "square doughnut" so that all the members are facing the center. This creates maximum participation and a feeling of involvement for all. Even when I'm dealing with a board meeting of thirty to forty people, I try to organize it as a square doughnut or in two four-sided or three-sided tiers so that the group is fairly close together, all within earshot of one another, and facing the center. Even with very large groups, I work hard at trying to create a physical arrangement that is comfortable and promotes maximum involvement. It's essential to plan in advance for blackboards, easels, and audio-visual equipment; and to check electrical outlets, microphones, public address systems, and so on. Also, don't forget the arrangements for water and coffee service.

Check the meeting room well in advance. The day before the meeting be certain that someone has the work order, knows you are coming, and knows what the arrangements are to be. Then check the meeting room one hour in advance of the meeting. I do this even with breakfast meetings. My experience is that 50 percent of the time there is a breakdown in the arrangements. The blackboard will be there, but no chalk. There won't be an extension cord for the projector, or the electrical socket will be wired with the lights so that when the lights go out the projector also goes out. Or the public address system won't work, or perhaps someone forgot to provide a microphone. And it happens at least 10 percent of the time that the meeting room isn't set up at all, and the only person around never heard of you or your damned meeting.

If your meeting is in a hotel, by all means check the bulletin board to be sure that the meeting time and place are clearly identified. I'll make a private bet with you that at least half of the time the bell captain or the catering department will have listed the wrong meeting room or the wrong time, and at least 25 percent of the time they will have forgotten to list you at all. It is always a mystery and frustration to me that hotels which make so much of their money from meetings generally handle them so poorly. This is why it's essential to doggedly check the arrangements a day in advance and in person an hour in advance.

Abide by Murphy's Laws:

What can go wrong will go wrong.
If unattended to, it will only get worse.

Don't let the chairperson or staff dominate the meeting. If either or both take up all the time, they may feel good at the end of the session, but they'll be talking to themselves at the next meeting.

Keep the group informed between meetings. This includes getting the minutes out quickly, reporting to the committee on action taken on their recommendations by the executive committee or board of directors, and sending thoughtful notes sharing interesting bits of information or news of the organization's activities. Whatever it is, a deliberate, thoughtful, ongoing effort to let the members know they are important and are appreciated will pay off.

Give the group a sense of accomplishment and momentum. The original charge to the group should have been realistic enough so that there can be a regular sense of accomplishment. If large tasks are broken down into bite sizes, the group can have a feeling of getting somewhere. Be sure that the members do gain a sense of movement and have the satisfaction of accomplishment. Committees and boards often suffer from a feeling of vagueness or vastness, and it takes considerable effort to provide the members with some feeling of tasks well done.

Keep it interesting. Deliberately plan part of the agenda for the purpose of giving the group a feeling of being in the know, having a chance to learn some of the exciting things that are happening in the field, or knowing more about what the organization as a whole is doing. I learned a lot from a president who insisted that every meeting should include a section which he labeled "the entertainment." It was his deliberate and successful policy that every meeting should include a film or speaker or some presentation to take the group away from the immediate tasks and give them a sense of excitement and being in the know.

Pay attention to the niceties. Take time to figure out how to make your meetings pleasant. For instance, people say how much they appreciate having large name cards placed in front of each person attending the meeting. Send the committee list with each agenda. Include nicknames and women's first names. This may seem like duplication, but people do forget names and like to review the list in advance.

Occasionally hold your meeting in a special setting. This doesn't mean it has to be in a fancy club. It might be in one of the facilities which relate to the group's efforts. The National Mental Health Association encourages local boards to meet at least once a year in the state hospital serving the community.

Provide a regular mechanism for board acknowledgment of committee progress. This kind of thoughtfulness makes a big difference to committee members, who inevitably wonder if their efforts are really noticed and really do achieve results. Thank a committee when its work is done and express appreciation to those who are going off the committee. It's hard to anticipate all the things that add up to the niceties and to thoughtfulness; but unless presidents, committee chairpersons, and staff members take time to project themselves into the place of the members, the rush of everyday events will continue to preoccupy them, and important opportunities to develop a closer feeling of camaraderie and family will be lost.

All the basic rules apply to board meetings. In addition, there are special considerations. The board of directors has to have an overview of the mission, goals, progress, and problems of the agency, which means that a part of board meetings has to be given to this kind of review. It can be partly accomplished by a *written* report of the president, including a report of progress toward the annual agenda (the one-year plan).

One of the most important roles of the board is to establish the priorities and directions for the organization. This means that a reasonable amount of time must also be given to discussion and, when appropriate, to approval of the annual agenda, the annual budget, and the five-year plan, and to regular determination of progress on those plans.

Because the board's decisions are so central to an agency's effectiveness, it is all the more necessary that the agenda and related material go out in advance. The board members should have an agenda in their hands at least a week in advance of the meeting. The supporting material should not be so voluminous that it will not be practical for board members to gain a grasp of the issues. This means that a good deal of work will have to be done by the president and executive director to reduce complicated issues to their essence. Some organizations throw in all the minutes of intervening committee meetings and then add insult to injury by having the chairperson read the minutes.

Don't expect that every board member is going to read everything, although if the material is distributed well beforehand, you'll be surprised at how many will. People who have a particular interest in a subject will carefully prepare for the discussion. The presentations and discussions should start with the assumption that people have read the material in advance of the meeting, and it should become an embarrassment for members to ask questions or make comments which clearly indicate they have not done their homework.

Carefully identify the reason for having each item on the agenda. Certain items will be there for important information purposes. Other items will be there for the board's consideration and disposition. One can't accurately predict which items will get fast action and which ones will require extensive debate. You may recall Parkinson's law that the smaller the item the greater attention it will be given. He uses the example of the board which quickly passes on the purchase of a multimillion-dollar nuclear reactor and then gets hopelessly bogged down in a discussion of purchasing garbage cans. He says that this is because everybody knows about garbage cans.

Provide a suggested timetable. This obviously will be adjusted to the board's interest, but at least it will provide some indication of the items which seem to require fuller consideration.

The board agenda and resource material should include intelligible financial reports—an income and expense statement, balance sheet, and budget status report.

Limit the executive director's report. For example, only occasionally do I make an extensive report to the board of directors. I consider that if my job is properly done, the reports of the various committees, task forces, and other officers will cover most of the business that needs attention. Occasionally I may want to share management considerations or special observations with the board. It's my impression that if I do not constantly dominate the board discussions, then the information and issues I *do* bring to the board will carry more weight. I shudder at the meetings I attend where the executive director and other staff members carry the ball so totally that the board members are left completely uninvolved, limp, and glassy-eyed.

Most membership organizations hold an annual meeting, which can and should be a special occasion. It's probably accurate to say that most annual meetings are dinner meetings and that by the time the group is finished with the meal, the reports, the elections, the out-going president's comments, the in-coming president's comments, the awards, and the responses of those honored with awards, those members still present are numb, disengaged, and dreading the main speech, which is still to come.

Annual meetings should be exciting and stimulating and should provide a significant thrust to the organization's major business. For these reasons, the basic rules governing all meetings given in the first few pages of this chapter are particularly important. In addition, here are some other important considerations:

- **Treat the voting membership as an important part of your organization.** The annual meeting is an important time for the voting members to be involved and informed about your future plans.

- **Provide enough time for what needs to be done.** If you really line up all that can (and should) be done at the annual meeting, it is almost a certainty that it can't be reduced to a dinner meeting unless, as is too often the case, you are prepared to go well into the night. Instead, given enough advance notice, people will set aside a Saturday or a weekday or at least an afternoon topped by a really fun-filled and interesting dinner without all the business being crammed in. To do this: (1) adopt a time schedule and stick to it; (2) leave time for questions, discussion and debate; and (3) provide an advance agenda with written reports. (Include information on award winners, nominating committee recommendations, and summaries of the actions called for.)

- **Relate the meeting to the basic thrust of the association.** It's surprising how often organizations will choose themes and speakers which do not fit into or contribute to the mainstream of their current efforts. It's almost as though annual meeting committees were divorced from the basic organization. Often the pattern is to come up with a catchy theme and a principal speaker that do not take advantage of the tremendous opportunity to use the annual meeting as an occasion to push the organization's basic projects.

- **Plan carefully for awards and recognition.** The annual meeting is a time when an organization can honor those who have served its cause. Be careful, though, not to present so many awards that the meaning is diminished. The awards can be listed in a printed program. In some cases, many people may be included in an award category—for instance, volunteers who have contributed more than 100 hours to the organization. These people can be asked to stand up as a group. If you are trapped into doing everything at a dinner meeting, present some of the awards in advance and then be sure the names are listed in the printed program. It's also effective sometimes to spread the awards throughout the agenda. Except in unusual cases, don't introduce individuals who aren't present. I always have a sinking feeling when names are called for people to stand, then several of the people aren't present.

- **Select interesting locations.** It's not always possible to come up with an imaginative approach, but people do like to visit an interesting place. This can be either a new hotel or, at the other extreme, a facility that relates to the agency's work. Be careful about the expense, however. Increasingly, agencies are involving youth and the poor, and those $20 dinner tabs have a way of saying you don't really mean it. Consider, for a change, holding the meeting in a jail, state hospital, church, museum, campground, new synagogue, a mansion donated for the day, a community college, a movie theater or legitimate play-house, or even in city hall, a company's training facility, or any other place that's different, interesting, inexpensive, and perhaps educational.

- **Work hard at promoting attendance.** There should be early mailings to the voting membership and to a very carefully developed list of outside groups and individuals. A *personal invitation* should be ex-tended by officers and members of the annual meeting committee to the fifty outside people you are most eager to have present. It should be made clear that the board members are expected to be there. Voting members should also know they are expected to attend this one meet-ing each year. Committee members are part of the voting membership and they should be particularly urged to take advantage of this op-portunity to get a broader feel of the organization. Promoting atten-dance requires imagination and hard work, but the annual meeting can be a very significant event in terms of public exposure, community involvement, and agency thrust. Some members of the annual meeting committee should carry on an extensive telephone campaign to the board members, voting members, committee members, and others to promote attendance.

- **Take advantage of your publicity opportunities.** Some of your pro-motion efforts can be assisted by advance notices to the news media. However, these will simply support your promotion efforts and should not be considered as doing the promotion job itself. The many events which will be part of a really good annual meeting will provide pegs for advance stories and for media coverage during the meeting itself.

- **Spread the workload.** One of the reasons that annual meetings often don't achieve their potential is that the event is left largely to the staff. However, it's the kind of activity at which many board members will work very hard. The annual meeting should be a major volunteer responsibility. The committee should be a year-round operation with regular reports to the board of directors. The various assignments—involving publicity, registration, promotion, awards, and program—should be made to individuals or subcommittees. Obviously, staff backup is needed, but not nearly so much as we generally think. Clearly, the opportunity and responsibility to make the most of this annual event should not be curtailed because staff members don't have enough time. Most of the responsibilities can be carried by volunteers.

- **Pay special attention to arrangements.** Remember that "what can go wrong will go wrong." Make a careful list of all the physical arrangements and check them. If you don't, things will rapidly go wrong and Murphy's second law will come into play: "If unattended to, the situation will only get worse." Among the many things that can go wrong are:

—The microphone or speaker system won't work (or will squeal so badly that people will think they're experiencing a lobotomy);

—The awards will be in the wrong order (or else they won't get there at all);

—The president will introduce the head table from left to right when it's set up right to left; or

—The hotel will serve pot roast on Good Friday.

Don't be afraid of healthy controversy in meetings of committees, the board, or voting membership. If the cause is important, people will feel strongly about it but not always the same way. Let people debate and even argue, but keep it within the bounds and context of an organization's meeting. Don't be too quick to refer the issue to a committee or to try to mask very real differences. It amuses me when some well-meaning peacemaker will jump up and offer the observation that "they're really not that far apart," when the antagonists are at each other's throats, or "the two points are not mutually exclusive," when in fact the two arguments are opposite.

If the going gets too hot, fall back on *Robert's Rules of Order* to help organize the discussion and decision, but don't let that process take control of healthy exchange.

Once the matter has been decided, the volunteer and staff leaders must help the organization adjust quickly to the decision and get on with the more positive aspects of the agency's program and operations. A good organization, like a good manager, spends time on issues that it can do something about and doesn't waste time on issues it can't do anything about.

Obviously, peacemaking should be the order of the day, but once in a while it's not the best course to follow. Occasionally, it's better that people lose and move out of the mainstream. There is a great temptation in voluntary organizations to make up and to bring Charlie back into the chairmanship or to the executive committee to show him there are no hard feelings. This is usually the right thing to do, but sometimes it only perpetuates the underlying difference which was finally settled. There are times—not often, to be sure, but there are times—when it's better to let some people fall away or go away mad. This may not seem fair—a contradiction to the kind of spirit that voluntary organizations try to generate, but some people and some controversies are better moved out so the organization can concentrate on what the clear majority wants to do. Remember that an organization can sustain only so much controversy.

It is important to say a word about the annual meeting of national organizations. Much of what I said about annual meetings in general applies here, but the national annual meeting deserves special mention. It is the major vehicle by which national leaders can promote the spirit, thrust, camaraderie, and communication so necessary to the total organization. Often the board and even the national staff tend to take the annual meeting for granted. We don't realize the responsibility and opportunity it represents and thus we don't set aside enough time to do it imaginatively and well.

As the executive director of the National Mental Health Association, I talked each year with the staff about the importance I attached to the national annual meeting and the kind of preparation I thought was necessary to make it an experience people would go away from with new respect for the association, new pride in the organization, and a storehouse of information to apply back home.

We went over our service plans to identify the problems and aspirations of our local units and to match people for meals and social functions in order to promote optimal communication and informal consultation. We set up our cocktail hours in a "cocktails and conversation" format so that people could go to specific tables or booths to talk about subjects of interest to them. This not only broke the ice—which is so essential to do—but it also provided people with a good deal of information.

I'm sure it's the same with most national organizations, but the handbook governing all the technical arrangements for those annual meetings was a tome. It started with a selection of facilities and ran through several hundred pages, ending with instructions on providing tips to hotel employees who were particularly responsive. In between there was a collection of lessons learned that helped make certain that our meetings were professionally and thoughtfully done so that people went away with a confidence that their national association was well run and did care about them. This, in turn, instilled a greater spirit and commitment in our membership.

Not everyone can get to the national annual meeting and we tend not to realize how helpful it is for people to see the organization beyond the limits of their own chapters. Some national organizations no longer have a national annual meeting. For instance, the Girl Scouts of America meets every three years. That organization uses the first of the intervening years for regional meetings, and the second for development and discussion of the issues which will be decided in the triennial national meeting. I favor some such system because regional or sectional meetings give many more people a feeling of being part of something special.

Whether you are responsible for a task force or international conference, work hard at producing good meetings. They are the key to good decision-making, all-out follow-through, and maximum volunteer motivation. It's on the meeting ground that the quality of the organization is truly revealed.

12

Robert's Rules of Order— Demystified

Robert's rules of order can be very complicated—but almost always unnecessarily. Occasionally all that complexity is required—and that's why the *Rules* are extensive—but for most of us it comes down to some fairly simple ground rules that in turn are based on common sense and courtesy. These will get you through 99 percent of the situations you are likely to face.

Robert's Rules of Order begins with this basic rule of fairness: "American Parliamentary Law is built upon the principle that rights must be respected: rights of the majority, of the minority, of individuals, of absentees, and rights of all of these together."

There's one quick way you can be smarter about *Robert's Rules* than almost anybody else. You are about to become one of the rare ones who knows who Robert was! Poor Robert almost always gets left out, even by the show-offs who can recite which divided motions can't be amended. The next time one of them tries to bamboozle you with more knowledge than common sense, get him or her aside and casually ask who Robert was? Chances are, that will be one for you.

Robert was Henry Martin Robert, a young Civil War officer on the Union side, who later became a general and head of the Washington, D.C. District. He took on the task of codifying and simplifying the rules of procedure of the U.S. House of Representatives. The work was completed in 1876, at which time General Robert adapted those rules to fit other civic organizations.

Other rule books have been written but *Robert's* is still the basic text. Indeed, if your own bylaws or rules don't stipulate otherwise, it is standard practice, and the law in many states, that *Robert's Rules* shall be used in the resolution of internal differences.

I'll begin with the most common parliamentary procedures you are likely to need. Indeed, once you are a third of the way through this chapter, you'll have covered most of what you'll ever need to know and probably more than you want to know.

Starting at the most elementary level, this is the way a group formally makes a decision:

- One of the members will **move** that a decision be made (this is proposing that the board go on record in favor of a certain definite action).

- Another member of the group will **second** the motion which means "support" for the action proposed. (The second is necessary to be certain that the issue is of interest to more than one person.)

- Once the motion has been made and seconded there is **discussion, clarification,** and **debate.**

- When the subject has been covered fully, there is the **vote.**

- Prior to both discussion and vote, the person in the chair should **restate the motion** to be certain everyone knows what is being discussed and decided.

It may strike you as an enormous simplification, but for most committees and boards that's all you need to know: a motion, second, discussion and vote.

The next level involves a situation in which the group considers that it might want to make some changes in the motion as originally offered. In the course of the discussion it may become obvious that the motion doesn't quite say what the board now has in mind. This is the way that slightly more complicated scenario would unfold:

- The motion.

- The second.

- The chairperson restates the motion.

- Discussion, clarification, and debate.

- Someone suggests that the original motion be amended and another person seconds the idea. (At that point it will usually happen that the maker and seconder of the original or main motion will agree to the amendment even though a vote on the amendment has not been taken.

Technically, once a motion has been made and seconded it involves the whole assembly, but if no one offers objection to the amendment, no vote is usually taken.)

- If the persons who moved and seconded the original motion do not agree to the amendment or anyone else voices objection, then there is discussion, clarification and debate on the amendment itself.

- After the group has adequately considered the amendment, the chairperson restates the motion to amend and the group votes *on the amendment*.

- Once the amendment has been accepted or rejected, the group returns its attention to the original motion.

- If the amendment passed, the main motion would now be known as "the original motion as amended." If the amendment had been defeated, it would simply be the original motion.

- Debate would proceed on the original motion. It could be amended again, in which case it would be the new amendment that gets the informal or formal consideration.

- When the amendments have been disposed of, the board votes on the original motion (as amended, if that's the case). Although that is slightly more complicated, it is simply the group's way of deciding whether the original motion needed some changes before it reflected the combined view of what should be done.

- If the main motion is defeated, the same basic proposal cannot be brought forward again at the same meeting. That's to keep the losers from filibustering by bringing the same motion up again and again. (There is an exception. If one person who was on the winning side of the vote realizes that he or she may have made a mistake, such as misunderstanding what the motion called for, he or she can move for reconsideration, at which point the board decides whether to allow reconsideration.)

If you serve on a fairly informal board or committee that rarely gets involved in parliamentary procedure, don't bother with the rest of this chapter. For those who do participate in more involved board deliberations, including debates, there are some additional points worth knowing.

1. As obvious at it may be, it is important to know that if a motion is made and *not seconded*, the motion is automatically lost and nothing further should be said about it. If there isn't a second it means that the subject is not something the group wants to spend time on, and the individual who proposed the motion should not presume upon the group's good nature by commenting on the subject as though it had been accepted for discussion ("on the table").

For other trustees it's not a good idea to second a motion just to be nice. If you and the others don't want to spend your time on the issue, don't clutter up the agenda with it. If every person were free to bring forward his or her ideas and take up the group's time, you'd never get on with the more important considerations. *Robert's Rules* begins with the motion and second as a deliberate way of deciding if the matter is worth the group's time. By seconding a motion you don't care about, you may be nice to the mover but not very fair to the group.

2. Almost all motions can have only two amendments to them before a vote must be taken on at least one of those amendments. Otherwise everyone would get lost and the main motion would be obscured. For example: If the original motion and second call for spending $1,000 for new chairs around the conference table, one amendment may suggest changing the amount to $2,000 and a subsequent and separate amendment may propose that the money be spent for chairs *and* a new conference table. If any more amendments were allowed, you can see how people would get confused about what they are expected to decide.

Also, amendments must be "germaine," that is, they must relate to the subject of the motion that would be amended. You can't have an amendment that introduces a different issue.

3. A motion to amend can also be the subject of a motion to amend ("I move that the amendment be amended"), but there can be only one such motion to amend an amendment on the floor at any one time.

The debate and vote would first apply to the motion to amend the amendment. After that is disposed of, there can be fuller discussion and the vote on the amendment, and finally additional discussion and vote on the original motion (as amended, if the amendment was approved).

At the risk of laboring the point, let me provide a recap in the form of an example:

- "I move that we have a fundraising dinner and do it in June."
- "I second the motion."
- "We have a motion before us to have a fundraising dinner and do it in June. The floor is open for discussion."
- Discussion.
- An amendment: "I like the idea, but I wonder if we should tie the hands of the committee by stipulating June. Would the maker and seconder of the motion be willing to delete that reference to the month of June?"
- The maker and seconder may accept the deletion, and if no one else offers objection, discussion would proceed on the original motion without the reference to June.

- The maker and/or the seconder of the original motion or anyone else may not agree to the deletion and therefore not accept the amendment ("I like parties in June," he exclaimed!) In that case, if the person offering the amendment feels strongly enough about the issue to want a formal consideration of his or her idea, a motion would be made to amend the original motion by deleting the phrase "and do it in June."

- The amendment would require a second.

- The chairperson would state the motion to amend.

- Discussion, clarification, and debate would proceed *on the amendment.*

- After ample discussion, there would be a vote on the amendment; let's assume that the amendment "to delete June" passes. ("I hate you!" shouts the maker of the original motion.—Sometimes even Robert's rules don't assure courtesy.)

- After the vote on the amendment, the group returns to a discussion of the original motion.

- After ample consideration, the group votes on the original or main motion.

The amendment to "delete June" could have been amended if someone else had moved, "O.K. Let's not specify June, but let's stipulate that it has to be done sometime between April and July." ("How about the last day in May or any time in June?", pleads the originator, but the chairperson gavels him out of order.)

Usually the maker and seconder of the amendment and everyone else present will accept that kind of change without challenge and discussion and vote would proceed upon the original amendment. If they don't informally accept the change to the amendment, then the immediate discussion and vote are on the substitution of the phrase "sometime between April and July" in place of the phrase "and do it in June."

Once the substitution has been discussed and voted, the group would return to a discussion and a vote on the amendment. In cases such as this, the vote on the amendment to the amendment nullifies the need for the amendment itself. If the group has voted to hold the event "sometime between April and July," there's no need to vote on the "to delete June" issue. If, however, the amendment to the amendment lost, then it would be necessary to vote on the amendment "to delete June."

After the first amendment has been dealt with, the group would again return to discussion and consideration of the main motion.

By this point in my explanation, parliamentarians are probably on their feet hollering that I must explain the difference between "amendment" and "substitution," which I'll do at the end of this lesson.

4. For most votes, a majority of those present is all that's needed to approve or disapprove a motion. (This is called a "simple majority.")

Your bylaws and *Robert's Rules* may stipulate that certain votes require a two-thirds majority, such as for amendment of the bylaws (or impeachment of the president, who by this point would recognize any seconder).

A two-thirds majority is also required to suspend the rules, close nominations, or end debate. (For a fuller list there is a "Basic Chart of Motions." See Figure 1 on page 113.)

5. You'll frequently hear people say, "I move the previous question" or, "Move the question," or even "Question."

When a member of the board feels that discussion has gone on long enough, he or she can move that debate be ended—in essence saying, "I move that debate be ended and that we now vote immediately on the motion before us." The motion before the group can be an amendment to an amendment or the original motion. Calling for an end to debate is usually referred to as "the previous question."

If there is a second, there can be no debate on the motion to close debate, but two thirds of the group must vote for the motion. If they do, there must be an immediate vote on the issue at hand. If "the previous question" is not approved, debate on the issue at hand proceeds. After an interval, someone else can also move the previous question, but if the group doesn't feel that all the points or people they want to hear have been heard—or if they are not sick of the topic—they can again defeat the "question."

This is a pervasive misperception about "the previous question." Frequently one or more people will feel that the group is ready for a vote and will say "Question" or "Move the question." Then the person in the chair will assume that the group must therefore vote and will cut off further debate. Debate cannot be ended unless the group actually agrees.

The person in the chair can say something like, "Some people are ready to vote—does the whole group agree." If just one person disagrees or is waiting to say something, the debate continues. If those who called "Question" really mean it, they must formally move the previous question and see if two thirds of the group agree to end debate.

The maker of the motion being debated can't propose ending debate. Be alert also for those who have already had their say who want to deny the same chance to others.

When someone shouts "Question" it's appropriate for the chairperson to say, "I know several people still seem to want to speak to the issue and as a matter of fairness I will let the discussion proceed." If someone formally moves the previous question, even the person in the chair can't do any more than clarify what the group is voting on (closing debate) and that it requires a two-thirds vote.

6. Some other motions are not debatable:

- "Protest a breach of rules or conduct"
  (*"She's pulling my hair!"*)

- "Call for an intermission"
  (*"With all this coffee, doesn't anyone else need to . . . ?"*)

- "Complain about conditions"
  (*"This heat is so bad, my underwear is sticking!"*)

- "Avoid considering an improper matter"
  (*"I agree we should all be concerned about fluoridation, but after all, this is an association of grandmothers for planned parenthood!"*)

- "Confirm a decision by calling for a standing vote"
  (*"I know it sounded unanimous, but with this crazy person in the chair, it's the only way we're ever going to get to stretch."*)

- "Call for a point of information"
  (*"Are you out of your cotton-pickin' mind!?"*)

For fuller examples of nondebatable motions, see the "Basic Chart of Motions."

7. Voting can go from the very informal to formal. The chairperson may say something like, "There appears to be a clear consensus, and unless anyone objects, we'll assume that matter is approved." If that's not challenged, it would be considered an unchallenged vote. (In the original draft of this chapter, I said that "it would be considered a unanimous vote." The Master Parliamentarian who reviewed the chapter for me said that it is incorrect to assume that silence means support. Technically then, the only votes that can be recorded as unanimous are when each person actually votes on the same side.)

Very often there is call for a voice vote: "All those in favor, please say 'Aye.' All those opposed, please say 'No.'" Usually the decision is obvious. Frequently because most people seem to have voted "Aye," there is not a call for the "No" votes. That's not good practice. It's good for the group to see that votes are unanimous or unchallenged and it's equally important that people have a chance to register their dissent.

If the results of the voice vote are not clear or if it's the practice of the organization to try to make a record of how people vote, then there would be a raising of the hands for "Aye" and "No." Sometimes this is done as a standing vote.

If the vote is still not clear or if it is important that there be a clear record of votes, there can be an actual roll call, with each member asked to respond "Aye" or "No." If a person prefers not to vote, he or she can just say "Present."

In large gatherings, there can be a "count off." All those in favor stand up, and the chairperson designates a person to begin. That person says "one" and sits down, the next person says "two" and is seated, and so forth until all those who were standing have counted off and been seated. Then those voting "No" go through the same procedure. This is a clear way to get an actual count and to guarantee that no one is voting twice or not being counted.

At the extreme there can be a ballot. This is sometimes used in voting on nominees or on very sensitive issues.

Any member can call for any one of these voting procedures and it is up to the chairperson to decide. If he or she decides against such a suggestion, the group can go through the formal procedure of a motion, second, debate, and vote on whether to accept the voting procedure called for in the motion. Usually the chairperson goes along, unless it is a delaying tactic that the chairperson believes is fundamentally unfair to the group.

8. The Motion to Table is used often enough and has enough confusion surrounding it that you may want to have some briefing about it. If a board member feels that the discussion is not getting anywhere or that the group clearly does not want to decide the issue at hand (at least at that time), the individual can "move to table." This requires a second and is *not* debatable. Only a majority vote is required.

The move to table is often used to "kill" the matter, but others have the privilege of bringing it up again ("take it from the table") later in the meeting or at a future meeting. To take an item "from the table" requires a motion and a second, is not debatable, and can be approved by a simple majority.

Sometimes items are postponed to "a time certain," such as, "I move that this item be postponed until after we've disposed of these other matters" or "until the next meeting" or "until the budget has been developed." A motion to postpone is debatable.

The motion to table is a more deliberate challenge to the matter at hand. Some people really don't want to deal with the issue, and they want an immediate sense of the assembly. The motion to postpone is a more practical scheduling situation.

In preparation for the annual meetings of delegates to the National Mental Health Association, we included in the advance resource packets the "Basic Chart of Motions." Those meetings frequently involved complicated subjects and charged debates; we also frequently ran into self-styled parliamentarians. We wanted everybody to be on equal footing or at least to have readily at hand a chart that explained what was going on and what their rights were.

You may not want to bother with the "Basic Chart of Motions" that follows now (or ever!), but at least you know where it is in case you're involved in a meeting where some fuller orientation to *Robert's Rules* might be helpful.

The Channing L. Bete Company has produced a good primer called *The ABC's of Parliamentary Procedure.* Its "Parliamentary Procedure . . . at a Glance" is reproduced at the end of the chapter. It's not quite as detailed as the "Basic Chart," but gives a good overview of many of the basic procedures you are likely to run into.

If you're a perfectionist or a masochist, you can get your own full set of *Robert's Rules of Order.* The long-standing reference edition is *Robert's Rules of Order, Revised* published by Scott–Foresman and Company in Chicago. It includes

Figure 1. Basic Chart of Motions

	Second	Debate	Amend	Vote	Recon- sider	Inter- rupts
PRIVILEGED MOTIONS (high privilege motions)*						
Fix a time to which to adjourn	S	—	A	M	R	—
Adjourn	S	—	—	M	—	—
Recess	S	—	A	M	—	—
Raise a question of privilege	—	—	—	Ch.	—	I.S.
Call for orders of the day						
(Takes a ⅔ negative vote to prevent return)	—	—	—	Ch.	—	I.S.
SUBSIDIARY MOTIONS (assisting motions)*						
Lay on the table	S	—	—	M	—	—
Previous question (close debate)	S	—	—	⅔	R*	—
Limit or extend debate	S	—	A	⅔	R	—
Postpone to a set time (definite) (To make Special						
Order ⅔ vote)	S	D	A	M	R	—
Commit (refer to a committee)	S	D	A	M	R	—
Amend	S	D	Aa*	M	R	—
Postpone indefinitely	S	D	—	M	R-a	—
MAIN (or Principal) MOTION OR RESOLUTION*	S	D	A	M	R	—
RESTORATORY MOTIONS (main motions)						
Reconsider (the vote)	S	D*	—	M	—	I.P.
Rescind (repeal)	S	D	A	⅔*	R-n	—
Ratify (approve)	S	D	A	M	R-n	—
Take from the table	S	—	—	M	—	—
SPECIAL MAIN MOTIONS						
By-laws (amending or revising)	S	D	A	⅔	R-n	—
Accepting or adopting reports of committees	S	D	A	M	R	—
INCIDENTAL MOTIONS (incidental to the pending question)						
Demands or Requests (decided by the Chair)						
Point of Order	—	—	—	Ch.	—	I.S.
Parliamentary Inquiry	—	—	—	Ch.	—	I.P.
Miscellaneous Information or Requests	—	—	—	Ch.	—	I.P.
Division of Assembly	—	—	—	Ch.	—	I.P.
Withdraw a Motion (by motion S.M. R-n)	—	—	—	Ch.	—	I.P.
Withdraw a second	—	—	—	Ch.	—	I.P.
Question Quorum	—	—	—	Ch.	—	I.S.
Objections						
Objection to General Consent	S	—	—	M	R-n	I.P.
Object to Consideration of a Question	—	—	—	⅔	R-n	I.P.*
Appeal Decision of the Chair	S	D*	—	M	R	I.P.
Reading Papers—Object to	S	—	—	M	R-n	I.P.
Expediters						
Suspend Rules	S	—	—	⅔	—	I.P.
Choose Method of Voting	S	—	A	M	—	I.P.
Close Nominations or Polls	S	—	A	⅔	—	I.P.
Reopen Nominations or Polls	S	—	A	M	R-n	I.P.
Division of Question or Motion	S	—	A	M	—	I.P.
Consideration by Paragraph—Seriatim (Chair may						
suggest)	S	—	—	M	R-n	I.P.
Filling blanks	—*	—	—	M	R-n	I.P.

*NOTE: These motions hold the rank indicated with the main motion lowest in rank

LEGEND:

"S"   indicates a second is required.
"D"   indicates debatable.
"A"   indicates amendable.
"Aa*" under Amend indicates only two amendments can be pending at one time.
"M"   (Majority) or "⅔" indicates vote required.
"R"   that vote on motion may be reconsidered—if followed by a "n" only negative vote and if by an "a" only the affirmative vote.

"I.S." indicates may interrupt a speaker.
"I.P." indicates may interrupt a proceeding and usually a speaker with consent.
(*)   indicates there are one or more exceptions but these can be considered minor as basically the rule indicated applies.
(—)   indicates a "NO" under that particular heading.
"Ch." chair decides or rules.

a special section listing all the different types of motions alphabetically with a note indicating whether they are debatable, require a two-thirds vote, etc. There is also a paperback edition of *Robert's Rules* published by Spire Books, Fleming H. Revell Company in Old Tappan, New Jersey.

For some of you it might be helpful to talk briefly about parliamentarians. Usually it's sufficient that the chairperson has some grasp of the basic rules. It's probably more important for persons who regularly staff boards and committees to be reasonably familiar with *Robert's Rules*, at least to the extent of knowing the kinds of matters covered in the "Basic Chart" and "Parliamentary Procedures." I routinely recommend to staff members that one of the items in the file carried to all meetings should be a summary of parliamentary procedures.

Many organizations identify a particular board member as the informal parliamentarian. It's important to be sure that the individual in that role will be even-handed. It's equally important that the individual not get the group more deeply involved in parliamentary procedure than is necessary.

When major controversy is to be put before the board, or if certain types of meetings routinely involve very complicated or divisive matters, a professional parliamentarian should be at hand. In those cases the parliamentarian should not be a member of the board. The person chairing the meeting should do everything possible to put the issues out for full and adequate debate before the parliamentary maneuvering begins. Despite the good intentions of *Robert's Rules of Order*, their implementation often thwarts early consideration of the broad issues. Someone's always quick to jump in with a motion to amend, motion to substitute, motion to split, and all the other maneuverings which so often focus debate either on the parliamentary procedures themselves or on issues that may not get at the heart of the matter.

For the names of qualified professional parliamentarians in your area, you can write to:

National Association of Parliamentarians (NAP)
3706 Broadway, Suite 300
Kansas City, MO 64111
(816) 531-1735

American Institute of Parliamentarians (AIP)
124 W. Washington Blvd., Suite 144
P.O. Box 12452
Fort Wayne, IN 46863
(219) 422-3680

One of the best summaries of parliamentary matters I came across is called "Parliamentary Procedure At a Glance." It was put together by O. Garfield Jones at the University of Toledo in 1932. While giving ample attention to helping the reader work through the maze of what's possible, Jones emphasizes that "common sense is the essence of parliamentary rules; fair play is their guiding principle; reasonable discussion followed by prompt action is what they are devised to achieve."

Figure 2. Parliamentary Procedure . . . at a Glance*

To Do This:	You Say This:	May You Interrupt the Speaker?	Do You Need a Second?	Is It Debatable?	Can It Be Amended?	What Vote Is Needed?	Can It Be Reconsidered?
ADJOURN MEETING	"I move that we adjourn"	NO	YES	NO	NO	MAJORITY	NO
CALL AN INTERMISSION	"I move that we recess for . . ."	NO	YES	NO	YES	MAJORITY	NO
COMPLAIN ABOUT HEAT, NOISE, ETC.	"I rise to a question of privilege"	YES	NO	NO	NO	NO VOTE	NO (usually)
TEMPORARILY SUSPEND CONSIDERATION OF AN ISSUE	"I move to table the motion"	NO	YES	NO	NO	MAJORITY	NO
END DEBATE AND AMENDMENTS	"I move the previous question"	NO	YES	NO	NO	2/3	NO[1]
POSTPONE DISCUSSION FOR A CERTAIN TIME	"I move to postpone the discussion until . . ."	NO	YES	YES	YES	MAJORITY	YES
GIVE CLOSER STUDY OF SOMETHING	"I move to refer the matter to committee"	NO	YES	YES	YES	MAJORITY	YES[2]
AMEND A MOTION	"I move to amend the motion by . . ."	NO	YES	YES[3]	YES	MAJORITY	YES
INTRODUCE BUSINESS	"I move that . . ."	NO	YES	YES	YES	MAJORITY	YES

THE MOTIONS LISTED ABOVE ARE IN ORDER OF PRECEDENCE . . . BELOW THERE IS NO ORDER . . .

To Do This:	You Say This:	May You Interrupt the Speaker?	Do You Need a Second?	Is It Debatable?	Can It Be Amended?	What Vote Is Needed?	Can It Be Reconsidered?
PROTEST BREACH OF RULES OR CONDUCT	"I rise to a point of order"	YES	NO	NO	NO	NO VOTE[4]	NO
VOTE ON A RULING OF THE CHAIR	"I appeal from the chair's decision"	YES	YES	YES	NO	MAJORITY	YES
SUSPEND RULES TEMPORARILY	"I move to suspend the rules so that..."	NO	YES	NO	NO	$2/3$	NO
AVOID CONSIDERING AN IMPROPER MATTER	"I object to consideration of this motion"	YES	NO	NO	NO	$2/3$[6]	—[7]
VERIFY A VOICE VOTE BY HAVING MEMBERS STAND	"I call for a division" or "Division!"	YES	NO	NO	NO	NO VOTE	NO
REQUEST INFORMATION	"Point of information"	YES	NO	NO	NO	NO VOTE	NO
TAKE UP A MATTER PREVIOUSLY TABLED	"I move to take from the table . . ."	NO	YES	NO	NO	MAJORITY	NO
RECONSIDER A HASTY ACTION	"I move to reconsider the vote on . . ."	YES	YES	—[8]	NO	MAJORITY	NO

NOTES:
1. Unless vote on question is not yet taken.
2. Unless the committee has already taken up the subject.
3. Only if the motion to be amended is debatable.
4. Except in doubtful cases.
5. A majority vote in negative needed to reverse the ruling of chair.
6. A $2/3$ vote in negative needed to prevent consideration of main motion.
7. Only if the main question or motion was not, in fact, considered.
8. Only if motion to be reconsidered is debatable.

13

Fundraising

Almost every nonprofit organization needs money. This applies to fledgling organizations, groups in search of new sources of funds, United Way affiliated organizations that need to supplement their income through self-support, and many other organizations that need to raise money to support their existing programs or to carry out their plans for expansion.

Fundraising is hard work, but if you have a cause or program that deserves support and you're willing to work at it, you can raise money. Along the way, you and the organization will gain confidence, contacts, and camaraderie. One of the best expressions of all three comes from Booker T. Washington's experience in trying to raise money in the early days of the Tuskegee Institute. In the chapter on "Raising Money" from his book *Up From Slavery*, he says:

> While the work of going from door to door and from office to office is hard, disagreeable and costly in bodily strength, it has some compensations. Such work gives one a rare opportunity to study human nature. It also has its compensations in giving one an opportunity to meet some of the best people in the world—to be more correct, I think I should say *the best* people in the world. When one takes a broad survey of the country you will find that the most useful and influential people in it

are those that take the deepest interest in institutions that exist for the purpose of making the world better.

The fundraising commitment must begin with the board and must be high on the agenda of a significant number of the trustees. Not only must it be of high priority, it must also be high in status and recognition within the organization. That's not easy. If you're wondering how to get moving, you probably already know the problem of a board of directors not really recruited with fundraising responsibilities distinctly in mind. And if you're already getting most of your support from fees, contracts, or United Way, it's even harder to stir up real fundraising interest and urgency. Raising money takes dogged persistence, bullheadedness, salesmanship, year-round cultivation, board support and encouragement, a plan, an attainable goal, and lots of excitement—to wit, it's hard work. But if the board decides it is going to raise money and is willing to allocate at least 20 percent of its energy and resources to accomplish this goal, you can and will succeed.

It's fascinating to hear people today speak about the American Heart Associaton's success. They assume that the organization couldn't help but succeed. They will go on at great length about how the organization had a visible cause, leadership, fundraising staff, dollars to invest, and a basic fundraising blueprint; how the total association was organized and dedicated primarily to raising funds; and how, in the early 1950s, there was a wide-open climate for fundraising.

Thirty years ago the real picture was similar to that of most organizations today that are trying to figure out how to raise money. There wasn't a visible cause; heart attack victims looked so normal that there was no chance to get the kind of sympathy one could generate with a poster showing a child polio victim. We didn't have leadership; certainly we didn't have the community leaders with us. Most of the leaders were physicians, who took little interest in fundraising. We didn't have a fundraising staff—most of us were young idealists with far more fire than knowledge. We didn't have very many dollars, certainly not the kind of money necessary to prime the pump of a major campaign. We didn't have a blueprint for campaigning; indeed, we were floundering around trying to figure out whether to develop and sell valentines or go into the United Fund, raise money by mail or accept government grants. And the organization certainly didn't have a fundraising determination. In terms of fundraising climate, everywhere we went we were told that people were tired of working and fed up with being asked to contribute, and that we should look to the Community Chest for support. It was terribly difficult to get local groups interested in fundraising and convinced that they could do it.

In thirty years the American Heart Association has gone from that beginning to an annual income approximating $130 million.

What evolved during the 1950s was, first, that the local board was convinced that money had to be raised; then gradually came the recruitment of campaign chairmen who were willing to join up and give it a try, and a growing pervasive spirit for making each February's totals better than the February before.

As often happens, the darkest days turned out to provide some very real blessings. Throughout the 1950s and 1960s the American Heart Association was fighting to survive United Way's determination to take the association in or else to dry up its income sources. We lost a good many chapters, and we lost a great many board members. Indeed, we seemed to lose most of the bigger names we had tried so hard to recruit. It turned out, however, that those who stayed with us were a hardy lot. Contrary to belief, they were not often the significant community leaders. They were independent souls who were not frightened away and, by standing up and being counted, brought a verve, backbone, and determination to the agency which has been its true making.

The American Heart Association has grown rapidly, expanding its income and its sources of funds. Its 1983 income profile looked like this:

Income Source

Special Gifts	$ 9,904,639
Business	$ 7,679,037
Door-to-Door	$ 20,764,803
Special Events	$ 26,871,735
Memorials	$ 14,610,837
Other Income*	$ 15,712,402
Bequests	$ 32,287,860
National Office Direct Income	$ 187,528
Grand Total	$128,018,841

* Other Income includes Combined Federal Campaigns/Health Agency Drives, United Way, etc.

I often think of those early years, particularly when I hear all the same reasons why it can't be done today, and when I'm asked if I think an organization can raise money for general support or for a new program or affiliate.

Every time I'm asked by a board delegation if I think their organization can raise money, I repeat that they are in for some awfully hard work. I don't say this to discourage them. Indeed, I hope they'll push on, and I hope this applies to you. But if you're timid or your organization isn't really determined, you won't survive the obstacles, heartaches, and difficulties which, unfortunately, I can promise you are ahead. On the other hand, if you have a cause that deserves support and if you're willing to scratch, kick, and beg, you *can* raise money.

The procedure for getting a new or renewed fundraising effort underway should be something like this:

- **Convince your fellow trustees to make a full commitment.** I'll come back later to the board's fuller role.

- **Define the need.** This doesn't have to be an elaborate brochure, but define why you need money and try to come up with a needs goal. This shouldn't be "pie in the sky," but it shouldn't be too timid, either. What does your group really think it actually needs as a minimum to make a significant difference in the next three years?

- **Develop a fundraising plan.** Basically, a plan involves the following:

  a. *Identify the type or types of fundraising to be undertaken.* On the basis of consultation with other agencies, persons who have been involved in fundraising in the community, and consultants available to you from a parent organization, you will begin to get an idea of where your immediate potential rests. Don't scatter your shots too widely, but, as they say, don't put all your "begs in one askit" either. Later in this chapter, I'll talk about the various fundraising categories you can consider.

  b. *Establish a realistic goal for the first year.* Don't shoot immediately for your needs goal unless you have an angel or two in the wings or unless your needs are very modest. Set a goal that is attainable based on the sources of funds and the number of campaign workers it is going to be possible to recruit. Start small! Most campaigns tend to fall apart because the initial efforts are so ambitious as to be beyond the capacity of the organization. If a group becomes discouraged the whole effort quickly falls apart. On the other hand, if you set an attainable goal (and I don't mean that it has to be unduly modest) and you hit it, the organization will, in spirit and in fact, be on its way.

  c. *Determine exactly how many board members and other campaign workers you need to make the contacts necessary to raise that amount of money.* Here, too, be realistic. Determine the deployment of these campaign workers in terms of teams and the consequent need for captains and other leaders. Make the jobs bite size. Campaigns easily fall apart because unrealistic burdens are placed on too few people who either won't accept the jobs or don't follow through.

  d. *Set a firm timetable for recruitment, training sessions, campaigning, reporting, and recognition.* It will be terribly important to provide enough time. This doesn't mean that things can't be pulled together in a hurry, but if you're unreasonable, you just won't have time to do the job.

  e. *Decide on the budget.* It needn't cost an arm and a leg, but the campaign is going to cost some money and you have to be prepared to budget for the operation. If the budget won't cover what you're trying to do, you may be able to get some seed money from a corporation, foundation, or individual. More on this later.

- **Bring the plan back to the full board to get their firm support.** This includes approval of the budget, dollar commitments of support from individual board members, and guarantees of service. You may find at this point that some of the board members fall away, and you'll need to adjust your plans accordingly. Even though it's discouraging, it's better to have some shaking down at this point so that those remaining are as committed as you are to getting the job done.

- **Recruit the chairperson.** This is the most critical step. He or she needn't come from within the organization but should be someone who has a *demonstrated* capacity to accomplish the plan. Beware of talkers and, above all, don't seek a fast sell. This is one of the most important recruitment jobs you'll ever do.

- **Establish and keep to a regular schedule of training sessions and report meetings.**

- **Provide for recognition and awards.**

- **Put some of your best campaign volunteers on the board.**

- **Develop your second-year plan, with heavy involvement of those who participated in the first success.**

This all sounds very pat, and I certainly don't mean to suggest that, if one is willing to follow these steps, success is assured. However, there's a much better chance of getting there if this kind of proven pattern is followed.

Right from the start you'll wonder where you're going to find the volunteers to carry on the campaign. The answer is that your volunteers are out there, but you've got to scratch hard to find them. People want a cause and are willing to join up if you can only reach them.

What I said earlier on cold canvassing applies here, too. Many times I've gone into a community absolutely cold and have succeeded in recruiting a campaign chairperson. My pattern is to go to priests, ministers, rabbis, the mayor, the head of a service club, heads of women's groups, and persons who have worked in other campaigns. I ask them if they can identify people who may wish to take on the kind of job I have outlined, and it is rare that this pattern does not produce a chairperson. Each prospect I talk to who says no, I ask to be willing to help the chairperson who is finally recruited; so that even if I get several turn-downs, my next chances are improved because I've got a growing cadre of helpers already lined up.

You've got to look to your board of directors for help, but through sad experience I know that if someone on the board has not already come forward, the situation is not likely to change. However, go over the list carefully to be sure that many of them are lined up to help.

Actually, the chairperson will be the kind who can do a good deal of his or her own recruiting, but don't leave your recruit all alone and out on a limb. He or she can give only so much time; and since each chairperson is only one person, if you're going to make as large a step as possible in the first year, you're going to need a lot of helpers. Look to people who have been helped by the organization or who have shown some interest in the cause. If the jobs are, in fact, bite size, more people will be willing to help and will produce.

One of the greatest problems with fundraising and within nonprofit organizations generally is the confusion between the fundraising roles for board and staff. In terms of accountability, it is a board function, and it's a rare situation that the function can be delegated substantially to staff members. Sometimes, if it's entirely a direct-mail effort, a specialized staff working with highly sophisticated mail houses can handle it all. More often the campaign depends on contacts, and it's not realistic or reasonable to expect staff members to have most such connections.

The campaign therefore is always a board function. It can be delegated to a board committee consisting of board members and others with staffing by the chief staff officer or, if the position exists, the fundraising director. Every trustee should be expected to contribute and to raise funds within their means and contacts. The committee should be responsible to the board. If the head of the committee or drive is not a member of the board, he or she should be invited to all board meetings, even when the agenda does not call for discussion of campaign progress. Most agendas should include the topic.

One of the most inappropriate things a board can do is to call for increased income and leave it to the staff to produce; or to recruit the head of the drive and then turn back to the "real" work of the organization, which usually involves planning for new expenditures that the poor bloke isn't going to raise—not that way anyway.

The board is accountable—and the board leads. If it can't contribute or raise the funds, it must put together a campaign committee that can do the job and then back that group with every dollar, hour, and huzzah it can muster.

If your reaction, and maybe even the staff's, is to apologize for becoming too much like a fundraising organization—and maybe even to decline too much involvement because "we're essentially a program agency" or because "I'm here because I'm a program person"—cancel the campaign until and unless the tune is changed to "I'm a program person who knows how important this is, so how can I help?"

If your cause *really* needs the money but too many board members won't help, plan for turnover. If you think that's going too far, you turn over.

In the last few years of enormous financial crisis for so many voluntary organizations faced with government cutbacks, I've met with at least fifty board and staff delegations seeking advice on development. I start with the same encouragement I give in this chapter, but I also follow up quickly with how much work is in store. I indicate that their organization must be prepared to devote at least 20 percent of its resources to fundraising and that the board and chief staff officer will have to devote closer to one third of their time for the first year or two. Despite their apparent conviction, the reaction is rarely, "If that's what it's going to take, we'll do it!" In the majority of cases the reaction is rejection, anger, and insult.

Often the chief staff officer is most offended. Those physicians, social workers, historians, or former foreign service officers are deeply upset that I should undercut their professional status by putting them in such a substantial fundraising role. I always try to convey that fundraising is really a matter of the people who care about a cause and know it firsthand, telling the story with the same conviction that they tell it every day to colleagues, friends, and neighbors.

Most of these delegations leave shaking their heads, already thinking about finding more reasonable advice. Later, I hear that they have merged, reduced their focus substantially, closed, are looking for a new executive director, or have had their government funding restored. I can predict that in the interim they went into further deficit, or secured a grant from a foundation or board member to create the position of development director to whom they turned over the noxious assignment.

I know I'm being uncharacteristically direct here but it's deliberate. My primary message is to tell you how much you can do and to urge you to proceed with optimism. However, that would be irresponsible if I didn't couple it with the truest lessons I've ever learned in community organization, all involving what it takes to launch and sustain a significant fundraising effort.

I mentioned the process of hiring a development director. Right now institutions are willing to *pay* about anything for an experienced fundraising executive. In part that's because of the economic crisis, but also because boards and executive directors are willing to do almost anything to get someone else to perform their jobs. The good development directors are worth what they are being paid, but those very same specialists are good in large part because they know—and will tell you—that they can succeed only to the extent that the board and staff leadership are committed to and involved in the fundraising. It will not work for the board to assign the task to the executive director, and it will not work for the executive director to pass it on to the fundraising director. On the other hand, if the three work together as a team, the results can be terrific.

Along with more dollars, a major development effort achieves many other positive benefits, including community awareness and greater clout with government, which often means that the organization that raises a good deal of its own money has even greater ability to influence others who are important to both the program and the financial success of the agency's mission.

For the board member in a smaller organization, I've no doubt labored quite enough on the matter of experienced fundraising executives. Let me acknowledge quickly that most campaigns don't require a full-time trained fundraiser. Many groups find someone who can devote a realistic amount of time to the job. I advise these groups to look to effective women or retired persons who may not want full-time employment. You'll be surprised how much experience and ability are already out there in the community. Talk to other agency volunteers and staff, your United Way, and the community leaders who have been identified with major causes—they may be able to lead you to the right person.

Don't expect any staff person to function as the campaign chairperson, or to take the place of the efforts of your board members. The staff exists only to help the volunteers carry out the work of the organization. If you turn too much of the load over to staff members, the results are bound to be disappointing. It's the kind of volunteers you have in the campaign who are going to make the difference, and if they have some staff backup, they can make even greater use of the time they give.

Generally, I advise associations not to engage fundraising firms to serve as staff for ongoing community campaigns. Many of these groups are expert in planning and conducting capital gifts campaigns. Specialty firms and specialty departments of the larger firms are often skilled in direct-mail solicitation, bequest cultivation, church "every member" drives, special events, and many other fundraising categories. As such, they raise a great deal of money for voluntary organizations. I have tremendous respect for the ability of fundraising firms, notably those associated with the American Association of Fund-Raising Counsel. The only fundraising role I've generally found them not particularly suited for is staffing the annual community campaigns of such groups as voluntary health agencies. Many of the fundraising firms with whom I've worked are the first to point out that they are not geared to provide this service. Their experience and professionalism make them more expensive than most local groups can afford on a regular basis, and most local voluntary agencies don't have at hand or in early prospect sufficient community leadership to raise the sums which would justify the fees these firms have to charge.

I generally discourage groups from hiring a person whose full-time job is working part-time for several agencies (except in the area of special events, where many experts routinely help several different organizations). In my experience this arrangement rarely works well.

Build into your three-year campaign plan a firm estimate of staff needs and make the switch as soon as you can go to your own full-time person. This may be hard on the individual whose part-time efforts have brought you to that happy transition, but if you're going to grow and sustain the momentum, you will need an individual who is good and is employed full-time.

I know I seem to be preoccupied with the staffed operation, and many of you are ready to burst with exclamations of how much your organization already raises without staff. My rule of thumb is that, if a campaign is going to involve several fundraising categories and an annual goal of $50,000 to $75,000, some backup is usually needed. However, many organizations prove the exception.

Many organizations have board members who have more experience and savvy than most staff people, and those fundraising efforts are models of high yield and low cost. The basic rule is for the board to do everything possible on its own and to hire a staff only when that will help the volunteers reach even higher results.

Let me turn to the various categories of fundraising, beginning with a quick look at where the country's contributions come from.

In 1983, according to *Giving U.S.A.*, published by the American Association of Fund-Raising Counsel, Americans gave almost $65 billion to more than 500,000 nonprofit institutions and agencies. About 90 percent of the money came from individuals; of this amount, about one half came from individual contributors with annual incomes of $25,000 or less. This clearly represents good news for you, because it tells you that you probably have potential among the broadest possible pool of citizens in your community. That was the basic message that Booker T. Washington conveyed more than one hundred years ago. His concluding message in "Raising Money" was this:

> I have spoken of several large gifts to the school; but by far the greater proportion of the money that has built up the institution has come in the form of small donations from persons of moderate means. It is upon these small gifts, which carry with them the interest of hundreds of donors, that any philanthropic work must depend largely for its support. . . . In a large degree, it has been the pennies, the nickels and the dimes which have come from the Sunday schools, the Christian endeavor societies and the missionary societies, as well as from the Church proper, that have helped. . . .

The next most important sources of support are bequests, foundations, and business corporations, each representing approximately 5 percent of what is contributed each year.

Since individual causes and organizations differ so much, all I can do is present some of the fundraising categories so that you can get a feel for the possibilities. It will be important to work closely with experienced individuals and groups in the development of your own campaign plan, including the specific categories that you desire to pursue.

1. Special gifts. This is a pretty sophisticated kind of fundraising; it's been my experience, however, that you can often go to well-to-do people or to foundations or corporations with a specific plea for leadership gifts or start-up grants. I've seen a number of organizations go to ten or fifteen such sources and ask for $500 or $5,000 a year from each for two years as a means of getting this kind of campaign started. This of course means that you are going to have to replace this money with new gifts at the end of two years, but that is part of your gamble and commitment. When we started INDEPENDENT SECTOR, we turned to a number of foundations and business corporations for start-up assistance. With most, we asked for $30,000, with $15,000 for the first year, $10,000 for the second, and $5,000 for the third. We guaranteed that everything possible would be done to replace that "soft" or temporary money with "hard" dues from a growing number of members. During that first three years the board spent a good deal of its time and I devoted at least one third of mine to membership development and other fundraising efforts. When the grants ran out, the core budget was carried by dues income.

Beyond leadership or start-up gifts, you may well find that there are upper-income families who may surprise you by having quite an interest in your cause. Carefully develop your list and be certain that these people are seen personally. There will be a great temptation to say that a personalized letter going to five hundred such people is better than trying to see ten or fifteen personally, but don't you believe it.

Your campaign plan can include a growing list of such personal contacts each year so that at the end of five years you will have a fairly sophisticated special gifts campaign launched.

2. Community and family foundations. An experienced executive of an older organization or a trust officer can quickly identify the likely community and family foundations. These should be approached for leadership gifts or start-up grants, although some may be willing to provide an annual gift for several years and others may be willing to make at least a small contribution. Don't be timid—go to see them and tell them your story. Your heart may be pounding and your hands may be shaking, but your conviction will come through, and that is what often tips the scales.

Obviously, if a member of the board or campaign organization knows some of the individuals involved, this assistance should be used to its fullest extent—both as a door opener and to help sell the cause. In these categories, don't assume that someone won't give. Remember the story of Vivian Beaumont, who gave one of the major buildings which now stand in the Lincoln Center complex in New York. With dismay, one of her friends asked her why she had given her money to Lincoln Center and not to another theater with which the friend was identified, and Vivian Beaumont's surprised reply was, "Because they asked me!"

3. Door-to-door solicitation. Door-to-door campaigns are still one of the means of raising substantial sums of money. You don't have to organize the whole community or region, you can start with certain neighborhoods. If I had to go from point zero to the maximum dollars in the shortest possible time, I would still use the door-to-door campaign as the heart of my effort.

You can generally find people who have had experience with this kind of campaign who are willing to advise you—if not assist you—and they can often lead you to someone who will take on the task. Don't get too ambitious the first year—you'll begin to have dollar signs in your eyes when you think of the potential of reaching every house and when you hear what the American Cancer Society is raising by this method. If you are too ambitious to start with, the operation will collapse and it will be all the harder next year. Decide what part of the community you can realistically tackle the first year and be satisfied to bite off just that much, with the assurance that there will be other years.

4. Businesses. Business giving is the fastest growing side of philanthropy, and an increasing number of corporations try to assist with more than just cash, as important as that is. They donate equipment, provide for printing, contribute furniture, give low-interest or no-interest loans ("program-related investments"), encourage participation of their employees, and in many other ways help in the maintenance and development of community and national organizations. Alex Plinio, president of the Prudential Foundation, started out to write a paper entitled "Twelve Ways That Companies Help Voluntary Organizations with Other Than Cash Contributions." Each time he presents the paper, someone mentions types of giving that he left out. Now he's up to something like "Forty-One Ways. . . ."

5. Labor groups. Don't overlook the labor organizations. They have a history of significant generosity to worthwhile causes and may be quite sympathetic about helping a struggling new organization or launching a new effort by an existing organization.

6. Special events. Special events are probably the most ubiquitous of America's fundraising efforts. Special events are going on almost all the time and almost everywhere. These events include balls, bake sales, golf tournaments, walk-a-thons—an almost endless list of projects.

My own approach is usually to get clubs and organizations to put on special events for the cause. It's better to have many organizations putting on special events than to have your association trying to develop events. All this generates considerable publicity and attention, which can lead to gifts from the treasuries of the various organizations and to some volunteers from them.

Special events may well have a prominent place in your initial campaign plan as one of the fastest means of making some money. I'm inclined to caution you, however, about major dependence on any one special event. In the long run, they have a way of wearing out and ending up a somewhat fickle source of ongoing support. There are, of course, magnificent exceptions, but generally these are rarities and any one special event is not a secure way of funding an ongoing operation.

7. Testimonials. Many organizations use the testimonial approach. Some organizations raise a great deal of money this way and are able to sustain the operation. Most organizations, however, find it a means of raising immediate money for a special situation without the expectation that like sums can be generated each year.

The approach is to identify an individual who is esteemed and who deserves the honor. It's also necessary to pick someone who is sufficiently revered, feared, or central to people's economy that they will be willing to pay $100 or much more to honor him or her. These testimonials are usually dinners, and the emphasis is on selling tables to organizations, business associates, and others who are eager to participate in the testimonial.

8. Retail sales. Many organizations raise money through the sale of cookies, apple butter, flowers, magazines, aprons, Christmas cards, and a myriad of other objects. This can be an expensive proposition, so go into it with your eyes open. Many commercial groups will actively enlist your participation in selling their products, with a part of the profit going to your organization. Some of these arrangements can be very helpful to organizations, but generally they are primarily helpful to the companies promoting the idea.

9. Media appeals. Unfortunately, direct appeals for money through public media announcements have pretty much worn themselves out. Very little money is raised this way except for emergency or unusually dramatic appeals. It's almost certain that someone in your organization will suggest that this is the solution to your troubles, but I warn you that, although it will provide useful publicity, it probably will not provide significant income.

10. Direct mail. Direct mail has proven to be a very useful source of income for many organizations. A direct-mail approach usually requires a cause that has a broad appeal, but specialists can help zero in on an audience that fits your profile. This effort requires a very sophisticated, professional direct-mail specialist. You'll need money to have a field test done, and then if the field test is successful, you'll still have to expect the first year to come close to a washout with expenses equaling income. If renewal rates hold up for the second and third years, the net income for the cause can be substantial.

Direct mail tried through your own office to a wide constituency will not usually pay for itself. Many organizations have to discover this for themselves. It seems so natural that, with a cause as stirring as you believe yours to be, people are bound to respond to a heart-rending letter. It just doesn't happen that way.

11. Memorials and honorary gifts. Many organizations have successfully promoted memorial and honorary gifts. The American Heart Association has probably been the most successful in the area of memorial gifts. This falls naturally in their direction because of the unfortunately high proportion of deaths caused by heart disease. In 1983 memorial gifts constituted $15 million, which was 12 percent of the total American Heart Association income. If you're not in a death-related cause, however, memorials are not a likely source of substantial income. You may want to cite the success stories of some churches and synagogues, but I submit that their successes are also grounded in their unique relationship to death.

However, honorary gifts have been successfully promoted by many organizations. This takes very careful and long-term cultivation. It involves creating a habit among your own members and gradually among a widening circle of friends so that they automatically think of the honorary gift as a way of expressing special congratulations to people on the occasion of a birthday, baptism, marriage, bar mitzvah, anniversary, or holiday.

A growing number of people send a simple postcard at Christmas indicating that, in lieu of many Christmas expenditures, they have made a donation in the name of their friends to a particular charity.

12. Membership. Memberships represent a slow but very secure long-term source of support. In many campaign plans I've developed, such support starts low and rises steadily, while the special events category starts high but doesn't increase substantially. Membership dues should be at a high enough dollar amount to provide for regular service of the members and support for the programs. A minimum of $10 is wise, and if possible, I go to $25. Members should be recruited first from the board. Every board member should be at least a contributing member, if not a special giver. Then move to past board members, current committee members, the persons served by the agency, and those persons who have shown an interest in the cause. Watch the circles expand. As many potential members as possible should be approached personally. Until you have a chance to recruit a very wide group personally, you may want to approach some of the more likely prospects by phone or mail. Some organizations have been successful in setting up membership booths at conventions and meetings of other groups.

Set a specific goal in terms of the eventual proportion of the population you want to enlist as members. For instance, a local Mental Health Association strives to enlist and hold a minimum of one half of 1 percent of the population. This gives an organization something very specific to shoot at, and the goal can be divided into annual targets.

13. Bequests. A fast-growing source of donated funds is bequests. Bequests now constitute 5 percent of American giving, which is almost $5 billion. Bequest cultivation is a very sophisticated form of fundraising and obviously cannot be counted in your short-term fundraising plans. For organizations that are building long-term fundraising projects, however, a realistic proportion of the effort should be reserved for bequest cultivation.

Several years ago I was able to bring an unusual group together to provide guidelines for what I wanted to be a very serious, major, and successful bequest promotion for a local chapter of the American Heart Association. The group was assembled by the chief judge of the probate court and included other probate judges, trust officers of major financial institutions, and tax and estate lawyers. All were assured that they would not have direct fundraising responsibility, but would only provide a blueprint for the organization to follow. As so often happens when a group gets involved and interested, we were able to successfully recruit several of the individuals (obviously not including the judges) to lead the implementation.

In a series of three meetings chaired by the chief judge, the group produced the following blueprint, which was followed and very shortly began to provide substantial legacies. In the intervening years, the program has produced almost staggering results with surprisingly little effort.

1. Basic Assumptions

a. That a very small proportion of the Bar writes 75% of the wills that include gifts to charity.

b. That these lawyers are almost always community figures or seen by their clients as important in the community.

c. That most people who have money to leave are not certain which charities to consider.

d. That lawyers who are community leaders are frequently asked by will-writing clients to suggest examples of worthy charities or asked if certain causes are really okay.

e. That a bequest cultivation program is not as long-range as might be assumed, because most people write or amend wills when there is reason to be concerned.

f. That lawyers are interested and curious about heart disease.

g. That broad-scale mail campaigns with fancy brochures don't really make a dent.

2. The Program That Evolved

a. We used several members of the original group to form our bequest cultivation committee.

b. The committee screened the names of the will-writing attorneys. (I learned that these can be pretty quickly identified by checking on which lawyers in your community are members of the two relevant American Bar Association Sections dealing with taxation and estates.)

c. It turned out that there were about 170 such attorneys in a metropolitan area of approximately two million. We expanded our committee to include several more of the 170.

d. We held several meetings of the committee to help explain the problems of heart disease and the work of the American Heart Association.

e. Our basic approach was for every committee member to "adopt" twelve fellow will-writing attorneys. The assignment included:

(1) An initial luncheon or evening session. These were usually held at the committee member's club or home with the purpose of outlining: where we stand in heart disease control; how an individual

can protect himself; what the American Heart Association is; and a plan for future mailings.

(2) Once every year thereafter the committee member sent a personal letter to the attorneys for whom he or she was responsible. The mailings included the current annual report and other progress reports.

(3) The object was not hard-sell, but rather to be certain that the 170 will-writing attorneys were given a chance to know more about heart disease and the American Heart Association.

f. One of the basic steps the committee recommended was that every member of the board of directors of the association should include a bequest, however small, in his or her will.

Even this long list of campaign categories doesn't begin to cover all the possibilities, but it will give you some feel for the most likely things to be explored. I have not included any discussion of such devices as gift annuities, gifts of appreciated property, charity remainder trusts, and many other important sources of funds. These will generally not be applicable until you have built a corps of annual givers and committed supporters.

Don't try to tackle too many sources at once. When you finally decide which ones fit your organization, go after them with ferocious determination, and you'll find that the dollars will begin to multiply.

Fundraising doesn't have to cost much money, but raising money does involve certain costs. Most of the costs are the staff time applied to the fundraising operation. Usually only the very small campaigns or the very large campaigns can keep costs below 10 percent; the middle area becomes more expensive. Indeed, if you need staff members but are not at the point of attracting large gifts, the cost of the operation will almost have to be greater than 10 percent. This isn't unethical and shouldn't shock or deter anybody. My own gut reaction is that an ongoing campaign is ethical and justified if its costs are one third or less. If this means that your agency is able to raise a lot more money than it otherwise would, which results in further pursuit of its public mission, most givers will accept the morality and logic of that.

Some initial campaigns will cost even more than 30 percent. Direct-mail campaigns usually break even the first year, but if the field tests safely project that by the third year your renewals will be at a level so that your costs are down to the one-third level, I'd encourage you to go ahead. I've been involved in initial community campaigns that cost 50 percent. It bothered me, but on the other hand I knew that this was necessary to get the operation going and I knew that subsequent years' costs would drop to well below one third.

In some campaigns involving sales of goods, the costs may routinely run above 50 percent. This is all right so long as the givers are satisfied that they are simultaneously getting something they want and helping a cause. It's not fair if people are pressured into taking something they don't want or if the impression is left that most of the money will be going to charity. In some sales efforts, however, most of the money does go to charity, particularly if the sales items are donated.

Listed below are some of the specific standards on fundraising from the "Standards for Charitable Solicitations," issued by the Council of Better Business Bureaus. These might be helpful as you plan for and evaluate your fundraising activities, including costs and ethics.

Solicitations and Informational Materials

1. Solicitations and informational materials, distributed by any means, shall be accurate, truthful and not misleading, both in whole and in part.

2. Soliciting organizations shall substantiate on request that solicitations and informational materials, distributed by any means, are accurate, truthful and not misleading, in whole and in part.

3. Solicitations shall include a clear description of the programs and activities for which funds are requested.

4. Direct contact solicitations, including personal and telephone appeals, shall identify a) the solicitor and his/her relationship to the benefiting organization, b) the benefiting organization or cause and c) the programs and activities for which funds are requested.

5. Solicitations in conjunction with the sale of goods, services or admissions shall identify at the point of solicitation a) the benefiting organization, b) a source from which written information is available and c) the actual or anticipated portion of the sales or admission price to benefit the charitable organization or cause.

Fundraising Practices

1. Soliciting organizations shall establish and exercise controls over fundraising activities conducted for their benefit by staff, volunteers, consultants, contractors, and controlled or affiliated entities, including commitment to writing of all fundraising contracts and agreements.

2. Soliciting organizations shall establish and exercise adequate controls over contributions.

3. Soliciting organizations shall honor donor requests for confidentiality and shall not publicize the identity of donors without prior written permission. Donor requests for confidentiality include but are not limited to requests that one's name not be used, exchanged, rented or sold.

4. Fundraising shall be conducted without excessive pressure. Excessive pressure in fundraising includes but is not limited to solicitations in

the guise of invoices; harassment; intimidation or coercion, such as threats of public disclosure or economic retaliation; failure to inform recipients of unordered items that they are under no obligation to pay for or return them; and strongly emotional appeals which distort the organization's activities or beneficiaries.*

Without getting into the debate of how much public education is accomplished in fundraising campaigns, it's obvious that the larger the campaign, the more public awareness will be generated about the cause and organization. This helps in recruitment and also helps the organization to be identified as a source of help for the cause involved. It's my belief that the benefits do, in fact, affect the program pursuits of the organization. I am convinced that the 15 to 20 million persons involved in the American Cancer Society and the American Heart Association campaigns over the past thirty years feel some identification with these causes. They have probably read some of the educational material and, because they identify with the groups, they also know where to turn when information or help is needed.

An annual campaign provides impetus for telling the association's story, which is almost always very healthy for the organization. Even if it's only a membership effort conducted by an agency involved in the United Way, it's an opportunity to remind a growing number of people who you are, what you represent, what you can do for them, and what they can do for you.

Fundraising campaigns can be fun. They are almost always exciting. They provide a rallying point for the organization and in many ways lend an air of excitement to the whole operation. They're also hard work! And sustaining the effort year in and year out is particularly tough. You'll need to carefully and quickly promote volunteers up through the campaign organization (and surely from the campaign organization to the board), so there can be new blood and fresh leadership moving forward to share in the excitement of the campaign and thus be stimulated to carry the burdens of it.

One of the basic responsibilities of the campaign chairperson is to help recruit a replacement. This is also one of the president's responsibilities. Place the responsibility firmly with one of them, but make it clear that the other has got to stand ready to help and to see that it happens.

You must constantly seek ways to make clear to the workers how much their efforts mean. When I was director of the American Heart Association in Baltimore, every year we sent a New Year's card to each of the 7,000 to 10,000 block workers with a message something like this: *"During the Season of Good Will, we want to*

---

* Reprinted from "Standards for Charitable Solicitation," with permission from the Council of Better Business Bureaus.

thank you again for your wonderful service to your community as a Heart Association Volunteer."

Successful fundraising performance has to be acknowledged and applauded throughout the organization. Find every possible way to say "thank you" and to give people the warm feeling of accomplishment to which they are entitled. People want a cause. You have to help your people realize that they've got a good one, which is not only doing great things but is also grateful for the campaign volunteers' efforts. If you've achieved your goal, save some of the praise for the board, too.

14

Budgeting and Financial Accountability

B**Y THEIR VERY NATURE**, voluntary associations operate with public support and therefore have a responsibility to spend their money judiciously and to report on their expenditure to the public.

In a speech entitled "Responsibility of the Board Member of Voluntary Health Agencies," Marion Folsom, former Secretary of the U.S. Department of Health, Education and Welfare, said:

> It is definitely the responsibility of the individual lay Board Members to insist that their agencies cooperate in this program. The businessman can be especially helpful here. He should be sure that his agency is determining the cost of each of its services and is giving complete information to the public.

An organization that handles more than $5,000 should have an audit, and therefore is bound by the accounting practices spelled out in the various audit guides published by the American Institute of Certified Public Accountants. For example, there is an audit guide for health and welfare organizations. This guide is a companion piece to the *Standards of Accounting and Financial Reporting for Voluntary Health and Welfare Organizations*, published by and available from the National Assembly, National Health Council, and United Way of America. According to the *Standards* foreword: "Adoption and use of the standards presented in this publication will enable voluntary health and welfare organizations to report their income and expenditures uniformly and in terms the contributing public can understand." The other audit guides likely to be of interest to various readers are: *Audits of Colleges and Universities; Hospital Audit Guide (2nd Edition);* and *Audit of Certain Nonprofit Organizations Including Statement of Position 78-10.*

Even if your organization is not required to have an audit, you should consult an auditor to determine what requirements or practices are necessary to protect yourself, the organization, and the public.

In this chapter it will be assumed that your operation is sufficiently large to be audited and that there is probably a need to delineate the separate roles of the board and staff.

The standards are obviously important and provide substantial benefits for individual agencies and the voluntary field in general. The standards are appropriately designed to provide effective and uniform reporting to the public. However, they do not provide the basic information needed to effectively manage an agency. Thus, the system must be supplemented if a manager is to have the information needed to control and manage the agency and if the board is to be able to follow financial developments.

For example, the standards will provide the organization and the public with information about the organization's proportional expenditures in certain fixed functional categories such as community services, public health education, and fundraising. But the manager and board will need to know more specifically how the money is being spent within the agency for specific program and development activities. Within professional education and training, for example, they'll need to know what has been spent for nurses' seminars, traineeships, consecutive case conferences, and so forth. The "line" items (salaries, rent, professional fees, and so forth) required in the standards are necessarily broad so as to apply to many different organizations, and in that regard, too, they have to be supplemented.

Budgeting in voluntary agencies is always a frustrating process for financial and business people because it's difficult to move back the timetable so that a realistic budget will be at hand well before the beginning of the fiscal year. The income of an agency is often so uncertain that it's difficult to forecast before the end of one fiscal year and the beginning of another. Ideally, the closest one can come to an intelligent timetable is to have a budget prepared two or three months before the next fiscal year. Earlier projections are, of course, possible and often necessary for grant applications, United Way presentations, and other purposes, but generally a firm budget isn't in focus until very close to the beginning of the fiscal year.

Without getting into an exhaustive review of budget-making, it might be useful to comment briefly on the process of developing income and expense projections. Usually, leaders of voluntary operations are so close to the cause and so overwhelmed with how much needs to be done that they will overestimate income and underestimate expenses. The hardheaded realism of the treasurer and the finance committee is essential as an offsetting influence.

Income projections should be based on a practical and objective analysis of current sources of income, including a source-by-source and gift-by-gift review. This not only makes for practical budgeting but also provides sensible preparation for the degree of work necessary to renew gifts and grants and find new money. It's essential not to project substantial new income, or at least not to count on it, to cover fixed expenses. The usual approach for nonprofit agencies is to hope so desperately for new income that it's counted in the budget; then, when it doesn't materialize, the agency ends up with a deficit or horrendous cutback. The wiser approach is to have an opportunity for budget revision during the year to allow additions according to new income produced.

If you have a staff, expense projections are usually developed by the staff director. Here the incoming president should be carefully consulted and, of course, the treasurer and finance committee will be closely involved.

It is important that the finance committee never be allowed the authority to make decisions that rightfully belong to the executive committee or the board of directors. Many finance committees, in their efforts to cut or control expenditures, will make decisions about what activities should stay or go, which is beyond their authority. They should say to the president, staff, and board that the appraisal of income projections will not sustain the expenses budgeted. Then, if the board agrees with the finance committee's figures, it is up to the board and staff to decide where the cuts will have to be made.

The budget should be prepared early enough so that the full board of directors, or at least the executive committee, can be involved in its review and approval before the beginning of the fiscal year.

The format for the budget should include at least the following:

- a narrative summary of the year ending and the year ahead

- a five-year review of income and expenses

- a comparison of working fund activities and balances for the closing and prior years

- a proposed budget including, for each line item, the prior year's budget, the prior year's actual expenditures and income, and the recommended allocation for the coming year.

You will note that a narrative summary is recommended. I worked with one treasurer for six years and we had a perfect relationship, except once a year we would have our annual set-to over whether I would be allowed to do a narrative summary. This clashed with his banker's approach, but I knew the narrative was the only way that many board members would really grasp what the budget picture was all about.

The first item in the budgets I prepared for the American Heart Association and Mental Health Association was an estimated dollar value of the volunteer time contributed. It helped put the other budget items, particularly staff salaries, into perspective. My goal was to constantly increase the ratio of contributed time to staff salaries and other expenses. Although there are few comparisons available, I feel that a 5 to 1 ratio represents effective use of volunteers in relation to staff time. Obviously, this applies more to cause-oriented membership associations than to direct service organizations, but the exercise helps all nonprofit agencies to think hard about volunteer utilization.

It's important to put a good deal of information into the budget, including the detailed breakdown of the various line items. For instance, within the line item of employee costs, it is important for the board members to know the relative costs of basic medical, major medical, retirement, social security, unemployment insurance, and any other benefits that might be provided. Most board members won't want to get into that much detail, but at least it's there.

Budgeting dollars is only part of the necessary budgeting process. Budgeting staff time is perhaps even more important. Just as dollar resources have to be carefully directed toward the priorities determined by the board, so, too, must staff time. This sounds much more complicated than it really is. It's simply a matter of identifying the number of staff weeks that are available for actual work and matching these to the ongoing activities and special projects. If time sheets are coordinated with this, it's easy for a staff person to indicate the specific activities and projects to which time was devoted during the day. At the end of a month or quarter or year, it's possible to see if the staff time was actually spent in the patterns and on the priorities intended. This is an important way to help board and committee members to better grasp the current level of commitments. Otherwise, in the absence of this kind of specific information, boards and committees are almost too ready to add new projects or to assume that what they decided was priority is reflected by allocation of resources.

In addition to the board's own time, dollars and staff time are the two basic resources available to the board. They must be carefully measured and metered if they are to be directed in ways consistent with the agency's predetermined goals.

An organization should produce a monthly income and expense statement, balance sheet, and budget status report. These should go to the board of directors and to the executive committee in advance of their meetings. Copies should also be sent monthly to the finance committee.

The audit should also go the board with ample opportunity for discussion. At least some members of the board should fulfill the functions of an audit committee. Some organizations have a separate audit committee and others combine this with the work of the finance or executive committee.

The accounting firm of Price Waterhouse has an excellent publication called "The Audit Committee: The Board of Trustees of Nonprofit Organizations and the

Independent Accountant." The functions of the committee responsible for the audit are described as follows:

(1) Review of the financial statements with the independent accountants prior to recommending approval by the Board. The purpose of such a review is to determine that the independent accountants are satisfied with the disclosure and content of the financial statements and to obtain sufficient information from the auditors to facilitate analysis of the financial statements submitted to the entire board of trustees.

(2) Appraisal of the effectiveness of the audit effort. This includes a discussion of the overall approach to and scope of the examination, with particular attention focused on those areas where either the committee or the independent accountants believe special emphasis is desirable or necessary. The responsibility for determination of the scope of auditing necessary for the formation of an opinion on the financial statements resides with the independent accountants, and that decision must be left to them. For this reason, the committee should not ask for nor be given detailed audit programs.

(3) Determination through discussions with the independent accountants that no restrictions were placed by management on the scope of the examination or on its implementation. It is often appropriate for management representatives to allow the committee to meet alone at some point with the independent accountants. This is not intended in any sense to reflect adversely on the integrity of management; instead, it provides an additional margin of security in that there will be an opportunity for a complete interchange, without the inhibitions or restrictions that might exist if members of the management team were present. It also establishes for the record that the independent accountants were presented a chance to discuss with the committee any topics they might choose.

(4) Inquiry into the effectiveness of the organization's management of financial and accounting functions, through discussions with the independent accountants and appropriate officers of the organization. Particular attention should be paid to the adequacy of internal controls over contributions and other sensitive areas.

(5) Review of reports prepared by the independent accountants discussing weaknesses in internal control, organizational structure and operations and containing recommendations to improve such weaknesses. There should be careful consideration of the action taken by management on the independent accountant's suggestions.

(6) Recommendations of the appointment of independent accountants for the ensuing year. The actual appointment of the accountants should remain the responsibility of the full board. Management, through its day-to-day dealings with the independent accountants, normally is in the best position to evaluate the services provided, and its input to the committee should be given careful consideration when nominations for independent accountants are being considered. On the other hand, the committee should be certain that management's recommendations are objective and not designed to serve its own self-interest.*

One of the problems for both boards and staff is the need for several different kinds of financial statements: for example, (1) those required in the standards, (2) those developed for management purposes, and (3) additional statements in a format required by governmental bodies, the United Way, or others.

I reconcile the requirements for different financial reports by starting with the system and information I need to manage the agency. I make sure that this is not incompatible with the standards and that my year-end reports can be easily recast into the format required by the standards. Similarly, the records can be recast to provide special information required by the finance committee, governmental agencies, foundations, and others. But the basic point is the need for a system which is conducive to sound day-to-day management.

In an understandable preoccupation with meeting the required accounting standards, too many agencies are trying to operate with the information that comes out of that system, and it just isn't adequate.

Operating and reserve funds that are available for short-term investment should be invested in savings accounts, certificates of deposit, treasury bills, and certain categories of commercial paper. They should not be invested in common stocks. This includes all funds needed for operations or considered ready reserves.

When common stocks are received as current contributions and are considered part of operating funds or ready reserves, they should be sold at time of receipt. If the organization is fortunate enough to have endowment funds, these funds should be managed by a major financial institution selected by the finance committee and approved by the board of directors. The investment policy should be established by the board. This can include a "combined income" or "total return" plan whereby the association, in consultation with the financial institution, establishes a fixed income that will be drawn from both income and principal. This allows for investment of some substantial part of the fund in common stocks as a hedge against inflation. The finance committee should do an annual review of the fund, and members of the finance committee should be readily available to consider special advice from the financial institution.

---

* Reprinted from "The Audit Committee" with permission from Price Waterhouse.

In thirty years of nonprofit agency administration, I have had some pretty rude awakenings and learned some pretty sad lessons. Let me summarize these lessons from the school of financial hard knocks. The lessons and the consequences apply to both board and staff.

- **Budget realistically.** It's too easy to get carried away with unduly optimistic income projections and unrealistic expectations. The resulting deficits and the horror of the budget cutbacks—particularly those which involve personnel—gradually teach the lesson that it's better to face reality and disappointment during the budgeting process than later.

- **Get regular monthly reports and study them carefully.** These reports should include at the very least the income and expense statement, balance sheet, and budget status report. A situation can change rapidly, and unless caught early it is not reversible.

- **Be sure that the reports are accurate.** This may seem obvious, but I have lived with and through situations where, because of switchovers in accounting systems or problems of personnel in the accounting area, or just a plain poor accounting staff, reports have not been reliable. It's easy to assume that the staff director has a close enough view of the organization that the reports are not far out of kilter. Don't believe it! If there is any indication that the reports are not accurate, get that situation straightened out fast.

- **Insist on understanding the financial picture and the reports.** It's better to look silly than not to pursue a part of the financial picture or report which you don't quite understand. It's not sufficient that the executive committee understands it or the treasurer or the accountant. The board members are ultimately responsible, and *you* have to understand it. Staff and board should be sure that the books are organized in such a way that they help the staff director manage. It's easy to assume that by meeting the accounting standards or by supplying the finance committee with what it wants, there are enough financial reports and information necessary to manage the agency. Do it in such a way that the figures can easily be recast to satisfy the other requirements. Equally important is the need to be certain that the reports are in a form that the trustees can understand and that the trustees feel free to ask questions.

- **Establish a close working relationship with the auditor.** For the staff, day-to-day access to the auditor is essential. Provide a realistic sum in the budget over and above the cost of the audit so that the staff director can feel free to consult regularly with the auditor on many financial management considerations.

It's probably not practical for the board to work with the auditor, but the finance committee certainly should. If there is no finance committee then the auditors should meet annually with the executive committee or board. It has always been my practice that at least part of that annual session of the finance committee and auditors is conducted in an executive session (without staff present). That bothers some executive directors and even some finance committee heads, but in a nonprofit organization it's too easy for the trustees to get far removed from understanding the financial side of the enterprise. It's important that at least those trustees who serve on the finance committee have an opportunity to learn firsthand that there are no barriers to getting the frank opinion of the auditors about the financial statements, internal controls, and the degree of cooperation given to the auditors.

- **Involve the auditor in establishing, or at least approving, your internal systems, including controls.** It's not enough to assume that the auditors are satisfied with your systems and controls simply because they provide you with a clean audit. They may be assuming too much, and, because it is essential that this area be properly organized, it is wise to involve them in setting up the system or at least regularly examining it in detail. Although these functions are usually delegated to staff, the board must be certain that they are fully and regularly carried out.

- **Make the most of the interest and knowledge of the treasurer and chairperson of the finance committee.** They can help tremendously in interpreting agency operations and finances to the board of directors. They will be useful in handling short-term investments or helping line up bank loans during low cash flow. But, most of all, you will need their hardnosed, pragmatic, conservative fiscal judgment. They often provide unwelcome advice, but for that very reason it's important to have it immediately at hand.

- **Involve the key volunteer leaders in the development of the budget.** The budgeting function is often seen as an internal staff responsibility, but the person who will be serving as president when that budget is in effect can feel thwarted if he or she doesn't understand the budget and hasn't had an opportunity to see that it reflects priorities as the president and board perceive them.

- **Recognize how easily the budget can thwart or contradict the board's decisions on priorities.** The board can go through an elaborate process of determining new priorities, and yet if the budget follows the same old pattern, the resources of dollars and staff are not likely to be converted to the new pattern of priorities.

- **Provide for some cushion in the budget.** I know from experience how important it is. It's so hard to cut a proposed budget back to fit realistic projections of income that I am almost never able to build in a 10 or even 5 percent cushion. On the other hand, I know that it is not possible to anticipate fifteen months in advance what emergencies will occur in the following fiscal year. A budget should have a contingency factor of 5 to 10 percent to be allocated, in small amounts, by the executive committee or board of directors for the unanticipated needs that arise during the year.

- **Provide for some basic reserves.** Nonprofit agencies should have reserves equal to at least one half of one year's operating expenses, though not greater than one year's operating expenses. This provides funds during low cash flow, a cushion against the almost inevitable occasional deficit, and some breathing room for emergencies. All this, of course, is in addition to fulfilling the basic purpose of a reserve—to help the agency survive a truly catastrophic period.

- **Don't switch accounting systems until you are really on top of your information.** There is always a temptation to help solve a current accounting problem by moving to a new system. My experience has been that you had better be very certain that you are getting accurate information from your current system before you start major adjustments. For example, I've seen a number of agencies run into terrible difficulty during a transition to computer operations. It's essential to be getting accurate information from your current system before and until the new system is functioning fully. It happens too often that board members who come from sophisticated operations will want to modernize the operations sooner than the staff is ready. They'll graciously offer to have their own organizations provide some of the equipment or computer time and people who don't know very much about the operation will come in on a volunteer basis. I've even seen organizations switch over to an available software package largely because it is available and seemed to work for someone else without adequate consideration of whether it really fit. I had one board member send me to a week's training school which turned out to deal almost exclusively with large mainframe computers and other equipment utterly beyond our needs and finances.

- **Realize that voluntary agencies are never going to get rich.** Your people will sometimes wonder when that day will come when the agency won't be living hand-to-mouth or be facing an imminent financial crisis. I don't mean to unduly discourage you, but I don't think that the really effective voluntary agency dealing with a major public problem is ever going to be comfortable. The needs and pressures to do even more will always outweigh income. At least I know it's a way of life and I'm not periodically disappointed that the tables haven't yet been turned.

- ***Remember that deficits are hell!***

This chapter has not attempted to describe the sophisticated procedures appropriate for many organizations. They can be found in *Accounting Guide* and *Budgeting Guide,* published by the United Way of America. Many voluntary organizations are as elaborate and sophisticated as most businesses in their approach to financial planning, management of cash, decentralized budgeting, profit centers, and computerization of data that can provide trustees and staff with every possible analysis of financial operations and trends.

My purpose here is to try to provide you as a trustee with an understanding of the basic functions you must fulfill. However large or small the operation and however much sophisticated equipment is available to you, it still comes down to "What am I accountable for?" And at the top of the list is stewardship.

15

Evaluating Results

Voluntary agencies are usually so busy doing that there isn't time (or it seems a poor use of time) to become involved with serious evaluation. At some point, though, someone inside or outside the organization is going to want to know if the effort is reasonably successful. Then you'll be pressed to provide some justification and assurance. It is to be hoped that you, as a trustee, will be the first to ask.

A medical researcher, long active in voluntary agencies, has this wonderful description of how nonprofit groups generally evaluate their results: "Any group as bright as we are which has worked as long and hard as we have must have done a lot of good." Don't dismiss too hastily this pleasantly cynical characterization of our approach to evaluation. When those doubting Thomases begin to raise questions, you may well find yourself reacting instinctively, and maybe even a bit testily, with a rather subjective, "It must be the most obvious thing in the world that any group as bright as we are. . . ."

In "Better Performance From Nonprofits," Cecil Cannan Selby, former national director of the Girl Scouts, made somewhat the same point: "Another assumption, not invalid on its face but leading to many pitfalls, is that volunteering is a good in itself. Because I am a volunteer and doing something gratis for others, I am doing something good in itself, and anything I do in this role must be good."

There is the likelihood, however, that at some point this may not be good enough for some other members of the board or for some contributors, or maybe even for you. You will then want to have a more objective measurement of whether it's all worthwhile or whether at least you're getting all the results possible.

Evaluation doesn't have to be complicated. It can be as basic as deciding what you want to achieve by the end of the year and then figuring out later if you got there. At its simplest, evaluation starts with an attainable goal to be accomplished at a realistic date, with a prior commitment to stop what you're doing on that date and look back to see if your goal was actually reached. The sad reason so many organizations don't follow this simple procedure is that they don't even start out with a plan; therefore they don't have a specific goal or deadline to check back on. My formula is that fuzzy goals equal fuzzy evaluation, and unfortunately the combination usually adds up to fuzzy performance.

In Chapter 9, I said that much of the planning in our agencies is characterized by the attitude: "We're going to do as much good as we possibly can, and we can't be expected to do any more."

I also said that specialists in planning have a way of making the process so involved that we tend to dismiss their recommendations as being beyond the resources and sophistication of our voluntary operations. The same thing happens with evaluation.

If what you see when you look back isn't pleasing, you'll automatically begin asking why, and this will be the beginning of a more effective marshaling of resources to accomplish the things that really are most important.

At this point, any evaluators or planners reading this are probably tearing their hair out because their science has been stripped to such nakedness. Nevertheless, planning and evaluation can be easy, and it can be simple. Earlier I quoted the Peter Principle: "If you don't know where you're going, you'll end up someplace else." An evaluation sequel might be: "If you don't know where you've been, how do you know you were there?"

There should be a built-in mechanism for self-evaluation. As stated above, this can be as simple as at the end of the year taking a look to see if your goals have in fact been achieved. This is the most basic form of self-evaluation and should be a routine part of every organization's operations.

In addition, there should be some mechanism by which the board can periodically take a fuller look at the organization's operations and activities. For instance, this review should determine whether or not basic planning and evaluation are being done annually. You'll find that these, too, can be as simple or as complex as the operation itself.

Periodically—at least every five years—you should arrange for an outside evaluation. This is most easily arranged if you are part of a national organization. For various reasons, you may resist having representatives of a national board or staff do the evaluation. If that's the case, you can put together a team from your sister associations, which really constitutes a peer review. If that avenue isn't available to you, it shouldn't be difficult to put together a willing and able team from your own community. In every town there are scores if not hundreds of people who have had unusual success in nonprofit activities. Ask two or three of the best staff directors and most experienced board volunteers from other groups to perform this function for you. They will be proud to be asked.

An effective evaluation will depend on the degree to which measurable standards are at hand, which begins with knowing what constitutes acceptable performance and better.

In an invaluable article, "How Can Businessmen Evaluate the Management of Voluntary Welfare Agencies?" Earle Lippincott and Elling Aannestad state that *". . . if the basic organizational components of the agency are operating effectively, you can assume that the output is likely to be worthwhile."* They acknowledged that this isn't an exact equation, but they believe, for example, that ". . . if the Board and the basic committees are functioning—including regular meetings with quorums present—it is likely the agency is not wasting its time."

In looking for operating standards, Lippincott and Aannestad asked the following questions:

1. Are the Board and staff set up to work effectively?

2. How well defined are the needs served by the agency and its program for meeting these needs?

3. Are adequate financial safeguards and sound controls maintained for fundraising?

4. Is the agency's work related to that of the national organization and of other planning groups in the field?

5. Is the agency doing a good job of what it is set up to do?

6. How many other agencies are trying to do all or parts of the same job?

7. Does the agency function in proper relationship to government agencies?

When I was the director of the American Heart Association in California, we agreed with Lippincott and Aannestad that one can be encouraged if the basic operation seems to be functioning. We recognized, however, that this doesn't assure that the end product is really good or is even as good as it should be. Therefore, we added two elements. First, we identified the *basic* activities that we believed a chapter of the American Heart Association should be handling well. Second, we acknowledged that one of the great things about voluntary agencies is their role as innovators. Obviously, certain activities can't be anticipated, so we gave a whopping one third of the total score to those unusual things that the chapter might be doing over and above the basics.

As a result, the standards were divided into three parts: (1) "Basic Organization" (such as board makeup, meetings, and turnover), (2) "Basic Activities" (such as an information and referral program, and at least one seminar for general practitioners each year), and (3) "Additional Activities." A chapter was evaluated every three years by a peer group of board members from other chapters. This had many intended and desirable results, but it also had a side benefit: the board members doing the evaluation learned a good deal about how to improve their own chapters.

Most of your basic standards are probably already at hand or are suggested by the standards performance published by the Council of Better Business Bureaus (CBBB) and the National Charities Information Bureau (NCIB). I included these in the beginning of Part II, in discussing the role of the board and board members, because, as I said, "It is helpful to start with the standards of performance by which organizations are held accountable and then work backward to how the board can be sure that the organization passes those tests." I feel strongly about this point and hope you will consider pages 20 and 21 as central to the subject of evaluation as well.

One of the hardest things to set standards for and to measure involves program performance. A new project is unfolding that will be helpful to many of you. The NCIB is involved in a "Program Effectiveness and Efficiency Project" (PEEP), which is designed "to establish specific goals and measurable objectives against which actual results can be compared." At this stage it involves a two-part questionnaire designed for use by grantseekers to be more specific in their proposals and reports to grantmakers so that both have the benefit of these statements of intended and actual results.

The first part of the questionnaire relates to pre–grant-period questions:

1. What are the general, long-term goals of your proposed project (or program or organization)?

2. Within these goals, what are your specific, short-term, measurable objectives against which you will be able to compare and evaluate actual results at the end of the grant period?
   a. That is, recognizing long-term measures may not be feasible by the end of the grant period, what are your projected short-term measurable benefits, outcomes, or impacts? For example, 50 per cent or more of the individuals served will be helped or get better?
   b. And, if applicable, what are your budget-based unit-of-service costs or other projected efficiency measures?

3. To achieve these goals and objectives, what specific activities are planned?

4. What is the itemized budget for the project (or program or organization)?

5. What data collection and evaluation procedures do you have in place so you will be able to answer the post–grant-period questions (see questions 6 through 10 below)?

The second part covers the post–grant-period questions:

6. Did you carry out each proposed activity as planned? If not, why not? (see question 3.)

7. How do your actual expenses compare with the budget? (see question 4.)

8. Based on the data you have been able to collect so far, how do the actual results compare with your measurable objectives? (see question 2.)

9. In addition to the above measurable results, what other progress have you made toward achieving your goals? (see question 1.)

10. Did you, or will you, use this information in your planning, budgeting, monitoring, evaluation or other management activities to improve your program effectiveness? If so, how?

The National Executive Service Corps (NESC), made of retired business executives who are available to provide management assistance to voluntary organizations, has started to define what is "the bottom line" for nonprofit organizations. This is how they suggest a board can get a sense of profit or loss.

These are the questions that will help you assess a nonprofit organization. Add up the answers. You'll find they lead you to . . . **"THE BOTTOM LINE."**

1. What is the mission?

2. What is the evidence that the mission is necessary and important to those served and not redundant in terms of other community efforts?

3. What is the evidence that individual programs to achieve the mission are effectively and efficiently carried out?

4. What plans and priorities have been established which realistically recognize the organization's mission, management and financial capabilities?

5. What is the evidence that the Board—as a whole and individually—fulfills its obligations?

6. What budgetary and management procedures have been established to accomplish the mission and assure accountability?

One of the frustrations for business people serving on voluntary organization boards is that it is so hard to define and measure success. Despite the good efforts of NESC, nonprofits will never have the simple measure of corporate bottom-line profits. A serious consequence is that too many nonprofit organizations assume therefore that other business standards and practices don't apply either. In her article "Better Performance from Nonprofits," Cecile Cannan Selby says that "the same businessman who would not conceive of going into the toothpaste business without identifying the merits of his products, identifying the market to which the product must be sold, and developing a plan to bring the product to market will work in a voluntary organization without taking the same steps with respect to its 'product.' "

In *Management Control in Nonprofit Organizations*, Robert M. Anthony and Regina Herzlinger of the Graduate School of Business Administration at Harvard put it this way:

> All organizations use inputs to produce outputs. An organization's effectiveness is measured by the extent to which outputs accomplish its objectives, and its efficiency is measured by the relationship between inputs and outputs. In a profit-oriented organization the amount of profit provides an overall measure of both effectiveness and efficiency. In many nonprofit organizations, however, outputs cannot be measured to quantitative terms. . . . The absence of a satisfactory, single, overall measure of performance that is comparable to the profit measure is the most serious management control problem in a nonprofit organization. (It is incorrect to say that the absence of the profit *motive* is the central problem; rather, it is the absence of the profit *measure*). . . .

One of the large problems facing boards in attempting to evaluate performance is the confusion about how much voluntary organizations should be like business. Business men and women who have not served extensively with voluntary organizations will so desperately want the organization to mirror what they know best and to come closer to a "bottom line" that they will be extremely impatient with their nonprofit organizations. This has led them, in fairly significant numbers, to assume and claim that voluntary organizations generally are managed poorly. It has become routine to hear such observations as, "These do-gooders and bleeding-hearts just don't know how to manage" or, "If we could just get more management discipline into these cause-oriented organizations, they would be far more effective."

It's my own observation that these perceptions are inaccurate and unfair. Voluntary organizations are like businesses and other human institutions in that about one third are models of excellence—beautiful examples of caring and daring and innovation and efficiency. For what they are supposed to be in our pluralistic

society, they are our models of excellence. One third are average—good to fair—
and one third are poorly managed and generally ineffective.

Senator Robert Packwood, who chaired the Senate Commerce Committee
and therefore has had a good opportunity to observe all three sectors, says that
on the basis of his regular dealings with government, business and the nonprofit
world, he finds that foundations and voluntary organizations are by far the most
reliable—that is, the most certain to do what they were established to do and
what society expects of them.

Management consultant Peter Drucker was once asked by a business reporter,
"What's the most effective organization with which you've ever worked?" Obviously, the inquirer assumed that the answer would be a business corporation
such as General Electric or Xerox or Hewlett-Packard. Drucker thought a moment
and replied, "the Girl Scouts." The reporter laughed and said that he hoped
Drucker would be willing to give a serious answer, and Drucker responded that
he was absolutely serious in believing the Girl Scouts were the most effective
group with which he had worked. He pointed out that if you took that many
dedicated volunteers, with a professional staff oriented and trained to increase
the usefulness of the volunteers, and you pointed all of that energy and commitment toward an important social purpose such as the development of women and
girls, those were clearly the ingredients for effectiveness and excellence.

That episode points up a large part of the misunderstanding about excellence
in voluntary organizations. Before we can judge performance, we have to have a
clearer grasp of what we're looking for. In the case of nonprofit organizations, we
need to have a much better grasp of the uniqueness of these organizations, both
in the social role they fulfill and in the ways they do it. If we simply apply "bottom-
line" efficiency as our standard, we fail to distinguish the special characteristics
of dynamic voluntary organizations. Nonprofit organizations can learn a great
deal from businesses about good management, bottom-line discipline, people development, evaluation of results and much more, but these are often not their
primary ingredients for excellence.

In his article, "Managing the 'Third Sector,' " which appeared in the October
3, 1978, *Wall Street Journal*, Drucker said:

> By now, however, the Third Sector has become so important, so big
> and so costly that we need to focus on how it is being run. Performance,
> effectiveness and productivity of the service institutions will increas-
> ingly matter. And they will also become increasingly difficult. Precisely
> because they have grown so much the service institutions require more
> and better management—and they require different management.

He added:

> Both the businessman and the civil servant tend to underrate the dif-
> ficulty of managing service institutions. The businessman thinks it's all
> a matter of being efficient, the civil servant thinks it's all a matter of

having the right procedures and controls. Both are wrong—service institutions are more complex than either businesses or government agencies . . .

I've worked with some chaotic, break-all-the-rules community organizations that management consultants think are the epitome of poor management, but which I found to be perfect examples of dynamic associations that are mobilizing people to deal with a very real need or aspiration. Management people will tend to focus on the fact that the organization doesn't have bylaws or hasn't been keeping minutes, or is living hand to mouth, but a community organizer will see citizens mobilizing other citizens to really make a difference. A great many voluntary organizations are both dynamic *and* efficient, but if I had to settle for one characteristic, it would be the former.

Even in larger organizations, there's a tendency to overlook the unique functions of citizen service, advocacy and education. When I was National Director of the Mental Health Association, new board members from the corporate side would invariably react that the board was too large, that there were too few internal administrative staff members, or that, for efficiency, we should consider merging with the retardation association. They didn't understand the need to achieve maximum feasible involvement and the need to keep citizens mobilized around causes they care passionately about.

There's one area of strain between voluntary organizations and their funders that would be humorous were it not so serious. Rarely are voluntary organizations allowed to build a realistic reserve, and even one year of deficit budgeting is viewed as a clear indication of poor management. Yet, even the best businesses have deficit years, and foundations will sometimes spend more than income to fulfill important obligations or take advantage of vital leads. But woe to the voluntary agency manager who, though dealing with urgent causes, has a year or two of red ink.

There is great interest of late in the book *In Search of Excellence: Lessons From America's Best Run Companies* by Thomas Peters and Robert Waterman, in which they describe some of the sensitive and sensible ingredients of good management. At the heart of their book is the chapter entitled "Back to Basics," which includes these sub-headings:

- Managing Ambiguity and Paradox
- A Bias for Action
- Close to the Customer
- Autonomy and Entrepreneurship
- Productivity Through People
- Hands-On, Value-Driven

- Stick to the Knitting

- Simple Form, Lean Staff

- Simultaneous Loose-Tight Properties

These subheadings describe the attributes that have characterized the best of voluntary organizations for hundreds of years. Their *primary* chapter is even entitled "Man Waiting for Motivation"!

Cecile Cannan Selby has examined the similarities and differences between profit and nonprofit organizations. Her findings help to remove the excuses proffered by nonprofit organizations when they should be performing in a "business-like" way, but she also helps us to understand the areas where comparisons are not practical or fair. She says:

> The altruistic, cause-related motivation that gives nonprofit organizations their great strength can be their downfall if it is not understood and appropriately handled. If these organizations are treated as illegitimate rather than legitimate, their innate operational differences from those in business will emerge as functional weaknesses. The uniqueness of this sector must be built on, and management techniques and related training programs that are adapted to nonprofits' special characteristics must be better developed.

The three "key differences" that Selby finds between nonprofit and profit organizations are (1) "the bottom line"; (2) "the confusion in direct-line accountability" (for example, she asks, ". . . in a board appointed program committee on which volunteers serve, is it the committee or the staff that is accountable for the function and can staff be accountable for what volunteers fail to do?"); and (3) "the mixed allegiance of many professionals in voluntary organizations who do not see themselves as part of the organizational hierarchy, at least in terms of accountability." She cites as examples the university professor and other intellectuals and artists who have their "own sense of creative integrity—an accountability that can override all others."

She concludes by calling for nonprofit organizations to be more effective *but* not always with the business model in mind:

> "In using the term *nonprofit*, which refers to a financial balance sheet only, perhaps we obscure the essence of this sector of our society, which is indeed to be profitable to citizens, business and government—to benefit its constituents, its clients and its employees. This sector has found, and one hopes we'll continue to find, new and better ways to preserve and enhance pluralism, voluntarism, and the distinctiveness of art, intellect and charity."

While I agree entirely with Selby, I also know that your likely frustration and mine is that we are not well along in defining those differences and determining how to measure excellence in such intangibles as the promotion of pluralism or art. In "Evaluating Nonprofit Activity" (from *The Nonprofit Organization Handbook*, edited by Tracy D. Connors), David Horton Smith says that people hide behind the statement, "You can't quantify virtue and helpfulness," but he asks how we really know if "the virtue really helps anybody?"

If evaluating nonprofit activity in general is difficult, it gets downright tormenting when you try to determine the results in programs related to advocacy, citizen education, good government, or other intangibles. With tongue in cheek, Robert H. Anthony and Regina Herzinger suggest that the way to measure the output of religious organizations might be "souls saved per pew-hour preached." Paul Ylvisaker of Harvard's Graduate School of Higher Education takes that a step further and says, "It's hard to evaluate the success of a church when you're denied access to the final judgment!"

The usual response to this difficulty is either to do nothing or to change the program focus toward more measurable activities just because they are measurable. In the first draft of the United Way of America's Services Identification System (UWASIS), there was a commendable attempt to quantify all program activities, but the colossal early mistake, later corrected, was to give the most measurable functions the highest priority. Advocacy and public education efforts were assigned the lowest ranking. When those of us in the mental health field challenged this overly simple determination, United Way acknowledged that advocacy was our most important service; but by then many local United Ways were penalizing us because they too had gone overboard on the "body count" emphasis.

Even when an organization can point to major advances in the directions of its advocacy and education programs, it's hard to prove cause and effect. Some organizations grossly exaggerate their impact on, say, a school board or Congress. Where is the middle ground?

If you're trying to change attitudes, it is now possible to conduct before and after "level of knowledge surveys" to see what change there has been on actual votes on appropriations or rulings. If you aren't sure whether your activities have made the difference, you can interview the school board members or Senate staff members who are likely to be candid. If you really want to get an objective report, use specialty firms who can develop and conduct impartial interviews.

If you don't know how to evaluate a rather involved activity, turn to your college sociology department or other social scientists who are likely to be quite skilled and helpful in identifying ways you can get more objective readings of your results.

You can also turn to various publications for advice on objective evaluation. For example, David Horton Smith, in "Evaluating Nonprofit Activity" (in *The Nonprofit Organization Handbook*, edited by Tracy D. Connors), shares these helpful observations:

Social science research makes it quite clear that although we may all be pretty good at evaluating other people and programs with which we are familiar, we tend to overestimate the worth of ourselves and our own programs, organizations, contributions, and so on. I may be able to evaluate your contribution fairly accurately and you may be able to do likewise for me, but we would both probably fail to be objective about ourselves. That is why physicians do not try to treat themselves.

Hence, the next step up the quality continuum is to have the evaluation of an informed, unbiased outside observer. Just by having an outsider— one not directly involved with the program or organization being evaluated—one has guaranteed a certain amount of objectivity, other things being equal. The problem, of course, is to make sure that the outsider gets enough or has enough information about your NPO program in order to make an *informed* evaluation. Yet even if this matter of informing the outside evaluator/rater is dealt with successfully, there are still likely to be various idiosyncratic biases that characterize the single outside evaluator. Still, the process of engaging and working with a single outside evaluator can have a great positive impact on an organization, especially if his/her visits bring together people and groups who do not normally meet or who do not discuss evaluation seriously if they do. Similarly, the single outside evaluator can lead the program/ organization to begin to gather new and better data on themselves, consider alternative programs, spell out goals and priorities more clearly, and so on.

Fortunately, social science research has been able to show a simple solution to this problem. It turns out that if you take the evaluation of several informed outside observers, their individual biases tend to cancel each other out to a substantial degree so that their collective evaluation (submitted individually and independently—by secret ballot, so to speak) is very reliable on the whole. Experiments have shown that the largest gains in objectivity and reliability of evaluation are made as one goes from one informed outside observer to, say, five. After that, additional members of the panel are still important up to about ten or twelve raters. Beyond this point, there is relatively little to be gained by simply adding more raters to the panel or team.

There are many today who argue for an *even* higher level of planning and evaluation. René Debós has called for the "development of social goals." He decries the piecemeal "ad hoc approach to solutions to human problems" which, he says, is no longer tolerable. He believes that it is no longer appropriate for scholars to avoid a coordinated centralized approach to long-term needs and their solutions on the old grounds that individual scientists must be left unencumbered. In essence, Debós believes that we should not be asking, "Where is science taking us?" but, instead, we should be asking, "How can we manage science so that it will take us where we want to go?" To do this, he says, we first need to decide our social goals. As an example of a sound goal, Debós suggests that by the year 2000 we may have decided that it should be routine for all persons to have a 100-year life span including an opportunity for health and happiness. Along this same line, when Walter Mondale was in the Senate, he introduced legislation to develop a National Social Report, which would more exactly define the basic social goals that we as a nation should establish. These approaches are obviously designed to better articulate relative social needs. An integral part of the effort is to define the goals so that specific programs to achieve them can be developed and an evaluation of progress and results can be created.

Evaluation can be sophisticated and technical, and both planning and evaluation are vital management skills which, in complex operations, will need to be carried to a very technical level. The only reason they were stripped of some of their status earlier in this chapter was to make the point that most things boil down to common sense, and if people can start there, they actually will get started.

For larger and more complex organizations, the planning and evaluation process will require the skills of a specialist to take advantage of the refined methods that have been developed for more scientific examination and determination of goals, the quantification of these goals, and an exact evaluation that automatically identifies the impediments standing in the way of maximum fulfillment of goals.

When he was Secretary of Defense, Robert S. McNamara and his fellow Ford "whiz kids" brought planning and evaluation to a high level, and their procedures have been further refined and applied throughout the Federal government, up to and including the human services agencies. Organizations that secure government contracts and grants to provide services to people are now required to present their objectives and goals in mathematically defined units of service, providing indications of dollar cost per unit and human value per unit.

The seemingly calculated approach by the Federal government and others to an appraisal of relative human needs strikes many people as substituting scientific procedures for moral judgments. At some point, however, someone has to be able to provide a clearer picture of which programs can have what impact on what degree of human suffering. It is much to be hoped that these facts will be served up to thoughtful, sensitive human beings who will also exercise humaneness in making value judgments about human needs. At least this combination will be an improvement over the irrational approaches that have been used so often to identify priorities and support programs.

Another example of advanced evaluation involves the accreditation standards and evaluations of such groups as the American Association of Museums and the accrediting bodies related to secondary schools and colleges and universities. In the case of museums, over the years peer groups have agreed on "basic standards" and "standards of excellence," and each museum is visited by an accrediting team at least every ten years to see if it meets or continues to meet the standards.

United Way of America has published a series of guides under the title "House of Accountability," including a much-improved revision of UWASIS, "Standards of Excellence" (guidelines for the "ought to be" of United Way organizations), the "Needs Assessment" mentioned in the chapter on planning, and a new book on evaluation and accreditation.

The sophisticated arrangements I have been talking about are obviously beyond the needs and resources of most voluntary organizations. It is important to make clear that, however simple or complicated the nonprofit endeavor, there have been developed and continue to be developed competent ways to measure the results.

Coming back down the scale toward the reality most of you face, there is a procedure that will apply in a great many organizations that is generally referred to as "determination of key results." In "Planning and Management in Nonprofit Organizations" (in Connors' *The Nonprofit Organization Handbook*), John O. Alexander lists six "key result areas" and provides "indicators" (of progress) for each. His checklist appears at the end of this chapter.

For the board's evaluation of its own accountability and leadership, I recommend taking another look at the "governance" section of the Better Business Bureau's "Standards for Charitable Solicitations" and the National Charities Information Bureau's "Basic Standards in Philanthropy."

The best checklist I've found for evaluating the board's own performance was developed by Father Thomas J. Savage of The Cheswick Center. The checklist, originally published in "The Cheswick Process: Seven Steps to a More Effective Board," is also reproduced at the end of this chapter.

The inclusion of Cheswick's board checklist underscores how important I believe it is for boards to evaluate their own performance. It's the most important phase in the whole review process. As you move out to the broader organization, I hope I've provided some guidelines and examples for that fuller review.

One quick way to take a look at your organization might be to match yours against a profile of effective voluntary organizations that I developed after years of trying to figure out why some voluntary organizations failed and others succeeded. The successful ones have these characteristics:

- A cause worth getting excited about.

- An ability to generate funds to do the job.

- Programs that can in fact do something for the cause.

- Adequate attention to morale in order to keep the undertaking spirited and vigorous even when the immediate tasks are not.

- Appropriate emphasis on increasing the number of citizens involved.

- Ability to keep the volunteers in charge even after the operation is staffed.

- Flexibility to respond effectively to new problems and opportunities and to fit the profile of "ad-hocracy," which must increasingly characterize the useful ongoing organization.

- A capacity to keep the real mission in focus no matter how frenzied things become or how great the pressure to move into new areas. This means that all important decisions are made with the organization's "reason for being" kept clearly in the forefront.

- Vision to see beyond the horizon, along with a sensitivity to human needs and an almost contradictory toughness to build an organization capable of translating the vision and sensitivity into change.

Despite the fact that planning and evaluation can become exceedingly complicated and sophisticated, they start with the basics of articulating goals, establishing timetables, and looking back at a later date to evaluate the progress or lack of it.

In the future, you will be able to say, "Any group as bright and dedicated as we are, which has worked as long and hard as we have *and which has been so conscientious in evaluating our results*, has obviously done a great deal of good."

Congratulations and thank you.

You're special.

Figure 3.   What Are the Things We Must Do Well?*

Key Result Area	Indicators
Constituent service	Attendance Inquiries Cases handled Requests for information Requests for service Documented complaints Number of meetings, events, or services performed Different or new geographic participation Different types of services by participation
Volunteer, member, and board participation	Number of volunteers active Number of voluntary days/hours Percent increase/decrease of voluntary participation Type of voluntary participants Percent increase/decrease of members Member dropouts New members inducted Members on active committees and working groups Number and types of services to members Member turnover rates Participation of board members on active committees and service functions Number of board meetings Number of board resignations Board attendance at meetings
Staff performance	Staff grievances Staff turnover Ratio staff to administration Ratio staff to clients or individuals served Ratio staff to total income/expense Staff absenteeism Resignations versus terminations
Financial management	Cost per unit of client service Cost for membership fulfillment Cost for repair and building custodial services Cost ratio of staff to administration Cost ratio of services by type Grants received Cost of grants administration Membership dues paid Amount of delinquent membership dues Ratio staff to income Total income Expense for consumable items Expense for equipment Expense for building, purchase or lease
Legislative effectiveness	Number of contacts with legislative leaders Amount of favorable versus unfavorable legislation Appearances before legislative groups to testify Legislation influenced
Public and media relations	Press releases published versus issued Favorable versus unfavorable press coverage Newsletter/bulletins issued to general membership or constituents

*Reproduced from "Planning and Management in Nonprofit Organizations," by John O. Alexander, in *The Nonprofit Organization Handbook*, edited by Tracy Daniel Connors, with permission. © 1980, McGraw-Hill, Inc., New York, NY.

Figure 4. Board Self-Evaluation Rating Schedule*

Rating Schedule	Excellent	Good	Fair	Poor	Unnecessary	No Opinion
Legal Framework						
1. Statements in the governing documents (charter, deed of trust, by-laws, etc.) setting forth the function and duties of the board are:						
2. Statements in the governing documents outlining the role and responsibilities of individual members of the Board are:						
3. Conformance of public warranties of the institution, express or implied, as evidenced by catalogs, guarantees, advertisements, solicitations, etc., to statements in the governing document is:						
Structure of the Board						
1. The size of the Board in relation to the needs of the institution is:						
2. The spread and balance of the Board as regards age, interest, and points of view are:						
3. The usual method of selection of new board members is:						
4. Retirement provisions for board members are:						
5. The committee structure of the Board is:						
Comprehension of the Board						
1. Understanding by board members of the purposes and objectives of the institution is:						
2. Comprehension by board members of the Board's role is:						
3. Comprehension by board members of their responsibilities is:						
4. Understanding by board members of the legal requirements and stipulations under which they act as a Board is:						
5. The Board's recognition that mere compliance with the law does not assure good management is:						
6. The Board's knowledge of and familiarity with the institutional structure of the institution is:						
7. The Board's perception and understanding of key factors in the success of the institution is:						

162

Figure 4—continued

Rating Schedule	Excellent	Good	Fair	Poor	Unnecessary	No Opinion
8. The Board's comprehension of the interests of the several constituencies with which the institution deals is:						
9. The supply of information regarding external developments—legal, economic, sociological, statutory, etc.—that may affect board decisions which is furnished board members is:						
10. Board members' degree of interest in and knowledge of: Education is:						
Broad economic development is:						
Politics is:						
International affairs is:						
Accounting is:						
Finance is:						
Marketing is:						
Administration is:						
Technology is:						
Other (as appropriate to the institution)						
11. The Board's comprehension of the present position of the institution in: The "industry" is:						
The community is:						
12. Ability of the Board to sense the role of the institution five years in the future in view of current social, economic, and political developments is:						
13. Familiarity of board members with provisions in the by-laws protecting or indemnifying them in the event suits are brought against them personally is:						

Practices of the Board

1. The Board's manual of Policies and Procedures is:

Figure 4—continued

Rating Schedule	Excellent	Good	Fair	Poor	Unnecessary	No Opinion
2. The frequency of Board meetings in relation to organizational needs is:						
3. Attendance of board members at meetings is:						
4. The pre-meeting package of informational material forwarded to the Board in preparation for meetings is:						
5. Financial and other reports presented to the Board, appraised in terms of:						
Intelligibility, are:						
Completeness, are:						
Conformity to the needs of the Board, are:						
6. Record-keeping of board meetings is:						
7. Conformity of board records with legal requirements is:						
8. The method by which the Board receives the report of the outside auditors, including the opportunity to discuss the report with the auditors, is:						
9. The Board's practices as regards: Amendments of by-laws are:						
Election of officers are:						
Designation of officers' salaries, bonuses, and fringe benefits are:						
Establishment of committees and their mandates are:						
Grants of powers of attorney are:						
Changes in reserves are:						
Establishing or altering pension plans are:						
10. Methods by which the Board periodically established short or long-run goals for the institution are:						
11. Procedures used by the Board in educating and indoctrinating new members are:						
12. The use of key executives in making presentations to the Board is:						

Figure 4—continued

Rating Schedule	Excellent	Good	Fair	Poor	Unnecessary	No Opinion
13. The use of inspection trips by the Board into different departments, plants, and locations is:						
14. Statements in the by-laws and resolutions of the Board governing the conduct of individual Board members in respect to attendance at meetings, conflicts or interest, term of service and retirement, use of confidential information, annual disclosure to other board members of changes in occupation or professional and financial connection are:						
Performance of the Board						
1. Performance of the Board in formulating short- and long-run goals for the institution is:						
2. The Board's ability to monitor its own accomplishments and progress is:						
3. The performance of the Board in achieving objectives: Set one year ago is:						
Set three years ago is:						
4. Standards of performance expected by the Board for: The several parts of the institution are:						
The institution as a whole are:						
5. Standards used by the Board to measure performance by: Individual parts of the institution are:						
The institution as a whole are:						
6. Ability of the Board to measure the progress of the CEO toward achieving institutional objectives is:						
7. Ability of the Board to acquire external, objective opinion regarding the institution's progress is:						
8. Cooperation among board members and ability of the Board to act as a team is:						

Figure 4—continued

Rating Schedule	Excellent	Good	Fair	Poor	Unnecessary	No Opinion
Committees						
1. By-law provisions or resolutions of the Board stating functions, duties, and limits of authority of committees are:						
Executive Committee:						
Academic Affairs Committee:						
Audit Committee:						
Property Committee:						
Finance Committee:						
Other Committees:						
2. Form of committee report is:						
3. Method of receiving, approving or amending, and recording reports is:						
Board Meetings						
1. Format of the agenda for board meetings is:						
2. Extent to which board members do their "homework" and are prepared for meetings is:						
3. Quality of discussion at meetings is:						
4. The division of time at meetings between routine matters of the institution and long-range planning is:						
5. The division of time at meetings between day-to-day matters of the institution and long-range planning is:						
Relations with Management						
1. Understanding of the areas reserved for board decisions is:						
2. Distinctions between Board Business and Administrative and Academic Prerogatives are:						
3. The Board's working relations with administrative staff are:						

*Reproduced from "The Cheswick Process: Seven Steps to a More Effective Board," by Thomas J. Savage, S.J., with permission. © 1984, The Cheswick Center, Boston, MA.

Part III

*For More Details:
A Reading and
Reference List*

THIS LISTING of additional reference sources is offered for those who want more information on various aspects of nonprofit board work. For easier reference, we have divided the list into four sections:

- Section A lists resource materials that are currently available and are likely to remain so for at least five years. Publishers' addresses are provided to facilitate ordering materials.

- Section B lists books which are no longer in print but which have gained sufficient circulation to be available in many state, university, and public libraries.

- Section C lists sources cited in the text.

- Section D lists some of the growing number of organizations and publishers currently producing materials about the nonprofit sector.

Our listing is not intended as a definitive reading and reference list; the closest anyone has come to that is the bibliography prepared by the Minnesota Office of Volunteer Services in cooperation with the University of Minnesota. Because our list could not be complete, and because some people will be surprised and even upset that we've missed some of their favorites, we thought of leaving the list out altogether. For all its limitations, however, we felt that it might at least serve its intended purpose as a starting point "for more details."

In our effort to identify good resource materials, we learned that the important topic of board development has not achieved sufficient status to have generated its own body of literature. In fact, the whole topic of the independent sector can still be characterized as in a "pamphleteering" stage or, in the jargon of librarians, as "fugitive" or "ephemeral" material. The literature is still a long way from giving the sector the intellectual underpinnings it deserves.

Brian O'Connell

Ann O'Connell

A. REFERENCE MATERIALS IN PRINT

As of late 1984, these materials were in print and, according to their publishers, will remain available for at least five years.

Adult Education Association of
U.S.A.
1957 *Better Boards and
Committees.*
AEA
1206 16th Street, NW,
Suite 301
Washington, DC 20006
1956 *Working with Volunteers.*
(AEA above)

Aid Association for Lutherans
1980 *The Shape of Things to Come:
1980-1990. A Report from The
National Forum on
Volunteerism.*
AAL Branch Operations
Appleton, WI 54919
(also: Volunteer,
1111 North 19th Street,
Arlington, VA 22209)

Allen, Kerry Kenn
1981 *Will Volunteering Survive?*
Volunteer: National Center
for Voluntary Action
1111 North 19th Street
Arlington, VA 22209

Allen, Kerry Kenn; Chapin, Isolde;
Keller, Shirley; and Hill, Donna
1979 *Volunteers from the
Workplace.*
Volunteer: National Center
for Voluntary Action
1111 North 19th Street
Arlington, VA 22209

American Institute for Certified
Public Accountants.
1974 *Audit Guide for Health and
Welfare Organizations.*
AICPA
1211 Avenue of the Americas
New York, NY 10036

American Society of Association
Executives
1975 *Principles of Association
Management.*
U.S. Chamber of Commerce
1615 H Street, NW
Washington, DC 20062
1982 *Fundamentals of Association
Management: The Volunteer.*
ASAE
1575 I Street, NW
Washington, DC 20005

Anthony, Robert N., and Young,
David W.
1984 *Management Control in Nonprofit Organizations, 3rd ed.*
Richard D. Irwin, Inc.
1818 Ridge Road
Homewood, IL 60430

Association of Governing Boards of
Universities and Colleges
1982 *The Board's Role in
Accreditation.*
AGB
1 Dupont Circle,
Suite 400
Washington, DC 20036
1982 *Trustee Liability Insurance,
1982.*
(AGB above)

Axelrod, Nancy R.
1982 *A Guide For New Trustees.*
Association of Governing
Boards of Universities and
Colleges
1 Dupont Circle,
Suite 400
Washington, DC 20036

Barry, Joseph K., and Mundt,
Charles
1973 *Financial Management Hand-
book for Associations, rev. ed.*
U.S. Chamber of Commerce,
Association Division
1615 H Street, NW
Washington, DC 20062

Bennett, Paul
1973 *Up Your Account–ability:
How to Up Your Serviceabil-
ity and Funding Credibility by
Upping Your Accounting
Ability.*
Taft Corporation
5125 MacArthur Boulevard
Washington, DC 20016

Berger, Peter L., and Neuhaus,
Richard J.
1977 *To Empower People: The Role
of Mediating Structures in
Public Policy.*
American Enterprise Insti-
tute for Public Policy
Research
1150 17th Street, NW
Washington, DC 20036

Bete, Channing L., Company, Inc.
1979 *The ABC's of Parliamentary
Procedure.*
Channing L. Bete
Company, Inc.
South Deerfield, MA 01373

Bortin, Virginia
1981 *Publicity for Volunteers: A
Handbook.*
Walker and Company
720 Fifth Avenue
New York, NY 10019
(also: Volunteer:
1111 North 19th Street,
Arlington, VA 22209)

Bradford, Leland P.
1976 *Making Meetings Work: A
Guide for Leaders and Group
Members.*
University Associates
8517 Production Avenue
P.O. Box 26240
San Diego, CA 92126

Broce, Thomas E.
1979 *Fund Raising: The Guide to
Raising Money from Private
Sources.*
University of Oklahoma
Press, Norman, OK
Order: Harper & Row, Order
Department,
2350 Virginia Avenue,
Hagerstown, MD 21740

Brown, Courtney, and Smith, Everett
1957 *The Director Looks at His Job.*
Columbia University Press
136 South Broadway
Irvington-on-Hudson, NY 10533

Callaghan, Christopher, and Connors,
Tracy, editors.
1982 *Financial Management for
Non-Profit Organizations.*
American Management
Association
P. O. Box 1026
Trudeau Road
Saranac Lake, NY 12983

Caparosa, Carol A.
1984 *Building Better Boards for Community Organizations: Final Report.*
American Association of Community and Junior Colleges
1 Dupont Circle, NW, Suite 410
Washington, DC 20036

Cass, Rosemary Higgins, and Manser, Gordon
1976 *Volunteerism at the Crossroads.*
Family Service Association of America
44 East 23rd Street
New York, NY 10010

Chapin, Isolde, and Mock, Richard
1979 *New Faces in Public Places.*
Volunteer: National Center for Voluntary Action
1111 North 19th Street
Arlington, VA 22209

Chapman, Terry; Lai, Mary; and Steinbock, Elmer
1984 *Am I Covered for . . . ? A Guide to Insurance for Non-profit Organizations.*
Consortium for Human Services
P.O. Box 1183
San Jose, CA 95108
(also: Volunteer, 1111 North 19th Street, Arlington, VA 22209)

Child Welfare League of America, Inc.
1957 *The Board Member of a Social Agency: Responsibilities and Functions.*
CWLA
300 Raritan Center, CN 3103
Edison, NJ 08818

1976 *Guide for Board Organization in Social Agencies.*
(CWLA above)

Cleary, Robert E.
1980 "Something Personal About It."
AGB Reports 22, 2 (March-April 1980): 39–42. Association of Governing Boards of Universities and Colleges
1 Dupont Circle, Suite 400
Washington, DC 20036

Connors, Tracy D., ed.
1980 *The Nonprofit Organization Handbook.*
McGraw-Hill, Inc.
1221 Avenue of the Americas
New York, NY 10020

Conrad, William R., Jr., and Glenn, William E.
1983 *Board of Directors: Self-Assessment.*
Voluntary Management Press
P.O. Box 9170
Downers Grove, IL 60515

1983 *Effective Board and Committee Meetings.*
(VMP above)

1983 *The Effective Voluntary Board of Directors.*
Swallow Press
Ohio University
Scott Quadrangle
Athens, OH 45701

Council of Better Business Bureaus, Philanthropy Advisory Service
1982 *Standards of Charitable Solicitations.*
Council of Better Business Bureaus
1515 Wilson Boulevard, Suite 300
Arlington, VA 22209

Craig, Dorothy P.
1978 *Hip Pocket Guide to Planning and Evaluation.*
Learning Concepts, Inc.
Order: University Associates, Inc.,
P.O. Box 26240,
San Diego, CA 92126

Crimmins, James C., and Keil, Mary
1983 *Enterprise in the Nonprofit Sector.*
Partners for Liveable Places
and The Rockefeller Brothers Fund
1290 Avenue of the Americas,
Room 3450
New York, NY 10104
(also: Volunteer:
1111 North 19th Street,
Arlington, VA 22209)

Dale, Duane, and Mitiguy, Nancy
1978 *Planning for a Change: A Citizen's Guide to Creative Planning and Program Development.*
Citizens Involvement Training Project (CITP), Amherst, MA
Order: Volunteer,
1111 North 19th Street,
Arlington, VA 22209

Davison, Betsy
1968 *Guide to Board Training.*
Association of Junior
Leagues of America, Inc.
825 Third Avenue
New York, NY 10022

Dorsey, Rhoda M.
1980 *Institutional Planning.*
Association of Governing
Boards of Universities and Colleges
1 Dupont Circle, Suite 400
Washington, DC 20036

Ellis, Susan J., and Noyes, Katherine H.
1978 *By the People: A History of Americans as Volunteers.*
Energize Publications
5450 Wissahickon Avenue,
Lobby A
Philadelphia, PA 19144

Fischer, Frank, and Sirianni, Carmen, eds.
1984 *Critical Studies in Organizations and Bureaucracy.*
Temple University Press
Broad and Oxford Streets
Philadelphia, PA 19122

Flanagan, Joan
1982 *The Grass Roots Fundraising Book.*
Contemporary Books, Inc.
180 North Michigan Avenue
Chicago, IL 60601
(also: Youth Project,
1555 Connecticut Avenue,
Washington, DC 20036
and Volunteer,
1111 North 19th Street,
Arlington, VA 22209)
1981 *The Successful Volunteer Organization.*
W. Clement and Jessie V.
Stone Foundation
111 East Wacker Drive,
Suite 510
Chicago, IL 60601
(also: Contemporary Books, Inc.,
180 North Michigan Avenue,
Chicago, IL 60601
and Volunteer,
1111 North 19th Street,
Arlington, VA 22209)

Flathman, Richard
1982 "The Rights of Volunteers,"
in *Volunteerism in the Eighties,*
edited by John D. Harman.
University Press of America
4720 Boston Way
Lanham, MD 20706

Frey, Ann, and Lindeman, Patricia
1981 *Evaluation Concepts and
Agency Self-Evaluation Methods.*
United Way of America, Inc.
United Way Plaza
Alexandria, VA 22314

Fund-Raising Institute
1982 *Success with Volunteer Boards.*
FRI
Box 365
Ambler, PA 19002

Gaby, Patricia V., and Gaby, Daniel M.
1979 *Nonprofit Organization
Handbook.*
Prentice-Hall, Inc.
Route 9 West
Englewood Cliffs, NJ 07632

Gale, Robert L.
1984 *Building a More Effective
Board.*
Association of Governing
Boards of Universities and
Colleges
1 Dupont Circle,
Suite 400
Washington, DC 20036

Gardner, John W.
1965 "How to Prevent Dry Rot."
Harper's Magazine, Vol. 231
(October, 1965).
Harper's Magazine,
Reprint Service
2 Park Avenue
New York, NY 10016

Gordon, Robbie
1978 *We Interrupt this Program . . .
A Citizen's Guide to Using the
Media for Social Change.*
Citizen Involvement Train-
ing Project,
University of Massachusetts
225 School of Education
Amherst, MA 01003
(also: Volunteer:
1111 North 19th Street,
Arlington, VA 22209)

Greenleaf, Robert K.
1975 *Trustees as Servants.*
Center for Applied Studies,
Cambridge, MA
(Order: Windy Row Press,
Grove Street,
Peterboro, NH 03458)

Gross, Malvern J., Jr., and Warshauer,
William, Jr.
1979 *Financial and Accounting
Guide for Nonprofit
Organizations.*
Ronald Press (John Wiley
and Sons)
605 Third Avenue
New York, NY 10158

Gross, Susan W.
1982 *The Ten Most Common Orga-
nizational Problems.*
Management Assistance
Group
1705 deSales Street, NW,
Suite 401
Washington, DC 20036
1983 *The Power of Purpose.*
(MAG above)

Gurin, Maurice G.
1981 *What Volunteers Should Know for Successful Fundraising.*
Stein and Day Publishers/ Scarborough House
Briarcliff Manor, NY 10510
(also: Volunteer,
1111 North 19th Street,
Arlington, VA 22209)

Haines, Mike
1977 *Volunteers: How to Find Them—How to Keep Them.*
Yellow Fire Press
3635 Buckeye Court
Boulder, CO 80302

Hanson, Pauline L., and Marmaduke, Carolyn T.
1972 *The Board Member: Decision Maker for the Non-Profit Corporation.*
Han-Mar Publications,
Sacramento, CA
Order: Volunteer,
1111 North 19th Street,
Arlington, VA 22209

Hardy, James M.
1972 *Corporate Planning for Non-Profit Organizations.*
Association Press,
New York, NY
Order: YMCA Program Resource,
1566 Carmen Drive,
Elk Grove, IL 60007
1984 *Managing for Impact in Non-profit Organizations: Corporate Planning Techniques and Applications.*
Essex Press
Erwin, TN 37650

Harper, Mary-Angela
1982 *User's Guide to the Handbook of College and University Trusteeship.*
Association of Governing Boards of Universities and Colleges
1 Dupont Circle,
Suite 400
Washington, DC 20036
1982 *Handy Companion to the Handbook.*
Jossey-Bass Publishers
433 California Street
San Francisco, CA 94104

Hesburgh, Rev. Theodore Martin
1980 "Reflections on Voluntarism in America." *Vital Speeches* 46 (June 1, 1980): 484–487.
Order: City News Publishing Company, Inc.,
Box 606,
Southold, NY 11971

Heywood, Ann M.
1982 *The Resource Directory for Funding and Managing Nonprofit Organizations.*
Edna McConnell Clark Foundation
250 Park Avenue
New York, NY 10017

Herzberg, Frederick
1966 "The Motivation to Work," in *Work and the Nature of Man.*
Thomas Y. Crowell,
New York, NY
Order: Harper & Row Publishers,
Keystone Industrial Park,
Scranton, PA 18512

Hilkert, Robert N.
1965 *The Board Member—
Opportunity for Service.*
Child Welfare League of America
300 Raritan Center, CN 3103
Edison, NJ 08818

Hopkins, Bruce R.
1980 *The Law of Tax Exempt
Organizations.*
John Wiley and Sons, Inc.
1 Wiley Drive
Attn. Order Department
Somerset, NJ 08873

Horgen, Gregory C.
1981 *Playing the Funding Game.*
Human Services
Development Center
929 Turquoise, Suite J-174
San Diego, CA 92109

Hummel, Joan
1980 *Starting and Running a Nonprofit Organization.*
University of Minnesota Press
2037 University Avenue, S.E.
Minneapolis, MN 55414

Ianotti, Lawrence W.
"Legal Responsibilities of
Trustees." *Philanthropy
Monthly* (June, 1978).
Philanthrophy Monthly
P. O. Box 989
New Milford, CT 06776

Ingram, Richard T. and Associates
1980 *Handbook of College and University Trusteeship.*
Jossey-Bass Publishers
433 California Street
San Francisco, CA 94104
(also: AGB,
1 Dupont Circle, Suite 400,
Washington, DC 20036)

Ingram, Richard T.
1980 *Trustee Orientation and Development Programs.*
Jossey-Bass Publishers
433 California Street
San Francisco, CA 94104
(also: AGB,
1 Dupont Circle, Suite 400,
Washington, DC 20036)

Jacobs, Jerald A.
1979 "Association Liability."
*Association and Society
Management* 11, 2
(February-March 1979).
Brentwood Publishing Co.
825 South Barrington Avenue
Los Angeles, CA 90049

Johnsen, Robert; Tobin, David; and
Bond, Jessie
1982 *Organizing for Local Fundraising.*
Center for Community Organizations,
Arlington, VA
Order: Volunteer,
1111 North 19th Street,
Arlington, VA 22209

Kotter, Philip
1982 *Marketing for Nonprofit
Organizations.*
Prentice-Hall, Inc.
Route 9 West
Englewood Cliffs, NJ 07632
(also: Volunteer,
1111 North 19th Street,
Arlington, VA 22209)

Langston, Stuart
1978 *Citizen Participation in America.*
D.C. Heath Co.,
Lexington Books
125 Spring Street
Lexington, MA 02173

Leibert, Edwin, and Sheldon, Bernice
1972 *Handbook of Special Events
for Nonprofit Organizations.*
New Century Publishers, Inc.
220 Old New Brunswick Road
Piscataway, NJ 08854

Lippincott, Earle, and Aannestad, Elling
"How Can Businessmen Eval-
uate the Management of Volun-
tary Welfare Organizations?"
Harvard Business Review 42, 6
(November-December, 1964):
870.
Order: Reprint Department,
Soldiers Field,
Cambridge, MA 02163

Lohmann, Roger A.
1980 *Breaking Even: Financial
Management in Human Ser-
vice Organizations.*
Temple University Press
Broad and Oxford Streets
Philadelphia, PA 19122

Lord, James G.
1984 *The Raising of Money.*
Third Sector Press
2000 Euclid Avenue
P. O. Box 18044
Cleveland, OH 44188
(also: Fund-Raising
Institute, Box 365,
Ambler, PA 19002)

MacBride, Marie
1982 *Step by Step: Management of
the Volunteer Program in Agencies.*
Volunteer Bureau of
Bergen County,
Bergen County, NJ
Order: Volunteer,
1111 North 19th Street,
Arlington, VA 22209

Marshall, Maxine
1980 *Volunteers: Hope for the
Future.*
Discipleship Resources
P.O. Box 840
Nashville, TN 37202

Mason, David E.
1979 "The Distinctive Nature of
Voluntary Organization
Management." *Voluntary
Action Leadership*
2 (Spring 1979): 40–42.
Order: Volunteer,
1111 North 19th Street,
Arlington, VA 22209

Mathiasen, Karl III
1976 *Confessions of a Board
Member.*
The Alban Institute
Wisconsin Avenue and
Woodley Road, NW
Washington, DC 20016
1977 *The Board of Directors of
Nonprofit Organizations.*
Management Assistance
Group
1705 deSales Street
Washington, DC 20036
1982 *No Board of Directors Is Like
Any Other.*
(MAG above)
1983 *The Board of Directors Is A
Problem.*
(MAG above)
1984 *Steering Nonprofits.*
(MAG above; published for:
Conserve Neighborhoods,
National Trust for Historic
Preservation,
1785 Massachusetts Avenue, NW,
Washington, DC 20036)

Mirvis, Phillip, and Hackett, Edward
  1983 "Work and Workforce Char-
       acteristics in the Non-profit
       Sector." *The Monthly Labor
       Review* (April 1983).
       Superintendent of Documents,
       Government Printing Office
       Washington, DC 20402

Morrison, Emily Kittle
  1983 *Skills for Leadership: Working
       with Volunteers, rev. ed.*
       Jordan Press P. O. Box 39101
       Phoenix, AZ 85069

Nason, John W.
  1982 *The Nature of Trusteeship.*
       Association of Governing Boards
       of Universities and Colleges
       1 Dupont Circle, Suite 400
       Washington, DC 20036

National Assembly of National
  Voluntary Health and Social
  Welfare Organizations, et. al.
  1974 *Standards of Accounting and Fi-
       nancial Reporting for Voluntary
       Health and Welfare Organizations.*
       National Assembly
       1346 Connecticut Avenue, NW,
       Suite 424A
       Washington, DC 20036
       National Health Council
       70 West 40th Street
       New York, NY 10018
       United Way of America, Inc.
       United Way Plaza
       Alexandria, VA 22314

National Charities Information Bureau
  1968 *The Volunteer Board Member
       in Philanthropy.*
       National Charities
       Information Bureau
       19 Union Square West
       New York, NY 10003

National Council of Jewish Women,
  Task Force on Voluntarism
  1978 *The Week the Volunteers
       Stayed Home (Program
       Package).*
       National Council of
       Jewish Women
       15 East 26th Street
       New York, NY 10010

Naylor, Harriet
  1973 *Volunteers Today: Funding,
       Training and Working
       with Them.*
       Dryden Associates
       Box 363
       Dryden, NY 13053
       (also: Volunteer:
       1111 North 19th Street,
       Arlington, VA 22209)

Newcomb, Betty
  1981 *Affirmative Action.*
       Association of Governing
       Boards of Universities and
       Colleges
       1 Dupont Circle,
       Suite 400
       Washington, DC 20036

Nordhoff, Nancy; Larsen, Jo; Barber,
  Putnam; and Craig, Dorothy P.
  1982 *Fundamental Practices for
       Success with Volunteer
       Boards of Nonprofit
       Organizations.*
       Fun Prax Associates
       711 Skinner Building
       Seattle, WA 98101
       (also: Volunteer,
       1111 North 19th Street,
       Arlington, VA 22209)

O'Connell, Brian
1976 *Effective Leadership in Voluntary Organizations.*
Walker & Company
720 Fifth Avenue
New York, NY 10019
1983 *America's Voluntary Spirit.*
The Foundation Center
79 Fifth Avenue
New York, NY 10003

Olenick, Arnold, and Olenick, Philip
1983 *Making the Nonprofit Organization Work: A Financial, Legal, and Tax Guide for Administrators.*
Prentice-Hall, Inc.
Route 9 West
Englewood Cliffs, NJ 07632

Partners, Inc.
1983 *Assessing and Improving Your Program.*
Yellowfire Press
1705 14th Street, Suite 199
Boulder, CO 80202
(also: Partners, Inc.,
1260 W. Bayaud,
Denver, CO 80223)

Payton, Robert L.
1984 *Major Challenges to Philanthropy.*
Independent Sector
1828 L Street, NW
Washington, DC 20036

Peters, Thomas J., and Waterman, Robert H., Jr.
1982 *In Search of Excellence: Lessons from America's Best Run Companies.*
Harper & Row Publishers
10 East 53rd Street
New York, NY 10022

Petersen, Sheila
1979 *Successful Community Fund Raising: A How-To-Manual.*
Caroline House
Ottawa, IL 61350
(also: Volunteer,
1111 North 19th Street,
Arlington, VA 22209)

Price Waterhouse
1980 *The Audit Committee: The Board of Trustees of Nonprofit Organizations and the Independent Accountant.*
Price Waterhouse
1251 Avenue of the Americas
New York, NY 10020

Public Management Institute
1980 *Board Member/Trustee Handbook.*
Public Management Institute
358 Brannan Street
San Francisco, CA 94107

Rainer, Judy
1980 *Helping People Volunteer.*
Marlborough Publications
P. O. Box 16406
San Diego, CA 92116
(also: Volunteer,
1111 North 19th Street,
Arlington, VA 22209)

Ramsey, William B.
1983 *How to Read a Nonprofit Financial Statement.*
Voluntary Management Press
P. O. Box 9170
Downers Grove, IL 60515

Robert, Henry M.
1967 *Robert's Rules of Order.*
Spire Books, Fleming H.
Revell Co.
Box 150
Old Tappan, NJ 07675
1984 *Robert's Rules of Order,*
Newly Revised.
Scott, Foresman and Co.
1900 East Lake Avenue
Glenview, IL 60025

Rutman, Leonard, and Mowbray,
George
1983 *Understanding Program*
Evaluation.
Sage Publications
275 South Beverly Drive
Beverly Hills, CA 90212

Saccamandi, Pat, and Host, Bobette
Reige, eds.
1981 *The Volunteer Skillsbank.*
Volunteer: National Center
for Voluntary Action
1111 North 19th Street
Arlington, VA 22209

Savage, Thomas J.
1982 *The Cheswick Process: Seven*
Steps to a More
Effective Board.
The Cheswick Center
11 Newbury Street
Boston, MA 02116

Scheier, Ivan H.
1980 *Exploring Volunteer Space:*
The Recruiting
of a Nation.
Volunteer: National Center
for Voluntary Action
1111 North 19th Street
Arlington, VA 22209

Schindler-Rainman, Eva, and
Lippitt, R.
1971 *The Volunteer Community.*
University Associates, Inc.
8517 Production Avenue
P. O. Box 26240
San Diego, CA 92126
1977 *Taking Your Meetings Out of*
the Doldrums.
(University Associates above)

Schoderbek, Peter P.
1979 *The Board and its*
Responsibilities.
United Way of America, Inc.
United Way Plaza
Alexandria, VA 22314
1979 *The Effective Use of*
Committees.
(United Way of America
above)

Selby, Cecily Cannan
"Better Performance from
Nonprofits." *Harvard*
Business Review 56, 5
(September-October 1978):
77–83.
Order: Reprint Department,
Soldiers Field,
Cambridge, MA 02163

Seymour, Harold
1966 *Designs for Fund-Raising:*
Principles, Patterns,
Techniques.
McGraw-Hill, Inc.
Princeton Road
Box 586
Hightstown, NJ 08520
(also: Fund-Raising Institute,
Box 365,
Ambler, PA 19002)

Shapiro, Samuel B.
1983 *Financial Incentives for
Association Executives:
The Theory.*
Foundation of the American
Society of Association Executives
1575 I Street, NW
Washington, DC 20005

Stringer, G. E., and Arsen, K. G.
1981 *The Board Manual Workbook.*
Volunteer Consultants
9015 Cliffside Drive
Clarence, NY 14031

Sumariwalla, Russy
1982 *Needs Assessment: A Guide
for Planners, Managers, and
Funders of Health and
Human Care Services.*
United Way of America, Inc.
United Way Plaza
Alexandria, VA 22314

Swanson, Andrew
1984 *Building a Better Board.*
Taft Corporation
5125 MacArthur Boulevard
Washington, DC 20016
(also: Volunteer,
1111 North 19th Street,
Arlington, VA 22209)

Tropman, John E.
1980 *Effective Meetings: Improving
Group Decision-Making.*
Sage Publications
275 South Beverly Drive
Beverly Hills, CA 90212

Tropman, John E.; Johnson, Harold
R.; and Tropman, Elmer J.
1979 *The Essentials of Committee
Management.*
Nelson-Hall Publishers
111 North Canal Street
Chicago, IL 60606

United States Chamber of Commerce
1976 *Association Committees.*
U.S. Chamber of Commerce,
Publication Fulfillment Office
1615 H Street, NW
Washington, DC 20062
1976 *Guidelines for an Association
Seeking a Chief Staff Executive.*
(U.S. Chamber of
Commerce above)
1977 *Association Bylaws.*
(U.S. Chamber of
Commerce above)

United Way of America
1979 *The Citizen Board in
Voluntary Agencies.*
United Way of America, Inc.
United Way Plaza
Alexandria, VA 22314

Unterman, Israel, and Davis, Richard H.
1984 *Strategic Management of
Not-for-Profit Organizations.*
Praeger Publications
521 Fifth Avenue
New York, NY 10175

Vineyard, Sue
1981 *Beyond Banquets, Plaques and
Pins: Creative Ways to Recognize Volunteers and Staff.*
Heritage Arts
1807 Prairie Avenue
Downers Grove, IL 60515
(also: Volunteer,
1111 North 19th Street,
Arlington, VA 22209)
1981 *Finding Your Way Through
the Maze of Volunteer Management.*
(Heritage Arts above)
(also: Volunteer above)
1984 *Volunteer Recognition Handbook.*
(Heritage Arts above)
(also: Volunteer above)

Volunteer Consulting Group
  1984 *How to Place Private Sector*
       Executives onto Non-Profit
       Boards of Directors, edited by
       Brooke Mahoney.
       Volunteer Consulting Group
       24 West 40th Street
       New York, NY 10018

Weber, Joseph
  1975 *Managing the Board of*
       Directors.
       Greater New York
       Fund, Inc.
       99 Park Avenue
       New York, NY 10157

Webster, George D.; Herold, Arthur
  L., and Dye, Alan P.
  1983 *Association Check List.*
       U.S. Chamber of Commerce
       1615 H Street, NW
       Washington, DC 20062

Webster, George D.; Oehret, Joseph
  B.; Panaro, Gerald P.; and Hazard,
  John W.
  1984 *Financial Incentives for Asso-*
       ciation Executives.
       American Society of
       Association Executives
       1575 I Street, NW
       Washington, DC 20005

Weiss, Carol
  1972 *Evaluation Research:*
       Methods of Assessing
       Program Effectiveness.
       Prentice-Hall, Inc.
       Route 9 West
       Englewood Cliffs, NJ 07632

Wilson, Marlene
  1976 *Effective Management of*
       Volunteer Programs.
       Volunteer Management
       Associates, Boulder, CO
       Order: Volunteer,
       1111 North 19th Street,
       Arlington, VA 22209

Wolfe, Joan
  1981 *Making Things Happen:*
       The Guide for Members of
       Volunteer Organizations.
       Brick House Publishing Co.
       34 Essex Street
       Andover, MA 01810
       (also: Volunteer,
       1111 North 19th Street,
       Arlington, VA 22209)

Wolfe, Thomas
  1984 *The Nonprofit Organization:*
       An Operating Manual.
       Prentice-Hall, Inc.
       Route 9 West
       Englewood Cliffs, NJ 07632

Young Women's Christian Association
  1978 *Board and Staff Working Together.*
       YWCA National Board
       726 Broadway
       New York, NY 10003

Zwingle, J. L.
  1981 "Conflict in the Board
       Room." *AGB Reports* 23, 4
       (July-August 1981): 23–32.
       Association of Governing
       Boards of Universities and
       Colleges
       1 Dupont Circle, Suite 400
       Washington, DC 20036

B. BOOKS AVAILABLE THROUGH LIBRARIES

These books are no longer available from publishers, but your library should be able to locate copies through state or national library systems.

Carp, Bernard
  1955 *Your Annual Meeting.*
       National Publicity
       Council for Health and
       Welfare Services,
       New York, NY

Cohen, Nathan Edward, ed.
  1960 *The Citizen Volunteer.*
       Harper and Brothers,
       New York, NY

Cornuelle, Richard C.
  1965 *Reclaiming the American
       Dream.*
       Random House,
       New York, NY

Dick, Jane
  1980 *Volunteers and the Making of
       Presidents.*
       Dodd, Mead,
       New York, NY

Houle, Cyril O.
  1960 *The Effective Board.*
       Association Press,
       New York, NY

Ilseley, Paul J., and Niemi, John
  1981 *Recruiting and Training
       Volunteers.*
       McGraw-Hill
       New York, NY

Nielsen, Waldemar A.
  1979 *The Endangered Sector.*
       Columbia University Press,
       New York, NY

Ramanthan, Kavasseri V.
  1982 *Management Control in Non-
       profit Organizations.*
       John Wiley & Sons,
       New York, NY

Scheier, Ivan H.
  1978 *Winning with Staff.*
       Volunteer, Arlington, VA

Sorenson, Roy
  1950 *The Art of Board Membership.*
       Association Press,
       New York, NY

Trecker, Harleigh B.
  1970 *Citizen Board at Work.*
       Association Press,
       New York, NY

C. BOOKS AND ARTICLES CITED IN TEXT

Adult Education Association of the U.S.A.
"Better Boards and Committees." Washington, DC: American Education Association of the U.S.A., 1957.

Alexander, John O.
"Planning and Management in Nonprofit Organizations," in *The Nonprofit Organization Handbook,* edited by Tracy D. Connors. New York: McGraw-Hill, Inc. 1980.

American Association of Fund-Raising Counsel, Inc.
Giving U.S.A.: 1983 Annual Report. New York: American Association of Fund-Raising Counsel, Inc., 1983.

Anthony, Robert N., and Herzlinger, Regina E.
Management Control in Nonprofit Organizations. Homewood, IL: Richard D. Irwin, Inc., 1975.

Axelrod, Nancy
A Guide for New Trustees. Washington, DC: Association of Governing Boards of Universities and Colleges, 1982.

Church, David M.
How to Succeed with Volunteers. New York: National Public Relations Council of Health and Welfare Services, Inc., 1962.

Cleary, Robert E.
"Something Personal About It." *AGB Reports* 22,2 (March-April 1980): 39–42.

Council of Better Business Bureaus.
"Standards for Charitable Solicitation." Arlington, VA: Council of Better Business Bureaus, 1982.

Curti, Merle
"American Philanthropy and the National Character." *American Quarterly* 10 (Winter 1958): 420–437.

Drucker, Peter
"Managing the 'Third Sector.' " *Wall Street Journal* (October 3, 1978).

Gale, Robert L.
Building a More Effective Board. Washington, DC: Association of Governing Boards of Universities and Colleges, 1984.

Gardner, John W.
"The Independent Sector," in *America's Voluntary Spirit*, compiled by
Brian O'Connell. New York: The Foundation Center, 1983.

Hardy, James M.
Managing for Impact of Nonprofit Organizations: Corporate Planning Techniques and Applications. Erwin, TN: Essex Press, 1984.

Herzberg, Frederick
"The Motivation to Work," in *Work and the Nature of Man*. New York:
Thomas Y. Crowell, 1966.

Houle, Cyril O.
The Effective Board. New York: Association Press, 1960.

Irwin, Inez Haynes
"The Last Days of the Fight for Women's Suffrage," in *The Story of Alice
Paul: And the National Woman's Party*. Fairfax, VA: Denlingers Publishers
Ltd., 1964.

Jones, O. Garfield
Parliamentary Procedures at a Glance. New York: Meredith Press, 1932.

Lippincott, Earle, and Aannestad, Elling
"How Can Businessmen Evaluate the Management of Voluntary Welfare
Agencies?" *Harvard Business Review* 42,6 (November-December 1964): 870.

McGuffey, William H.
"True and False Philanthropy," in *The Newly Revised Eclectic Reader* (1844).
Reprinted in *America's Voluntary Spirit*, compiled by Brian O'Connell.
New York: The Foundation Center, 1983.

Mirvis, Phillip, and Hackett, Edward
"Work and Workforce Characteristics in the Non-profit Sector." *The
Monthly Labor Review* (April 1983).

Nason, John W.
"Trustee Responsibilities," in *The Nature of Trusteeship*. Washington, DC:
Association of Governing Boards of Universities and Colleges, 1982.

National Assembly of National Voluntary Health and Social Welfare Organizations, National Health Council, and United Way of America
*Standards of Accounting and Financial Reporting for Voluntary Health and
Welfare Organizations*. Washington, DC: National Assembly of National
Voluntary Health and Social Welfare Organizations, 1974.

National Charities Information Bureau
"Program Effectiveness and Efficiency Project (PEEP)." New York:
National Charities Information Bureau, 1984.

"Standards for Voluntary Organizations." New York: National Charities Information Bureau, 1984.
The Volunteer Board Member in Philanthropy. New York: National Charities Information Bureau, 1968.

Nielsen, Waldemar A.
The Endangered Sector. New York: Columbia University Press, 1979.

O'Connell, Brian
America's Voluntary Spirit. New York: The Foundation Center, 1983.

Payton, Robert L.
"Major Challenges to Philanthropy." Washington, DC: Independent Sector, 1984.

Peters, Thomas J., and Waterman, Robert H., Jr.
In Search of Excellence: Lessons from America's Best Run Companies. New York: Harper & Row, 1982.

Price Waterhouse
The Audit Committee: The Board of Trustees of Nonprofit Organizations and the Independent Accountant. New York: Price Waterhouse, 1980.

Robert, Henry M.
Robert's Rules of Order. 1915. Old Tappan, NJ: Spire Books, Fleming H. Revell Co., 1967.

Robert, Henry M.
Robert's Rules of Order, Newly Revised. 1915. Glenview, IL: Scott Foresman and Co., 1984.

Savage, Thomas J.
The Cheswick Process: Seven Steps to a More Effective Board. Boston, MA: The Cheswick Center, 1982.

Selby, Cecily Cannan
"Better Performance from Nonprofits." *Harvard Business Review* 56,5 (September-October 1978): 77–83.

Smith, David Horton
"Evaluating Nonprofit Activity," in *The Nonprofit Organization Handbook,* edited by Tracy D. Connors. New York: McGraw-Hill, 1980.

Sumariwalla, Russy
Needs Assessment: A Guide for Planners, Managers, and Funders of Health and Human Care Services. Alexandria, VA: United Way of America, 1982.

Washington, Booker T.
    "Raising Money," in *Up from Slavery: An Autobiography,* 1901. Reprinted in *America's Voluntary Spirit,* compiled by Brian O'Connell. New York: The Foundation Center, 1983.

Weber, Joseph
    Managing the Board of Directors. New York: Greater New York Fund, Inc., 1975.

Zwingle, J. L.
    "Conflict in the Board Room." *AGB Reports* 23,4 (July-August, 1981): 23–32.

D. PUBLISHERS AND ORGANIZATIONS THAT PRODUCE MATERIALS ON THE NONPROFIT SECTOR

This list is limited to groups that specialize in nonprofit topics, have an extensive list of available titles, and are likely to produce new materials for at least the next five years.

Action
806 Connecticut Avenue, NW
Washington, DC 20025

Adult Education Association (with
Adult Education Program of
Syracuse University), Leadership
Series
Syracuse University Printing
Services
125 College Place
Syracuse, NY 13210

Aid Association for Lutherans
Branch Operations
Appleton, WI 54919

American Association of Fund-
Raising Counsel
25 West 43rd Street, Suite 1519
New York, NY 10036

American Education Association (of
USA)
663 Fifth Avenue
New York, NY 10022

American Management Association
Trudeau Road, P. O. Box 1026
Saranac Lake, NY 12983

American Red Cross
2025 E Street, NW
Washington, DC 20037

American Society of Association
Executives
1575 I Street, NW
Washington, DC 20005

Association of Governing Boards of
Universities and Colleges
1 Dupont Circle, Suite 400
Washington, DC 20036

Association of Junior Leagues, Inc.
825 Third Avenue
New York, NY 10022

Association and Society Management
c/o Brentwood Publishing Co.
825 South Barrington Avenue
Los Angeles, CA 90049

Association of Voluntary Action
Scholars
S-126 Human Development
Building
Pennsylvania State University
University Park, PA 16802

Association of Volunteer
Administration
P. O. Box 4584
Boulder, CO 80306

Center for Community Change
1000 Wisconsin Avenue, NW
Washington, DC 20007

Center for Creative Management
(Voluntary Management Press)
4800 Prince Street
P. O. Box 9170
Downers Grove, IL 60515

Center for Responsive Governance
1000 16th Street, NW
Washington, DC 20036

The Cheswick Center
11 Newbury Street
Boston, MA 02116

Child Welfare League of
America, Inc.
67 Irving Place
New York, NY 10003

Citizen Involvement Training Project
225 School of Education
University of Massachusetts
Amherst, MA 01003

Council for the Advancement and
Support of Education
11 Dupont Circle
Washington, DC 20001

Council of Better Business Bureaus,
Philanthropic Advisory Service
1515 Wilson Boulevard,
Suite 300
Arlington, VA 22209

Council on Foundations, Inc.
1828 L Street, NW
Washington, DC 20036

Energize Publications
5450 Wissahickon Avenue
Philadelphia, PA 19144

The Foundation Center
79 Fifth Avenue
New York, NY 10003

Foundation for Public Relations
Research and Education
Nonprofit Management Series
310 Madison Avenue, Suite 1816
New York, NY 10017

Fundemensions
1511 K Street, NW, Suite 611
Washington, DC 20005

Fund-Raising Institute (FRI)
Box 365
Ambler, PA 19002

Grants Magazine
896 Singing Trails
El Cajon, CA 92021

Grantsmanship Center
1031 South Grand Avenue
Los Angeles, CA 90015

Heath Publications
125 Spring Street
Lexington, MA 02173

Hoke Communications, Inc.
Fund Raising Management
Magazine
224 Seventh Street
Garden City, NY 11530

Human Services Development Center
P. O. Box 161809
Sacramento, CA 95816

Independent Sector
1828 L Street, NW
Washington, DC 20036

Institute for Nonprofit Management
Training
1244 Maryland Avenue, NE
Washington, DC 20002

Institute for Voluntary Organizations
175 West Jackson Boulevard
Chicago, IL 60604

Jossey-Bass Inc.
Publishers
433 California Street
San Francisco, CA 94104

Journal of Community Action
1100 17th Street
Washington, DC 20036

Lincoln Filene Center for Citizenship
Tufts University
Medford, MA 02155

Management Assistance Group
1705 deSales Street
Washington, DC 20036

Minnesota Office of Volunteer
Services
500 Rice Street
St. Paul, MN 55155

National Association of Accountants
for the Public Interest
45 John Street, Suite 808
New York, NY 10038

National Charities Information
Bureau
19 Union Square, West
New York, NY 10003

National Committee for Responsive
Philanthropy
810 18th Street, NW
Washington, DC 20006

National Council of Jewish Women
15th East 26th Street
New York, NY 10010

National Executive Service
Corporation
622 Third Avenue
New York, NY 10017

National Grant Development
Institute
1135 North Garfield
Pocatello, ID 83204

Nonprofit Management Association
1052 West Sixth Street
Los Angeles, CA 90017

Philanthropy Monthly
P. O. Box 989
New Milford, CT 06776

Plenum Publishing Company
233 Spring Street
New York, NY 10013

Public Management Institute
358 Brannon Street
San Francisco, CA 94107

Public Relations Society of America
845 Third Avenue
New York, NY 10022

Sage Publications
275 South Beverly Drive
Beverly Hills, CA 90212

The Support Center
1709 New Hampshire
Avenue, NW
Washington, DC 20009

Taft Corporation
5125 MacArthur Boulevard, NW
Washington, DC 20016

United States Association Executive
2607 24th Street, NW
Washington, DC 20008

United States Chamber of
Commerce, Association Division
1615 H Street, NW
Washington, DC 20062

United Way of America
United Way Plaza
Alexandria, VA 22314-2045

University Associates
8517 Production Avenue
P. O. Box 26240
San Diego, CA 92121

Voluntary Management Press
4800 Prince Street
P. O. Box 9170
Downers Grove, IL 60515

Volunteer Consulting Group, Inc.
24 West 40th Street
New York, NY 10018

Volunteer Management Associates
279 South Cedar Brook Road
Boulder, CO 80302

Volunteer: National Center for
Voluntary Action
1111 North 19th Street
Arlington, VA 22209

Yellow Fire Press
1705 14th Street
Boulder, CO 80302

Young Men's Christian Association,
Program Store
Box 5077
Champaign, IL 10022

Appendix

MINUTES OF OUR LAST MEETING

Association Office
October 26, 1984

PRESENT

Rodney Russell, *Chairperson*
Harry Gonzalez, *Treasurer*
Mrs. Jeffrey (Effi) Black, *Secretary*
Hon. Peter Paul Henderson, *Founder,
First Chairperson, and Chairperson
Emeritus* (79th consecutive
meeting)
Carol Archer
Louella Buckminster
George Colberg
Pat Greenlaw
Rev. Bryant Horsinger
George Horton
Bruce Knight

Harriet Lortz
Kathleen O'Reilly
Alan Scala
Joseph Shapiro
Beth Trister
Paul Widen
Lucas Zukert

Staff:
Jack Neal, *Executive Secretary*
Paula Masonowitz, *Office Manager,
Administrative Assistant, Assistant
Secretary, and Assistant Treasurer*

ABSENT

Penelope Mitchell, *Vice-Chairperson*
(absent again!)
Samuel Fales (excused for personal
reasons)

Gladys Pepper
Vincent Wenski
Cyrus Yarbrough
Felice Workenthrader

Mr. Russell opened the meeting at 8:07 P.M. and immediately turned the meeting over to me, Mrs. Jeffrey (Effi) Black, Secretary of the Board of Directors, for reading of the minutes of the last meeting. I announced that copies would be distributed at the conclusion of the reading. Mr. Scala asked if they could be distributed immediately so that we might dispense with the reading. I pointed out to Mr. Scala—as I had on several previous occasions—that *Robert's Rules of Order* requires a reading of the minutes. I also indicated that I had gotten out of a sick bed to fulfill this duty.

Mr. Russell suggested that we compromise by distributing the minutes in advance but still go ahead with the reading and everyone agreed. Mr. Scala, in a rare display of cooperation, complimented the chairperson for having the diplomacy to propose what he called a "Read Along." He suggested that for our next meeting we put it all to music and call it a Minute Minuet. Everyone chuckled. Mrs. Lortz said any composition as long as my minutes couldn't be called a minuet. Nobody laughed. I read the minutes.

The chairperson next called on the Treasurer to give the financial report.

Mr. Gonzalez said that income for the first six months was only $73,000, but projected receipts for the second half were $809,000. Ms. Trister asked if this was realistic, but Mr. Gonzalez pointed out that as Treasurer, he dealt with expenses, not income. Ms. Trister apologized.

The Treasurer did say he had heard indirectly that fundraising looked terrific. George Colberg asked if this was reflected yet in the financial statements. Mr. Gonzalez asked our Executive Secretary, who said that bookkeeping was a little behind because our one-day-a-week bookkeeper-dictaphone transcriber-telephone operator and general handy person had been on maternity leave and had just had a little boy. Everyone clapped and agreed to a resolution to send a letter of congratulations to the proud parents. A committee was appointed to select a gift.

The bookkeeping situation prompted Mr. Colberg to ask if we had an audit yet for 1983. Jack apologized saying we still don't, but added that we have to be patient because the service is being done for free by Mrs. Workenthrader's husband, who used to be an accountant, but who is now in the Peace Corps and is away a lot.

Mr. Colberg asked whether Mr. Neal or Mr. Gonzalez had any general idea of what the income looked like in the three and one-half months since the June 30 statement. Jack deferred to the Treasurer, who said that as manager of the branch where the association did its banking, he was aware that deposits were dropping off and that the Executive Secretary had inquired what a line of credit was. Other than that, he didn't know and would have to defer to the Fundraising Chairman. Mr. Widen said he would prefer waiting to give his report until there was a more positive atmosphere.

Jack Neal said he didn't want to ignore some rough patches in our financial picture, but that he could confide to the Board that he had heard from an attorney in town that the association might be getting a nice bequest. In answer to questions, Jack said he didn't know absolutely how much or how soon. This prompted Mrs. O'Reilly to ask if we knew whether the benefactor was dead yet. Jack said he had felt it was too delicate a question to ask. The Honorable Peter Paul Henderson, Founder, First Chairperson, and Chairperson Emeritus, said he would check around to see if he could find out who it was and, if still alive, whether we could hope that events might still help our cash flow this year. Everyone expressed appreciation.

Mr. Gonzalez said that on the expense side, things looked much better—that we were only 16 percent above the same time last year. Mr. Knight said this was indeed good news, but didn't he recall that we had cut the budget by about 20 percent? The Treasurer acknowledged we had, but explained that just because a Board cuts the budget, doesn't mean that expenses go down. There was a long, thoughtful silence.

Mrs. Archer said she didn't know much about finances, but was she close to the mark in guessing that with income so far below expectations and expenses so far above budget that the picture was somewhat negative?

To get specific, Mr. Colberg asked the Treasurer how he, from a banker's perspective, would view the situation if income for the last half was only as good as the first half and if expenditures remained at their current level. Mr. Gonzalez, responding in the professional spirit in which the question was asked, replied, "Stinky."

In terms of figures, he indicated that the shortfall would be about $475,000.00 against reserves of $19,875.53. Mrs. Masonowitz, the Assistant Treasurer, asked what a line of credit was.

To put things on a more positive track, Mr. Russell asked the Fundraising Chairman to report.

Mr. Widen explained that there were some disappointments. To begin with, the Special Event with a half million dollar goal fell short. We had not been able to get Bob Hope, Frank Sinatra, Jack Benny (Mr. Widen complained that staff had not told him that Benny was dead), or their backup, President Reagan, and that they had to settle for Merty Pink, the first woman deejay at Station WOLP, who turned out to be less of a drawing card than hoped. The event raised $783.87. Expenses were $1,113.53. But Mr. Widen indicated that, "We got great publicity for the association, so the overall effort should be viewed as a long-term investment."

The direct-mail solicitation also came up short. Mr. Widen and his advisers had assumed that with the emotional pull our cause represents, plus the power of this Board and the success of so many less worthy mail campaigns, that we didn't need the ridiculous expense of a direct-mail firm or the loss of precious time in test marketing; so Mr. Widen had volunteered to write the letters himself and to have them reproduced on his mimeograph. He reminded the Board that he had asked all of them to take a supply home and to mail them to all their friends. As of the meeting date, all of the returns were not in (13 of the 24 Board members had not yet mailed theirs) but, being realistic, this part of the campaign would have to be viewed as a failure. The costs so far, not including staff time, were $1,756 and income was $98, not including an "in-kind" gift by the Fund-raising Chairman's own company. This gift was valued at $2,500 for reproduction, proofreading, messenger delivery, etc. Everyone thanked Mr. Widen for his personal generosity.

Actually, not everyone. Mrs. Buckminster asked Mr. Widen if the expenses included any reimbursements to his firm. Mr. Widen asked that the Chairperson rule the question out of order and rude and hurtful. Fortunately, Jack Neal stepped in to volunteer that Mr. Widen had given a great party for the guys and gals in his shop and in the association, all of whom had done most of the work on the mail appeal. Mr. Neal said that this extra effort on behalf of the campaign added spirit and thrust to the 1984 Drive and, therefore, was not only in good taste, but entirely within accounting standards. Besides, he said many of the hors d'oeuvres were donated.

Mr. Zukert asked what the average contribution was from the letters the Board members themselves had sent out. The answer was $3.26. There was extended discussion whether this was the result of the Board members not having the right friends, not having enough friends or, for the 13 who had not mailed any letters, no friends at all. After a heated exchange, it was agreed to refer the issue to the Nominating Committee.

Mr. Widen then reported on the part of the Drive involving contributions from the Board members themselves. He reminded the group that it was an axiom of Board membership that the Board exists to provide "wisdom, work, and wealth." The Honorable Peter Paul Henderson, Founder, First Chairperson, and Chairperson Emeritus, reacted, as he had on previous occasions, by saying that he found the phrase crass and undignified. Mr. Widen indicated that it was not necessary for Mr. Henderson to remind the Board of the value of his years of service involved in founding the association and guiding it to its current level.

The advance gifts solicitation from the Board was to have been the "leadership" part of the Drive, but was not yet underway. It has been the major subject of seven Board meetings. Most recently, the Board has not been able to agree on whether there should be a suggested level or standard for contributions from the Board. This issue, in turn, has been subdivided into two issues:

1. Should the time given by Board members be considered in lieu of cash?

   Mr. Russell, our Chairperson, is on record as saying that ordinarily the dollar value of volunteer time should not be considered, but that in his case there should be an exception, particularly in light of how much time he is having to spend at the task. (It is assumed this would apply to the demanding office of Secretary also.)

2. Should "in-kind" gifts be considered?

Mrs. Archer has, on several occasions, reminded the group that while it had been a pleasure to host the Board's Christmas dinner at her lovely home, it was still an expense which her husband's tax deduction hadn't begun to cover. Mr. Shapiro told her that on that basis, he hoped the flowers the Board had sent had been treated as income.

The resulting exchange was ruled off the record, but it led to a suggestion that the Board clarify its legal liability coverage.

Mr. Russell gave his regular speech about harmony and the joy of working together in a great crusade. (Please see any previous minutes for exact wording.)

After a cooling-off break, Mr. Widen continued his fundraising report. He said there had been a few other setbacks. The telethon had turned out to compete with an unexpected seventh game of the World Series. To compound the problem, it had been carried on a cable channel not yet hooked up in our town (but several people as far away as Charles County had said it came through loud and clear). The net loss was $9,828.41. Though the Fundraising Drive Head described the total as a disappointment, he felt that the experience and exposure would stand the association in good stead. He also said we may want to consider expanding to Charles County to take advantage of the softening up already accomplished there.

The door-to-door campaign had run into a discouraging obstacle. Mr. Widen and his campaign advisers had given long and careful consideration to the choice of a time when absolutely the most people would be at home, and they had been fortunate to get a permit for that very day. Mr. Widen indicated with some pride that obviously no one else had been alert enough to come up with the idea. The only down side and the disappointing aspect was that they had never in this world believed that 95 percent of their volunteers would be so disloyal as to also stay home on Super Bowl Sunday. The net loss was $13,870.

Mr. Widen summarized that all in all it hadn't been nearly as good a year as hoped. He said that perhaps in the remaining two and one half months they would be able to try some additional gimmicks. Mrs. Greenlaw said that she didn't think the association could afford any more fundraising.

Mrs. Lortz asked permission to bring up a timely matter and, with the Chair's assent, reintroduced her stale idea for an auxiliary. This time she emphasized the favorable fundraising role that other auxiliaries play for their organizations. With that comment, several Board members became rigidly alert. Mrs. Lortz said that there were certain ironclad rules necessary for the success of an auxiliary that, if followed, could result in thousands, and eventually, maybe millions of dollars for the association. She said that if this organization would provide the seed money to set up the auxiliary and would allow the auxiliary to be totally autonomous, she could guarantee results and might even be willing to head it herself. Mr. Gonzalez asked if the income of the auxiliary would go to the association and the answer was decidedly affirmative, but only after the auxiliary's own projects were fully funded and endowed.

Mr. Colberg asked what the auxiliary would do. Mrs. Lortz responded that it would have its own by-laws, officers, board, bank accounts, and, as soon as possible, staff and office. "But what would it do?" Mr. Colberg persisted. Mrs. Lortz explained that until the auxiliary was established and its officers and board were in place, it would be inappropriate to speak for them.

The matter of an auxiliary was tabled.

Mr. Russell said it was time for committee reports.

He, himself, reported for the Executive Committee, saying only that they had met eleven times since the last Board meeting and had worked very hard on behalf of the Board. Mrs. Archer asked if he could give some examples of what they had been doing, but Mr. Russell explained that because the Executive Committee deals with so many sensitive matters, its meetings have to be off the record. He apologized, but indicated that as experienced volunteers, he was sure they would understand.

Mr. Scala asked who was on the Executive Committee, but was told the list is secret. He was assured that many of its members were present at the table at that very moment. A tingle shot through the room. Mrs. Buckminster asked if the Executive Committee had conducted an annual evaluation of Mr. Neal's performance. Mr. Russell said he would not be revealing a confidence to say that they had, but that he could not say more than that. Mrs. Buckminster probed to learn what the Executive Secretary's current salary was. Her brashness was greeted by gasps from the older members.

A few inexperienced Board members joined in going beyond their appropriate authority and asked for at least the general salary range. In a spirit of cooperation and camaraderie, Mr. Russell said that although he could not answer the question directly, he would give the Board three guesses. "Under $100,000?" asked Archer. "Yes," said Russell. ("Thank God," said Colberg.)

"Does the figure we're talking about include benefits?" asked Zukert. "Yes," said Russell, but added "That's question two." "Foul," cried Zukert.

"Is it between $20,000 and $50,000?" asked Knight. "Generally," said Russell.

And just before he closed discussion, Greenlaw queried, "Next time, can we play twenty questions?"

In the absence of the Vice-Chairperson, Mrs. Mitchell (who had missed 3 out of the last 5 meetings, 6 of the last 10, and 19 out of 30), Mr. Shapiro gave the report of the Personnel Committee.

The Board referred to them the disagreement between the Executive Secretary and Mrs. Mitchell over who should approve sick leave. The Committee, recognizing that Mrs. Mitchell has had much more personnel experience than the Executive Secretary, recommended that all personnel decisions reside with her.

Because of the sensitivity of the issue, the staff was asked to leave the room and the Board quickly approved the Committee report. (While in executive session, the Board also voted to move the office, give a raise to "great old Paula," and revise the letterhead.)

The Committee also reported on its position on maternity leave. They said that because the current staff were all over forty, with the exception of Beverly, the one-day-a-week bookkeeper-dictaphone transcriber-telephone operator and general handy person who had already just had a baby, there was no need for a policy and therefore the matter had been tabled. The Board approved but said that should anyone get pregnant, the matter should come up again. Mr. Zukert said that when the issue is discussed the idea of coverage for paternity should also be considered. Mrs. O'Reilly snapped that if a man is involved in paternity, the association has no obligation whatsoever, and the matter was dropped.

There was a brief report of the Annual Meeting Committee. The Governor had been invited to speak but so far no answer had been received. Because the day was getting closer we needed to have a backup. Mrs. Greenlaw pointed out that this was exactly the same situation the organization had faced ten years in a row and that the Governor hadn't showed up yet. Mr. Knight pointed out that this year the Governor was a Republican. Mr. Scala wanted to know "What the hell does that have to do with his showing up?" Mr. Knight said it was generally recognized that Republicans are more responsible. Mr. Russell reminded the group once again that we were nonpartisan.

When the group considered a substitute, just in case the Republican Governor didn't show up, it was obvious that we should turn once again to our Founder, First Chairperson, and Chairman Emeritus, who was persuaded to stand in for the Governor. This would be the tenth year in a row that our community would have an opportunity to learn of the founding and earliest days of our association. When discussion turned to an award for the speaker, Mr. Peter Paul Henderson discreetly left the room. In his absence, it was agreed that we would have the plaque made up for the Governor, but ask Hardy's Sport Shop to be ready to switch the simulated brass plate on the award at the last minute.

The next report was from the By-Laws Committee with Ms. Trister reporting for Mr. Fales who was absent (due to personal circumstances—different from the personal circumstances that kept him from the last meeting).

The Committee presented its seventeenth draft of the proposed By-Laws revisions, now stretching over four and one-half years of study. At the Board's last meeting, some had objected to the language of proposed amendments to Article XXCVI, Section 78c (Removal of Committee Members) because it might have been construed to provide a Committee Chairperson with arbitrary authority to dismiss members who were consistently in the minority.

The new revised proposal included a new phrase: "Consistent losers, no matter how often on the wrong side, are protected by due process." To underscore this point, the Committee had added a parenthetical phrase: "This sacred institution, under God, shall neither be ruled by the tyranny of the majority nor the tyranny of the minority."

That amendment, as revised, was officially moved and seconded. During discussion, it was pointed out that the use of the term "minority" could be misread and that therefore it was moved to add the word "numerical" in front of both "minority" and "majority" wherever they appear. The motion to amend the revised amendment to the By-Laws was seconded.

Ms. Trister reminded the Board that the By-Laws Committee had spent two evenings crafting this revised language and that she was not sure she and Mr. Fales could hold the Committee together much longer if the Board continued to behave like a board of editors rather than a board of directors—and on that basis, she flatly rejected any such amendment. Several members applauded.

Mr. Widen sympathized with the By-Laws Committee, but said that in the spirit of democracy, By-Laws should reflect the will of the governed. Several members clapped (including two who already had applauded the previous speaker). In that larger spirit, Mr. Widen offered an amendment to the amendment to the revised amendment to the By-Laws which read, "Minorities reflected by numbers, race, ethnic origin, gender, sexual preference, or Christian denomination."

Mr. Zukert pointed out that not all religions are Christian and, therefore, he moved that in the amendment to the amendment to the revised amendment to the By-Laws, "Christian denomination" be struck. In that same spirit, Mrs. Lortz moved that in the parenthetical section, the phrase beginning, "This sacred institution, under God . . ." be dropped because it flew in the face of separation of church and state. Mr. Widen agreed to accept her suggestion as part of his motion, but the seconder to Mr. Widen's motion did not and, therefore, Mrs. Lortz asked that as a matter of principle, she, as a Christian herself, be the one to move that the whole parenthetical clause be stricken.

A howl of protest erupted. Rev. Horsinger offered a Solomon-like solution in the form of a substitute motion which proposed that in the amendment to the amendment to amend the revised By-Laws, instead of striking the words "Christian denomination," the word "religion" be substituted. Mrs. O'Reilly shouted that she sympathized wholly with Rev. Horsinger's intent, but that it left a loophole wide enough for the devil himself to drive through. She asked if he would accept an amendment to his substitute motion so that instead of just "religion" the phrase would be: "God-fearing religions, definitely not including some of the new weirdo cults." There was strong applause. Before Rev. Horsinger could reply, Mrs. Lortz was on her feet demanding that everybody was out of order until her motion for precedence could be addressed.

To bring order to the chaos, the more experienced George Horton moved the previous question, but his intent was frustrated when Lucas Zukert asked which of the nine previous questions he was talking about. Pandemonium prevailed.

Finally, Ms. Greenlaw, shouting louder than the others, demanded a point of personal privilege and, when recognized, said "I move that I'm lost." Mr. Scala asked if she would accept an amendment so that it would say "We are all lost" and said authoritatively that *Robert's Rules* gave this motion the highest order. Mrs. Lortz challenged whether a motion "that we are all lost" had a higher standing than a motion for highest precedence and Mr. Horton assured her it did.

Ms. Trister said that because this item was only the first of sixteen recommendations of the By-Laws Committee to be considered by the Board that evening, she hoped that the Board would be willing for her to take all of these ideas back to the Committee and to come forward at another meeting with a proposal incorporating all of the various motions and ideas. Mr. Widen said if they could do that, they could leave God in wherever they wanted.

The Chairperson said that unraveling all these motions would have to start with the person who made the last motion being willing to be the first to back off so that the matter could be referred back to the Committee and so forth down through each of the people who had made a motion. Mrs. O'Reilly said she would obstruct the process unless she was guaranteed that a Catholic would be added to the By-Laws Committee. In the interest of peace and sanity, Mr. Russell guaranteed that every person who had made a motion had a right to be certain that an individual of his or her political, philosophical, religious, or sexual preference would be represented on the By-Laws Committee. On that basis, the unraveling proceeded.

Ms. Trister announced that the second item the By-Laws Committee was bringing before the Board related to whether the organization should use the term Chairman, Chairwoman, Chairperson, or Chair. Before she could offer her first motion, Mr. Russell gave the Board its choice of a recess, adjournment, or dissolution and fled the room.

On reconvening, the Chairperson said that in the interest of a change of pace, he was taking the privilege of moving ahead to the idea of having a "Board Retreat." Mr. Zukert kicked off the discussion about a one- or two-day "retreat" when all the Board members would go off together to some secluded place to have a good block of uninterrupted time to really think about the state of the association and to get to know each other better. Mr. Knight was concerned that his wife would be terribly upset about his participating in such a co-ed venture. Ms. Greenlaw said his wife had no idea how safe she was.

Mr. Shapiro wanted to know what exactly would be accomplished during a retreat. Mr. Zukert pointed out that all of the Board's regular meetings were so taken up with the kind of important matters we had been discussing that evening that there was never a chance to really "brainstorm" or engage in "blue skying." Mrs. Archer wanted to know how you got that kind of a process going and Mr. Zukert indicated that most often it just starts with people talking off the top of their heads. Mrs. Archer reacted by saying that that was not something this group need to go away for two days to get good at.

Mrs. Zukert asked the group to put aside immediate considerations and to try to see the idea from the point of view of the Board members getting to know each other's strengths and weaknesses. Mr. Gonzalez said that might be pressing our luck.

Ignoring these immediate doubts about the process, Mr. Zukert asked the group where such a session might be held. Four locations were suggested, but the reactions were so violently divided that Mr. Zukert concluded that a group which couldn't decide on the location for a "retreat" probably wasn't ready for one.

The final report for this meeting was by the Evaluation Committee and was presented by Mrs. Buckminster. She pointed out that the Committee deliberately included some "hard-nosed businessmen" as well as a number of social scientists and others who were used to getting to "the heart of the matter." She assured the Board that the language of the Committee was laced with such concrete terms as "bottom line," "cost-effectiveness," and "management by objectives" and that this was one evaluation where just doing good was not good enough. For example, she said that one of the businessmen had been particularly helpful in pointing out that our program of public education would always defy quantitative analysis and therefore we should drop any pursuits that can't be measured in specific body counts.

Rev. Horsinger interjected that it was wrong for a voluntary organization to sell its soul for the sake of doing something just because it can be measured. Mrs. Buckminster responded by asking the Reverend why he thought the Girl Scouts sell cookies.

Mr. Colberg said that if the churches had more doers and fewer worshippers, or more sales than prayers, there would be a more business-like approach to God and a lot more souls could be saved per minister. The Reverend seemed moved by this admonition and asked what specific ideas there might be to implement the idea. Mr. Colberg said he couldn't be specific, but there was no doubt in his mind that all churches and other nonprofit organizations with all their bleeding heart do-gooders would be much better off if the people working in them had MBA degrees rather than their abstract training in divinity, archeology, social work, or library science. He capped his point by asking, "How many bibles has theology ever sold?".

Mr. Russell asked what this hard-nosed Committee had concluded and Mrs. Buckminster said that the findings of their two-year evaluation could be summarized as follows: "Any organization made up of such bright people, who are so dedicated and who have worked so hard, must be doing a great deal of good."

Some Board members wept.

On that positive note, the meeting was adjourned at 11:16 P.M.

Respectfully submitted,

Mrs. Jeffrey (Effi) Black
Secretary of the Board of Directors

Attested:
Brian O'Connell
October 26, 1984

Index